D1525356

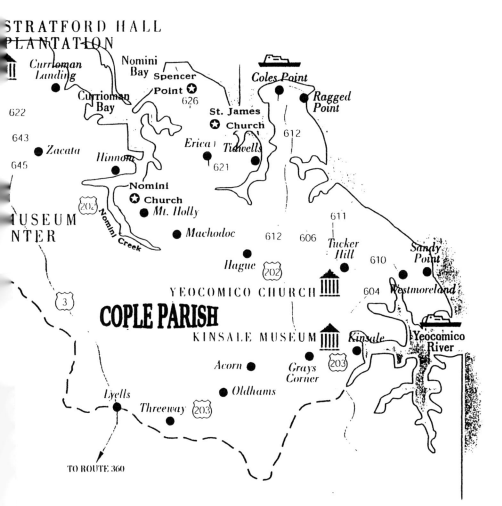

VER

STRATFORD HALL
PLANTATION

Currioman
Landing

Nomini
Bay

Spencer
Point

626

Coles Point

Ragged
Point

Currioman
Bay

622

St. James
Church

643

Zacata

Erica

Tidwells

612

645

Hinnom

621

Nomini
Church

MUSEUM
NTER

202

Nomini Creek

Mt. Holly

Machodoc

612

606

611

Tucker
Hill

Sandy
Point

Hague

202

610

3

YEOCOMICO CHURCH

604

Westmoreland

COPLE PARISH

KINSALE MUSEUM

Kinsale

Yeocomico
River

Acorn

Grays
Corner

203

Lyells

Oldhams

Threeway

203

TO ROUTE 360

The Life

of

Cople Parish
1664-1964

in

Westmoreland County, Virginia

Bertha Lawrence Newton Davison

HERITAGE BOOKS
2008

HERITAGE BOOKS

AN IMPRINT OF HERITAGE BOOKS, INC.

Books, CDs, and more—Worldwide

For our listing of thousands of titles see our website
at
www.HeritageBooks.com

Published 2008 by
HERITAGE BOOKS, INC.
Publishing Division
100 Railroad Ave. #104
Westminster, Maryland 21157

International Standard Book Numbers
Paperbound: 978-0-7884-1227-1
Clothbound: 978-0-7884-7094-3

Dedication
To
BLAKE TYLER NEWTON
1889-1977

"A lifelong member of Cople Parish and descendent of earliest Parishioners of the Parish. He served more than half a century on the Vestry, holding at one time or another all offices of that body; for many years Trustee of the Parish, Delegate to the Council of the Diocese of Virginia, elected a delegate to seven Trienniums to General Convention of the Episcopal Church in America.

While serving Christ and his Church, he was also a servant of the people of the Commonwealth of Virginia and the Northern Neck as State Senator, Superintendent of Schools of Richmond and Westmoreland Counties and President of the State Board of Education.

We remember him as a leader and supporter of the efforts for the advancement of good learning, the conducting of Confirmation classes, the promotion of the rule of law, justice and grace; many works of charity and constructive services in our community and in the Commonwealth. He exemplified in his life the teaching of Holy Scripture, that with the fruits of Heavenly Benediction came Love, Joy, Generosity, Goodness, and Faith.

NOW, THEREFORE, BE IT RESOLVED, that the Communicants, Rector, Wardens and Vestry of Cople Parish give thanks to Almighty God for Mr. Newton's unstinting service to God and His Church, and for the good example he left for us; and also pray that ancient prayer: "Eternal rest grant unto him, O Lord, and may light perpetual shine upon him".

Copied from resolutions in the minutes of the Vestry of Cople Parish printed in *Virginia Churchman* July 1977.

TABLE OF CONTENTS

The original pagination has been maintained for the body of the text.

Chapter

FOREWORD

This history of Cople Parish, founded in 1664 in Westmoreland County, Virginia, is of particular interest because it provides a continuing testimonial to the application of ecclesiastical and political concepts in a specific geographical area. In its nearly three hundred and fifty years, the life of the Parish has paralleled and influenced the evolution of the American social experiment through the resilience and devotion of its people to the practice of their beliefs.

My interest in researching this history was spurred by an awareness of the need for a documented chronological account, my eighty years of association in the Parish and my desire to create a memorial to my father, the Honorable Blake Tyler Newton, whose family has lived in the Parish since its inception.

Because the formal records of the Parish prior to 1849 have been lost, this work includes extensive research of source materials found in documents of the Episcopal Diocese of Virginia, The Virginia Historical Society and the Westmoreland County Clerk's office, Montross, Virginia. The appendices provide bibliographical and genealogical data for those researching family and church information.

I was encouraged in this endeavor by historian J. Paul Hudson of the United States National Park Service, the Reverend Treadwell Davison, past president of the Northern Neck Historical Society, and Mrs. James Dall Brown of the Publications Committee of that Society's Journal. For their help and the ten years of encouragement of my children, I am very grateful.

ACKNOWLEDGMENTS

Without the help of the following people I could never have been able to compile this story of Cople Parish. My greatest source was the extensive research of the late H. Ragland Eubank and Mrs. Helen C. Tayloe. These papers were left in Richmond after The VIRGINIA WRITERS' PROJECT was discontinued and were about to be sent to the dump when the Rev. Treadwell Davison rescued them and brought them to Cople Parish. Many thanks to Captain and Mrs. William King for their help in locating a Publisher and their support all during the twelve years it has taken to get this material together. I am deeply thankful to the Westmoreland Clerk's Office in Montross and the Westmoreland County Museum.

The Rev. John Page Williams, the late Arthur Whittaker, Mrs. Cornelia Hayes, the William Taylor family, Mr. and Mrs. Hally Tubman, Mrs. Lynn Norris, Mr. And Mrs. John Morrow and W. Fairfax Griffith shared their books, pictures and papers.

S. Bryan Chandler let me use his great grandfather, Hannabel Chandler's, diary and Mrs. Catherine Baltz sent me excerpts from the diary of John Newton Murphy. Miss Louise Sydnor contributed a notebook with minutes of the Woman's Auxiliary meetings during World War II which she had found in a pile of trash at an auction sale at Mr. Holly. The late Dr. Vernon Perdue Davis was a great help checking records at the Diocese of Virginia Mayo Memorial House in Richmond.

To my family I am very grateful for their support and help in many ways: To my daughter Be Herrera for getting me started and for writing the Foreword. To my son Marshall Davison for giving me courage to continue, to my daughter Lucy Treadwell Atkins for helping me type and to my son Treadwell Davison Jr. for proofreading through the years. To my late husband Treadwell Davison for his great help in deciding how to tell Cople's story.

RECORDS OF RECTORS OF COPLE PARISH

The Rev. John Scrimgour	1680-1691
The Rev. John Bolton	1692-1696
The Rev. Samuel Gray	1703-1708
The Rev. James Breechlin	1708-1722
The Rev. Walter Jones	1724-1733
The Rev. Charles Rose	1738-1761
The Rev. Thomas Smith	1764-1789
The Rev. James Elliot	1792-1811
The Rev. George Washington Nelson	1834-1840
The Rev. William Norward Ward	1840-1849
The Rev. Thomas S. Rumney	1849-1850
The Rev. William McGuire	1850-1852
The Rev. Edward McGuire	1853-1854
The Rev. Grayson Dashiel	1859-1859
The Rev. Charles Rederfer	1861-1866
The Rev. Andrew Fisher	1866-1868
The Rev. Dabney Wharton	1868-1873
The Rev. John Lloyd	1818-1876
The Rev. Pendleton Brooke	1879-1885
The Rev. Robert Funston Ward	1893-1894
The Rev. Austin Brockenbough Chinn	1894-1897
The Rev. Albert Rhett Walker	1898-1900
The Rev. Franklin Rideout	1900-1902
The Rev. Charles Gross	1902-1903
Augustus Davisson	1903-1906?
The Rev. Henry Lane	1907-1908 (supply)
The Rev. Arthur P. Gray	1908-1910
The Rev. Charles Crusoe	1910-1915
The Rev. Frederick D. Goodwin	1917-1930
The Rev. Clarence Buxton	1930-1945
The Rev. Earnest deBordenave	1946-1947 (supply)
The Rev. Francis Bayard Rhien	1946-1947
The Rev. William Byrd Lee	1948-1953
The Rev. Edward Morgan	1955-1960
The Rev. Macon Walton	1959-1960
The Rev. Lawrence Mason	1960-1964
The Rev. James S. Guy	1964-1986

Supply: Serves in the Parish while the Parish has no resident minister.
Interim: A minister that serves the Parish while the Search Committee searches for a new minister.
Advisor: A Clergyman that advises the Vestry during their search for a new minister.

Nomini Episcopal Church

Edward White Photographer
Kinsale - Va. 1999

FIRST FIFTY YEARS IN THE LIFE OF
COPLE PARISH

by BERTHA LAWRENCE NEWTON DAVISON*

"Walk about Zion, and go around about her, tell the towers thereof. Mark ye well her bulwarks, consider her palaces; that ye may tell it to the generations following."

Psalm 48: 12–13

Tucked between the two rivers that form the Northern Neck of Virginia in the lower end of Westmoreland County, Virginia lies Cople Parish, a special place in the hearts of many people.

When our forebears came to Virginia in the 1600's, there were no land boundaries so far as we know. As Government gradually assumed its responsibility, first under the Virginia Company and later as a Royal grant, land boundaries became very necessary. The new lands were divided into parishes in line with the English heritage of the early settlers.

The Parishes were set up as geographical boundaries, similar to counties in the scheme of things today. The early parishes were areas governed by vestries made up of the most important people for the welfare, political, and legal matters, as well as spiritual Church concerns.

Cople Parish was established in 1664 and is still Cople Parish today, and was also Cople Magisterial District until recently when it was divided into two Magisterial Districts.

Westmoreland County was carved from the "Mother County," Northumberland, in 1653.[1] In 1657, by enactment of the Grand Association, *Hening's Statutes* tells us "that it shall be lawful for the Commissioners of several Counties not yet laid out into Parishes with the consent of the inhabitants thereof to divide their counties into Parishes as by the Major part of said counties shall be agreed."[2] At that time the lower part of what is now known as Cople Parish was in Chicacoan Parish. This area was changed to Yeocomico Parish, and the upper part of Westmoreland county was Nomini Parish until 1664. Then on May 25, 1664, by order of the Court, Westmoreland was divided into three parishes. "From upper Mochodik (sic) downward to the foot of the western most side of Mr. Pope's Cliffs for the one Parish to be called Washington Parish . . . from thence to the north west side of lower

---

*Bertha Lawrence Newton Davison, a life-long resident of Cople Parish, has written the first of a three-part series about this historic parish.

1. Northumberland County Order Book 1652–1655, Book 1, p. 33.

2. Hening's *Statutes*, Vol. 1, p. 469, and Westmoreland County Order Book B, p. 31.

Muchodick (sic) River for another parish to be called Westbury,* thence to the lower end of the county for the third parish."[3] The lower end was to become Cople Parish, named in honor of Colonel Nicholas Spencer, Secretary of the Colony of Virginia, acting governor in 1683–85, President of Council, cousin of Lord Culpeper and son-in-law of John Mottrom.† Spencer was a Burgess from Westmoreland and church warden of the Parish; his birth place was Cople, in Bedfordshire, England. Colonel Spencer lived at "Secretary's Point,"[4] the present Albany Farm located in Machodoc Neck on the Nomini River. (In the 1990's this area is still inhabited by active members of the Parish. "Secretary's Point", now Albany Farm, is owned by Dr. and Mrs. Lloyd Griffith, and King Copsico is owned by the Hon. and Mrs. Tayloe Murphy, Jr.)

The Parish was established at the time of the Restoration Period just after Oliver Cromwell's Protectorate of England (1649–1659). During that time, the church had been in a state of flux in the colonies with many settlers coming over from Maryland to Virginia to escape religious problems. Many of these settlers were born and bred in the Church of England, wanting no part of the quarrels between the Catholics and Cromwell's Commissioners, nor their oppressive ways.

When Charles II was restored to the throne in 1661, he gave Governor Berkeley a set of instructions which formed the basis of the Colonial Legislature for the Church in 1662. The Enactment of the Legislature concerning religion in the colonies boiled down to three Acts that affected Cople Parish.

Act I

A church to be built or "Chapel of Ease" throughout the Virginia colonies to accomodate the people living in remote areas. Duty of Church wardens to keep Church in repairs, Provide Books and decent ornaments. (A greate Bible, two Common Prayer Books, Communion cloth and Napkins, Pulpit and Cushions)

Act II

Duties of the Clergy and his compensation. He should preach each Sunday in each Chapel of Ease in the Parish, if any, as well as his parish church. Twice a year

---

*Westbury Parish was absorbed by Cople Parish from all indication. No mention of it is on record after 1665 in the Westmoreland County Record books.

3. Westmoreland County Order Book 1662–1664, p. 32.

†The Mottram family is still represented in the Parish by Charles Mottrom Sanford, a prominent and valuable member of the Parish.

4. By 1668 definitely Cople Parish. Westmoreland County Wills and Deeds, Book 1, p. 346, Dec. 9, 1668 "John Payne of Cople." Folio D, Dec. 1668: Mrs. Frances Spencer's letter to Attorney L'Strange Mortant. "Know all men by their presents that I, Frances Spencer, wife of Nicholas Spencer of Nomini of Cople Parish in the County of Westmoreland in Virginia, etc."

administer the Sacrament of the Lord's Supper. Every Parish not having a minister to officiate each Sunday would make a choice of a grave and sober person of good life and conversation to read divine service every intervening Sunday at the Parish Church when the minister was any other place. It was made clear that neither the minister or reader* should teach any other catechism than that inserted in the book of Common Prayer. A record of official acts were to be kept by the Minister or Reader. An annual salary of 80 pounds should be paid every minister "to be paid in valuable commodities of the County; if tobacco at 12 shillings per hundred weight, if in corn, at 10 shillings per barrel. It was the duty of the church wardens to collect these dues, cause them to be brought to a convenient place and honestly pay them."

Act III

Vestries should be chosen by the major part of each Parish. Twelve of the most able men to serve as Vestrymen out of which number the minister and vestry would choose 2 church wardens yearly, and if a vestryman die or move from the Parish, the minister and vestry name another to take his place . . . and be it further enacted that only those persons who swear allegiance to His Majesty "and subscribe to be conformable to the doctrine and discipline of the Church of England" might serve.

Duties of the Vestries were very clear: moral, spiritual, political, and economic.† Church wardens had the care of the poor, widows and orphans, overseeing their welfare, placing them with proper masters and mistresses to whom they were apprenticed; repair of buildings and chapels; maintenance of minister; and moral behavior of people in the Parish. The Legislature also added to their duties the processing of every precinct, the boundaries of land and upkeep of the highways, not to mention monitoring attendance at services, the due observance of the Lord's Day, by attendance upon public worship, and refraining from travel, except in cases of emergent necessity is required under penalty of a fine of fifty pounds of tobacco.[5] The church wardens had quite a job.

A special proviso to Act III excluded "Quakers or other recusants, who out of nonconformity to the church, totally absented themselves from worship; for each month's absence they would be fined twenty pounds sterling. If these nonconformists absented themselves for a year, they would pay an added fine, 'security for their good behavior.' "[5a]

---

*Comparable to our present day Lay Reader.
†Throughout the history of Cople Parish, its members have been involved in the major issues of their time and have served as leaders in County, State, and Nation.
5. Hawks' *Ecclesiastical History of the United States of America*, Vol. I, pp. 66–68. Francis Hawks was Rector of St. Thomas Church, New York; his history was published in 1836.
5a. Ibid.

These first three rules of the Legislature of 1662 were followed as much as possible.

A chapel of Ease was already in place on the south side of Peirce's Creek and on the west bank of Nomini Creek across from land patented by Thomas Youell. A wooden church had already been built in Yeocomico Neck near Tucker Hill and was called Yeocomico Church. Therefore when Cople Parish was formed there were two buildings in place, one at the east end of the Parish and the other at the west.[6] The names were never changed and the Parish still worships at these locations today. A list of Vestrymen for Yeocomico congregation August 22, 1655, names Nicholas Jurnew, John Powell, and Richard Holden, all residents of this area.[7] John Powell and his wife patented land in 1650 and lived near the present Tucker Hill on the east side of Bonum's Creek. There is no deed to verify the story that Mr. Powell donated the land on which the first Yeocomico Church was built, but it is certainly a reasonable assumption, since he was one of the first vestrymen and lived close by.[8] It is interesting to note that when Luke Dine, Thomas Beatle and John Ward patented 330 acres of land on the northwest side of Yeocomico River on August 1, 1663, the Yeocomico Church building was cited as a landmark.[9]

Native American Influences

The Native Americans figure prominently in the story of the life of Cople Parish since two of the churches for over 350 years have borne Indian names. (St. James, Tidwells located on the Machodoc River, was organized in the Parish in the 19th Century.)

When Cople Parish was formed in 1664, the relations between local tribes and the colonists were friendly to a large extent because of the policy of acquiring land from them by purchase as well as by patent. In nearly every instance, the early Northern Neck planters negotiated with local tribes to acquire possession of the land they desired by agreement and consideration (a cow, a calf, an article of clothing) before obtaining a patent to the tract.[10]

---

6. Westmoreland County Wills and Deeds, p. 78, Oct. 10, 1662. (Action regarding Boundary of Property March 11, 1662, Westmoreland County Order Book appointing Constable for Nomini Parish soon to be Lower Parish.)

7. Northumberland County Order Book 1652–1655, p. 33. Court held Aug. 20, 1655, appointed Vestrymen for Yeocomico Congregation. The site was where the present Yeocomico Church stands near Tucker Hill where John Tucker had business in 1671. (His daughter married William Fitzhugh of Stafford.)

8. *Historical Atlas of Westmoreland County*, Virginia, by David W. Eaton, p. 73.

9. Northumberland County Patents 1663, Book 5, p. 299.

10. Northumberland County Order Book 1650–1652, p. 50. "The King of Muchcholas sale of Rhotanche (now Bonum's Creek) for and in consideration of three Machocoats in hand paid by John Earle, Richard Holden and Thomas Hales and three more to be paid by John Nott, John Powell and George Thompson which they will pay within ten days hath sold a necke of land lying between Euocomocoes [Yeocomico] River mouth and a creek joining to Muchcholas called Rhotanche and their heirs forever."

The colonists were careful to investigate any complaint of the Natives and to settle controversies, if possible, in such a manner as would be satisfactory to them. Because of these policies, peace mostly prevailed between the local tribes and the colonists throughout the settlement period. An example of such an agreement is on record in the Northumberland County Record Books:

"The Governor and Council directed the Commissioners of Northumberland 'to make inquiry concerning ye complaint of Mr. Allerton intruding a plantation upon them.' "

Those being intruded upon were the Indians who lived near Machodoc Creek. The Commission investigated and filed the following agreement:

"We under subscribed have made due inquisition . . . and doe find the said Indians and the Werowance (Chief Head) Pecatoan, to be well contented with the said Allerton's stay there, *so long as the land (whereon he liveth already cleared) be usefull . . . provided that no more houseing be built than what is now upon it and to keep his cattle and hoggs on the other side of Machoatic River* . . . in confirmation of ye promises ye said Pecatoan with his great men have likewise hereto subscribed a Machoatik Indian Town the 6th day of February 1656."

This document was signed by George Colclough, John Robers, James Hawleym, William Presley, William Nott, and by Peckatoan, Wonussacomen and Tahocks.[11]

By 1665, according to *Hening's Statutes*, Indian troubles were actively brewing in the Colony. Therefore, by Act of the Assembly, October 1665, it was decreed that the local tribes would not have power to elect within themselves or constitute their own Werowance or Chief Commander. Understandably this was not welcomed by the different tribes, adding to the unrest. Another Act, announced from the Grand Assembly at James City in 1667, enacted because of worsening relations with the natives, was as follows:

"An act for establishing a Fast, on August 27th, to be set aside strictly requiring all persons on that day to repair to their respective Parish Churches with fasting and prayers to emplore God's Mercy and deprecate the evils justly impending over us and be it further enacted that if any person or persons in contempt hereof shall be found on that day working, gaming, or drinking (unless if necessary only excepted) he or they so offending upon presentment of the Church wardens and proof thereof be

---

11. Northumberland County Order Book 1655, Aug. 22, 1655, Book 1, p. 33.

made to the Vestry shall be fined by them one hundred pounds of Tobacco, half to the informer, half to the poor of the Parish, and it is further enacted that all ministers in the Parishes where they reside be required to prepare themselves for the solemnizing that day.[12]

It is possible to surmise that this service was held in Cople Parish under this directive.

During Bacon's Rebellion (1676) prominent Cople Parish vestrymen were badly treated by the "rebels." Major Richard Lee, Col. Nicholas Spencer and Isaac Allerton all suffered at the hands of their neighbors because they had served on the Council for Governor Berkeley as Commissioners.

A petition by Isaac Allerton was brought against Joseph Hardige (sometimes spelled Hardwick), Richard Bartton, Thomas Oakley, William Head, and John Atwill complaining of harsh treatment that he, along with Colonel Washington and Colonel Spencer, suffered at the hands of the rebels, and asked for return of valuable goods stolen by the group. Three members of Cople Parish were on the jury when the petition was brought to court. They were John Newton, Sam Bonum and William Hardige. They signed their findings on August 25, 1677:

"The rebels, as the Commission's Report stated, received more than fair treatment from the local juries. They were asessed for the goods they'd taken only, without punitive damages."[13]

This seems to imply some of Cople's parishioners were in sympathy with Bacon's Rebels.

The Indians were still a problem in the 1690's. According to a local legend, the Gerrard family decided to build a home on land patented in 1662. This property was situated on Cherives Creek* at a point where Garner's Creek† and Jackson's Creek meet and flow into the Potomac River. This was known in the 17th Century as Gerrard's Reserve. The workmen encountered opposition from the tribe at Fort Hill‡ where they had an encampment up on the ridge, about three miles south of Jackson's and Garner's Creeks. There was such a constant barrage of raids against the carpenters and bricklayers, who were Marylanders, that the work had to be suspended, and the workers

---

12. Hening's *Statutes*, p. 264, 1665–1666.
13. Westmoreland County Deed and patent Book 1665-1677, pp. 301–302a.
*Now Jackson's Creek, so named in 1737 for Richard Jackson who lived there.
†At one time called Hurd's Creek on Patent in Eaton's Atlas.
‡The property is now the home of Fred Fairfax, Jr. and is across Rt. 612 from the 20th Century entrance to Burnt House Field.

returned home across the Potomac River several times. Perhaps the local tribes felt that building east of the "Narrows" where they had agreed to allow Allerton to live in peace in 1656, was breaking the pact, and things were getting a little crowded. The harassment was not successful in the end. The legend concludes that the Indians finally gave up, and the Gerrard family home was completed. The Indians melted into the forests and all we have left of the native culture are the beautiful names of the rivers and creeks of the area, and the Indian names of two churches of Cople Parish: Nomini and Yeocomico. An occasional arrowhead is discovered on the banks of the Potomac and in the fields when they are plowed. Pottery shards, axe heads, clay pipes and stems, bowls and grinding stones are found by serious collectors of Indian artifacts. References to Indian servants can be found in the Record Books of the County: one of these Indians "belonged" to the Rev. John Scrimgeour.[14] What a pity we have no record of what became of him. Chief Pecatoan is remembered because the area between Jackson's Creek and Bonum's Creek is called Pecatone Neck.

From the beginning Negroes played a large part in the life of Cople Parish. They were brought here by slave traders and sold to landowners who needed manpower to farm the plantations. Unlike the Native American, the African American has survived, in a climate not to be pointed to with pride by the English-American, but with admiration for their ability to carry on and to overcome the indignities of slavery. The Negro played a large part in the economy of the Parish and lives of both races have been woven together in a remarkable way. Mrs. Inez Johnson, whose family has been in the Parish for many generations, has written a very full account of black history which was published in *Westmoreland County, Virginia History* in 1983, and it is well worth reading for all the factual information it contains pertaining to this subject.

Early Clergy in Cople Parish (1664–1680)

Until Cople Parish acquired a full time rector in 1680, services were read by visiting clergy or clerks.

The Rev. David Lindsay, Rector of Chicacoan Parish (the present day St. Stephen's in Northumberland County), kept a watchful eye over his former parishioners. He probably held the first service in Nomini and also in Yeocomico. Mr. Lindsay was a faithful minister in his Parish until his death

---

14. Westmoreland County Order Book 1690, p. 122.

in 1667. He was buried in Cherry Point Neck, a spot in Northumberland County which still records his life on a tombstone.[15]

Mr. *Francis Doughty* took the oath as minister in Westmoreland County in 1661.[16] He became rector of Sittenbourne Parish (now Essex County) and Farnham Parish in what was then Rappahannock County (Richmond County today) in 1665 and he may have read services for Cople Parish during this time.

The Rev. John Waugh lived in upper Westmoreland in 1665 and was well known throughout the Northern Neck for many years. At one time he was rector of Overwharton Parish in Stafford County but there is no existing record of him listed as rector of Cople Parish. He was very active in the area and managed to get himself into all sorts of controversies.

He was witness to the will of Dr. Thomas Gerrard, Feb. 1, 1672.[17] During the period before Cople Parish had a resident minister, Mr. Waugh became involved in quite a heated dispute. It seems Restitute Whitstone, (granddaughter of Major John Hollowes and orphan of John Whitstone, an early Westmoreland County justice, fell in love with Matthew Steele, a man "of no estate." The Rev. Mr. Waugh happened to be in the Parish at this time and the young couple prevailed upon him to join them in Holy Matrimony at the home of William Spence on Nomini River on August 26, 1674, even though John Peyton, Restitute's godfather, had forbidden him to perform the ceremony. The court records state he married them "without a licience" and was fined the sum of 10,000 pounds.[17a]

Miss Lucy Brown Beale in her article, "Early Clergy of Cople Parish," states that "at this wedding of Restitute Whitstone and Matthew Steele a difference did arise between Richard Searles and Morgan Jones* . . . the echo of the Jones dispute still lingers, but we do not know whether the Rev. Waugh was called upon to quiet same or not."[18]

About this time Mr. Waugh was rector of Overwharton Parish in Stafford County but was still connected with Cople Parish, though not as a minister. In the 1674 Records we find:

15. *William & Mary Quarterly Historical Magazine*, Vol. XVI, pp. 136, 137.
16. Helen Crabbe Tayloe, unpublished research for W.P.A.
17. Westmoreland County Wills and Record Book, 1665–1677, p. 3.
17a. Westmoreland County Record Book B, 1665–1677, p. 217.
*Morgan Jones had a pottery kiln in the Nomini area in 1677. Mrs. Virginia Sherman, Westmoreland County Historical Preservation officer, gives a detailed description of this kiln in her chapter on archeology in the *Westmoreland County History* (1983) pages 93–94, concerning this 17th Century industry in Cople Parish.
18. *Northern Neck of Virginia Historical Magazine*, Vol. XVIII, p. 1745.

This indenture made this 28th day of December in the year of our Lord God 1674 between Jno. Waugh of Stafford Parish of Stafford County in the Colony of Virginia, minister, and Elizabeth his wife on the one part and Nathaniell Garland of Copely Parish in Westmoreland County and of the aforesaid Colony, Joyner of the other part. Witnesseth that the said Jno. Waugh and Elizabeth his wife, for and in consideration of the summe of seven thousand pounds of Tob. and cask to him in hand before the sealing and delivering of these . . . by the said Nath. Garland and his heirs, etc . . . forever and by these present have given, granted, & bargained & sold unto Nath. Garland . . . all the messuage [a dwelling house] . . . lying and being in Copley Parish in Westmoreland County in ye Colony of Virginia & by estimation two hundred & fifty acres of Land . . ."[19]

This document brought to a close the connections Mr. Waugh and his wife had with Cople Parish, at least those which are officially recorded.

Some Early Seventeenth Century Landowners in Cople Parish

The Ashtons, Sturmans, Hallows, Hardiges, Spekes, Burwells, Rosiers, Hutts, Broadhursts, Spencers and Youells all had property along the Potomac and Nomini Rivers, and their names figure prominently in the County Record Books of the 17th Century.[20]

Major Francis Wright, son of Richard Wright, Gentleman, and grandson of John Mottrom, the first English settler in Northumberland County, nephew of Mrs. Nicholas Spencer and vestryman of Cople Parish, is a good example of the type of citizen who made up the society of the Parish during its early years. He lived at what we know as Cabin Point. He is on record in Westmoreland County as Gentleman, Captain, Major, Surveyor, Attorney, Sheriff, and Justice of Westmoreland County, all very important positions of trust. Major Wright was educated by tutors in the Parish and was also educated in England, carefully guided by his illustrious uncle Nicholas Spencer. He married Anne, daughter of Colonel John and Anne Pope Washington.[21]

Daniel Hutt patented a large estate named Prospect Hill on Nomini Creek in 1662 and was named Justice for Westmoreland by the governor of the Colony on April 5, 1664, the year Cople Parish was formed.[22] It is recorded that among his fleet of ships was "The Mayflower." He operated several ocean going vessels between Europe and the Colonies, and was styled a "Merchant

19. Westmoreland County Deed and Order Book 1665–1667, p. 234 (Waugh's sale of land).
20. Eaton, *Historical Atlas of Westmoreland County, Virginia*, Patents, pp. 59–74.
21. *Northern Neck of Virginia Historical Magazine*, Vol. IX, pp. 796–800.
22. Eaton, *Historical Atlas of Westmoreland County, Virginia*, p. 70.

of London." His son, Gerrard Hutt, was a credit to his parents and to his grandfather, Dr. Thomas Gerrard, for whom he was named. He commanded a foot company in Westmoreland County and was a vestryman of Cople Parish, a distinguished position and also one that demanded service not only to the Church but to the community as well. The Hutt family still lives on land that he patented which is now part of Montross Parish. When Daniel Hutt died, his wife, Temperance Hutt, was left one of the wealthiest matrons of the Northern Neck. She married often and well, becoming in succession, Madam John Crabbe, Madam Appleton, Madam Washington, and when she died in 1712 she was Madam Blancheflower. It is interesting to find in her will the following: "1 feather bed, furniture, etc. to Ann Davis when 17 years of age; my grandchildren and the children of my two sons, Gerrard Hutt and Osman Crabbe, residue of estate."[23]

Bushfield Plantation was patented in 1665 by Richard and Thomas Bushrod.[24] The Bushrods were also transplanted New Englanders. In this area is Snake Island just off shore from Bushfield Plantation. The story is told in many versions that Pocahontas, the daughter of Powhatan, was held captive there in the early 1600's.

On the eastern side of Lower Machodoc Creek (or river as it is sometimes called) in 1662, Isaac Allerton, Jr. had patented a large tract of land,[24a] originally patented by Lewis Burwell, 1650, and Richard Turney, 1651. Allerton was in this area as early as 1656. He was born at Plymouth, Massachusetts, in 1630 of parents who had come over on the Mayflower. An early graduate of Harvard College (afterwards Harvard University), he came to Virginia and settled on Machodoc Creek and became very prominent in the affairs of the colony of Virginia.

Further up Machodoc Creek we have a record dated October 20, 1661,[24b] for 360 acres of land belonging to Walter English. The Englishes still own property in Cople Parish.

The famous Lee family established themselves in the area of Machodoc. Records show that Richard Lee, the emigrant, patented 2,000 acres of land on the upper east of Machodoc Neck as early as 1658. This property, named Machodoc, had originally belonged to John Mottrom. Richard Lee, the emigrant, never lived here, but his descendants established a home and the name of the family is preserved in Lee's Creek, a branch of Machodoc River.

---

23. *Northern Neck of Virginia Historical Magazine*, Vol. IV, p. 331.
24. Eaton, *Historical Atlas of Westmoreland County, Virginia*, p. 54.
24a. Ibid, p. 56.
24b. Ibid, p. 24.

Richard Lee's son John, who was studying medicine in London when his father died in 1664, moved to Machodoc and became the first of the Lees to live in Cople Parish.[25]

Richard Cole repatented 1,350 acres of land bounded on the west by Machodoc River and on the north and east by the Potomac River in August 1661 and named his property "Salisbury Park." This fellow was a very colorful character. According to the Westmoreland Records, he left instructions in his will for a "stone of black marble to be sent out of England with my coat of armour set in brass, and under it inscribed:

> "Here lies Dick Cole, a grievous sinner,
> That died a little before dinner,
> Yet hopes in Heaven to find a place
> to satiate his soul with grace."[26]

Whether or not his wishes were carried out we do not know, but perhaps somewhere along the shore at Coles Point near the Barnes family graveyard there is a marble slab set in brass buried beneath sand and bramble. Records also reveal that Mr. Cole's self evaluation of his moral standing was probably due to the fact that he had been in trouble for not attending church and had been fined by the Court for his backsliding.

In 1653 on the east side of what is now known as Cole's Point Neck, James Hurd patented land along the Potomac River to Hurd's Creek (now known as Garner's Creek). William Hockaday patented the land between Garner's Creek and Jackson Creek in 1653, assigned to and renewed January 9, 1662, by Dr. Thomas Gerrard.

Dr. Thomas Gerrard, father of Wilton's builder, was a Roman Catholic and lived much of his life in Maryland. His daughters, however, married Church of England adherents. Frances Gerrard married Thomas Speke and Temperance Gerrard married Daniel Hutt as already stated. Dr. Gerrard married secondly Rose Tucker, widow of John Tucker of Tucker Hill.

The neck of land between Jackson Creek and Jernew's Creek (now known as Bonum's Creek), was patented by Henry Corbin, Captain Peter Ashton, and William Thomas in 1660. Nine hundred acres of this land had been first patented by Nicholas Jernew in 1650. This area is now known as Pecatone Neck.

---

25. Ibid, p. 71.
26. Westmoreland County Clerk's Office Deeds, Patents. Part 2, abstracted and compiled by J. F. Dorman, Washington, D.C., 1973.

From Bonum's Creek along the Potomac River east to Lynch's Point, we find patents during the 1650's to 1665, in the names of Joan Philpot Powell, (widow of Robert Philpot) and John Powell, Samuel Bonum, Reynolds Wilkerson, Robert Jadwin, John Earle, Thomas Hayles, Richard Holden, William Walker and Luke Dine. On the west side of the Yeocomico River persons named Maunders, Garland, Nelms were patent holders in the 1660's.

The name Hardidge, or Hardwick, appears all through the early records of Cople Parish in the Westmoreland Record Books. The name is spelled first one way and then another; consistent spelling apparently was not a must in the 17th and 18th Centuries. William Hardidge, the son of William, who married a daughter of Thomas Sturman and secondly the daughter of Lt. Col. Nathaniel Pope, was a Justice of the Peace and Lt. Col. of Militia of Westmoreland County. His daughter and heiress was the wife of Col. Henry Ashton. Her tomb is at Nomini Bluffs with the tomb of Henry Ashton.

The landowners recognized the importance of good fellowship and community spirit. They did not neglect the lighter side of life, which led to the establishment, in 1670, of the "first country club in America," referred to in many publications as the "Banqueting House" or "Hall." The participants in the building of this structure wrote an agreement and signed it on March 30, 1670:

"Whereas it is enacted that once every four years there shall be a procession of the neighborhood, to every man's land for the plain marking and bounding out by line trees or other convenient boundaries to every particular person's divident or seat in which no course hath ever been taken by the County Court of Westmoreland. It is therefore mutually consented to and agreed upon by and between all and everyone of us for the better reservation of that friendliness which ought to be between neighbors that each man's line whereon any one of us is bounded, one upon the other, be remarked, and plainly set forth, by sufficient bound trees, and that in presence of each of us four, or our substitutes, between this present day, and the last of September next ensuing. Witness our hands and Seals this 30th day of March 1670.
Thomas Gerrard, J. Lee, Henry Corbin, Isaac Allerton"[27]

The men who signed this agreement were at one time or another wardens of Cople Parish, with the exception of Dr. Gerrard who was a Roman Catholic. No evidence has been found of a building site in the area (in the corner of the field to the left of Rt. 666 where it intersects with Rt. 606). This leads us to the conclusion the "Club" must have been a crude shelter

---

27. Westmoreland County Deed Book, p. 344.

which was probably in the shape of a pavilion, with sturdy poles of pine trees supporting a roof of pine boughs, and time has erased it from the area. Still the memory lingers on. In 1744 apparently a question arose concerning the actual existence of a building on this spot, since the following deposition was put on Public Record March 27, 1744, which certainly proves some sort of structure was erected in this place.

"The Deposition of Thomas Lee, Esq. above 50 years of age and sworn sayeth that he has been informed by persons of credit, that lived before the year 1670, that *there was a Banqueting House* erected in Pickatorn's Field, by Henry Corbin, Esq. Captain John Lee, Thomas Gerrard, Esq. and Mr. Isaac Allerton, in order to perpetuate the bounds of their lands and this deponent has been told by his father (who was brother to the said Captain John Lee and married to the eldest daughter of Henry Corbin, Esq.) that he have been at an entertainment in the said Banqueting House, and this dependent's father has mentioned to this Deponent some particulars that are in an ancient paper now produced in Court, which ancient paper is their Handwriting. This deponent was told by the late Col. George Eskridge that he had the agreement about the Banqueting House in His possession, he was then attorney to John Gerrard, who, as this deponent has heard, and believes, was the grandson and heir of Thomas Gerrard, Esq. and further this Deponent sayeth not. Thomas Lee." "At a Court held for the said County the 27th day of March, 1744, This Deposition of the Honourable Thomas Lee, Esq. being by the said Lee sworn to in open Court concerning the validity of the two proceeding Instruments of writing, is, on the motion of George Lee, Gent. admitted to Record.

Test: George Lee C.C.W."[28]

Soon after this friendly processing agreement was signed by the gentlemen who lived between Machodoc Creek and Bonum's Creek, Cople Parish lost two of its most prominent citizens. First, Dr. John Lee died in 1673. He had never married and his brother, Richard Lee, inherited his holdings in Cople Parish called *Machodoc*.[29] Richard became very important in the affairs of the Colony. He served on the Council of the Colony of Virginia, the House of Burgesses and as a Naval Officer and Collector of Customs in the District. He was Captain Lee in 1673 and by 1676–77 he was referred to as Major Lee. At this time he was serving with his neighbor, Isaac Allerton, in the House of Burgesses. He married Laeticia Corbin, daughter of Henry Corbin of Pecatone. Their son Thomas was the builder of Stratford Hall.[30]

Dr. Thomas Gerrard also died in 1673. His will asked that he be buried

---

28. Westmoreland County Deed Book 24, p. 182.
29. Westmoreland County Deeds and Wills, Vol. 14, p. 412.
30. Ibid.

by his deceased wife, Susanna (nee Snow), in Maryland. He left to his son, John Gerrard, and "loving deare wife Rose [Tucker]" his estate in Virginia, Maryland and England.[31] Dr. Gerrard's widow, Rose, then married Capt. John Newton (referred to as "Marriner" several times in the Court Records). Another friendly agreement, this time between John Gerrard of one part, his step-mother, Rose, and her husband John Newton of second part, is on record as follows:

"March 16, 1676 (1677) Articles of agreement between John Newton who married with Rose the relict of Thomas Gerrard Esqr., late of Machoatick in Westmoreland County and John Gerrard of Machoatick, Gent.

Thomas Gerrard did by his last will and testament devise his land at Machoatick to Rose for life and to Jno. Gerrard, being equally to be divided between themselves. The cattle, hoggs, horses, sheep and household stuffs together with the Negroes and other servants shall remain the proper use of that party in whose possession the same now are. The southeast halfe of the dwelling house above stairs and below, the dairy and kitchen and the 15 foot hen-house, the hogg-house, a 15 foot quartering house, having a shedd along the end of it, the northwest half part of the ba(illegible), the one halfe of the sixty foot tobacco house shall be to the use of John Newton during the life of Rose and all the rest of the housing and buildings upon the plantation to be belonging to Jno. Gerrard.

"The pasture now fenced in be mutually kept fenced and the ground within the fence are in common between the partys. The orchard as is now fenced in next the creeke and that part of the garden from the burying place to the house and so easterly to pales next the orchard shall belong to Jno. and Rose Newton during the life of Rose, and the rest of the orchard and garden to John Gerrard, and all the apple trees, quince trees, peach trees and cherry trees the north side the dwelling house without the orchard fence to belong to Jno. and Rose Newton.

The plantation called the "Levells" now in the possession of John and Rose Newton shall soe continue.

The south part of the plantation called "Poplar Knowle" as it is now divided with a fence and two forty-foot tobacco houses shall belong to John and Rose Newton during the life of Rose and the rest of the cleared ground there to belong to John Gerrard.

The new plantation in the neck [Wilton] shall belong to John Gerrard.

Either of the parties having a mind to build a plantation on any part of the tract of land not yet built or released shall have free liberty so to doe, provided the party so building and clearing do not in any measure prejudice the other in the quiet enjoyment of the plantation hereby appropriated to either.

Neither without the consent of the other shall admit any family in to any part [of]

---

31. Westmoreland County Will Book 3, p. 161.

the tract of land. The intent of this article is not to hinder either of the parties from
aliening or letting to lease the whole premises belonging to either of them.

John Newton, Rose (R) Newton, John Gerrard
Wit: Thomas Howson, Ja. Gaylard, John Newton
16 May 1677. Recorded"[32]

This agreement gives an authentic description of a plantation within the
Parish in the 1670's. These plantations were located in the area southeast of
Jackson Creek and not too far from Yeocomico Church. "Poplar Knowle" is
shown on a 1750 land survey as being just across the bridge north of
Yeocomico.

The Glebe lands and the First Rector of Cople Parish 1680–91

Glebe lands refer to property procured for the maintenance and housing of
clergy. The vestry attended to this rule of the Legislature. The land they
chose was part of the acreage which Thomas Youell patented on the Machodoc
River in 1653. This land was repatented by Richard Wright in 1658, and in
turn a parcel of this land was conveyed to the Parish by his son, Major Francis
Wright. There is no deed on record showing when the land was transferred
to the Parish but in a letter in 1683 Lord Culpeper stated:

"I know of four parishes in the Colony that besides house, glebe and perquisites are
really worth 80£ per annum: Viz: Middle Plantation Parish, where there is a new
Church built . . . that cost 800£, two parishes in Gloucester County and that Mr.
Secretary Spences lives in Westmoreland County. But I fear the last, when he leaves
it will not be worth it by a good deal."[33]

From this piece of information we can be sure the land had been acquired and
the house built by 1683.

By 1680 the vestry had procured the services of the Rev. John Scrimgeour
as the first rector of Cople Parish. Mr. Scrimgeour was the first of many
Scottish ministers to come to the area and serve the Church. He was a
member of a Colonial Scottish Jacobite family and was referred to as "John
Scrimgeour, late of Boyhill" by Lt. Col. Edgar E. Hume.[34]

Apparently Mr. Scrimgeour came to the Parish before the Glebe house
was built because he made his home with Secretary and Mrs. Spencer at
Secretary's Point, which was located on the western side of the neck of land

---

32. Westmoreland County Deeds and Wills, Oct. 1655, p. 103.
33. *William & Mary Quarterly Historical Magazine*, Vol. XXVII, p. 209.
34. *Virginia Magazine of History and Biography*, Vol. I, p. 244.

between lower Machodoc Creek and Nomini Creek near their entrance to the Potomac River. Here also was an Indian village known as King Copsico's Stronghold. The glebe lands were on the eastern side of this "neck."

Most plantation houses during the early period of Cople Parish history were built near the water, and "The Glebe" was no exception. It was situated on the beautiful body of water known as Lower Machodoc River and a creek now called "Glebe Creek." There was not a great distance to travel by boat from homes of the parishioners along the creeks and rivers of the area to Nomini Church located at that time on the west side of Nomini River.[35]

In 1682, during the early part of Mr. Scrimgeour's ministry, Halley's Comet made its appearance. This proved to be a good omen, for about this time the glebe house was built. A sturdy, two-story structure, "The house utilized oversized Flemish-bond brickwork with glazed headers, and was called a typical single-pile pre-Georgian Jacobean-style manor house, solid and commodious, but no great pretentions."[36] This building is still standing and is part of the present dwelling on the property known as *Glebe Harbor*. Should we assume the Spencer's house was used as a guide?

The parishioners lived for the most part all along the several fingers of land called "necks," bounded by rivers, creeks and little bays, winding in and out, and all connected to the great Potomac River. The roads of this period were nothing more than "horse and Foote paths."[37] Therefore the waterways were the highways of the day. It is possible to conjecture that the minister traveled to Yeocomico Church for services by boat, from Secretary's Point down the Potomac to the mouth of Bonum's Creek, then south on Bonum's, winding up that stream until he reached Tucker's Run, which was very close to Yeocomico Church.

Plantations had their own wharfs where sea-going ships and smaller vessels could anchor in the natural harbors so plentiful along the banks of rivers and creeks.

Mr. Scrimgeour attended to the management of the glebe lands, although he never actually moved into the glebe house. He resided at Secretary's Point until he died according to Westmoreland County Records.

It is clear the parishioners were a most interesting and capable group when Mr. Scrimgeour came to the Parish. There is no list of vestrymen for that period, yet it is safe to assume the officers of the church, wardens and vestry, were held by the leading men in the area. The settlers here at that time came

---

35. Westmoreland County Deeds and Wills, Oct. 1662, p. 78.
36. Norris, *Westmoreland County, Virginia*, p. 268.
37. Northumberland County Patent Book 5, p. 299.

from all sections of England. They were not all from the same class of society. They ran the scale from artisan, yeoman, indentured servant, to professional men. There were African slaves, and some Indians were members of households. Therefore the church wardens and vestrymen had a large task. (It was their duty to protect fatherless children and widows, to punish wrongdoers, settle disputes between neighbors, and apparently oversee the entire society of the Parish. Every soul who lived inside the bounds of the Parish was considered a parishioner.[38])

Judging from the Record Books in the Westmoreland County Courthouse, the citizen did enjoy setting the record straight with the help of the Court. It seems that one of the chief delights of several of the matrons was gossiping about their neighbors. This led to several court battles. These cases were the 17th Century soap operas which make fascinating reading if you are so inclined. The Rector must have had a lively time.

There was a thriving trade in tobacco, the main currency of the time. Every community had mill ponds where grist mills were kept busy grinding corn and wheat grown on the several plantations. These mills were very important land marks, and some of them were still used into the 20th Century on sites established in the 17th Century. In 1694 "William Paine partitioned the court for liberty to build a mill on the head of Bonum's Creek and, showing that he has land of his own intersecting on one side of Mr. Gawen Corbin, Mr. Corbin gave his consent that Wm. Paine could have one acre for his mill."[38a] This mill was very near Yeocomico Church.

It is often said that the more things change, the more they stay the same, and the problems of the seafood industry in the 1680's have parallels in our area in the present day. For instances we find in the records the following:

"From a long practice of indiscriminate and wanton practice of catching the fish which had been in such abundance in the river when the settlers came, it was now necessary to *forbid by law* the taking of them in the lower Rappahannock between November and May with gigg, harping iron or any other such like instrument."[39]

During the 1680's other governing problems were similar to the 1980's. General William Beale, in his "Annals of the Northern Neck," says: "Amidst misfortunes of the times, the planters whilst mourning over their hardships and bitterly complaining of the 'Supineness and perversity of Government'

---

38. Hawks' *Ecclesiastical History*, Vol. I, p. 66.
38a. Westmoreland County Order Book 1690–1698, p. 153, Oct. 31, 1694.
39. Hening's *Statutes*, p. 66.

were also putting forth strenuous efforts to redress their grievances. Col. Nicholas Spencer and Richard Lee of Cople Parish, both members of the King's Council, were especially active and influential in this direction. Their efforts to reduce the burden of taxation resulted in the discharge of the greater part of the soldiers employed in the Rappahannock and Potomac Forts, who returned to the peaceful pursuit of agriculture. Only twenty men with their officers were left in the different garrisons, and a part of these were regular soldiers of His Majesty's regiments. This reduction of the military force was soon carried still further, and in the latter part of 1682, the forts that had so long remained as a menace to the Indians and which offered protection to the planters were dismantled. Such was the peaceable disposition of the neighboring tribes at this time that only twenty well-mounted and well drilled horsemen from Stafford County were sufficient as a guard for the frontier."[40]

In 1689 Colonel Spencer died. This was a loss to the Parish and to the Colony of Virginia, as well as a blow to the rector. The Secretary was a close friend of Mr. Scrimgeour and a valuable member of the Parish.

Colonel Spencer died suddenly in Court at Jamestown without time to get his affairs in order which caused a great confusion over some state papers. The Executive Journals of the Council tell the story:

"Mr. Secretary Spencer, dec'd, in April General Court and several other times, carried from James City and had in his possession, several papers relating to the Government of this their Majesties' Colony and Dominion; and it being of absolute Necessity . . . that all papers whatsoever of that Nature should be registered in the Secretaries' office and there kept."[41]

The Council ordered "that Mrs. Frances Spencer, the relict and Ex't'r of said Mr. Secretary Spencer, should deliver all the said papers to Col. Isaac Allerton." Mr. Scrimgeour figured prominently in this controversy between the General Court and Frances Spencer, the Secretary's widow, over the "possession of certain State papers." This must have been difficult for the poor clergyman as he was caught in the middle because he resided with the Spencers. However, judging by later occurrences, Madam Spencer was able

40. *Northern Neck of Virginia Historical Magazine*, Vol. XVIII, pp. 1733–1734.
41. Executive Journals of Colonial Virginia, Vol. 1, pp. 123–124. April 26, 1689, Col. Spencer attended a meeting in Jamestown of the Council of the Colony which ordered a special celebration for May 24, 1689, to proclaim William and Mary King and Queen, which proclamation was prompted by the Royal Council (Virginia Magazine of History and Biography, Vol. 20, p. 5. Richard Lee and Isaac Allerton were at this Council.) Col. Spencer's will was proved in the Prerogative Court of Canterbury, England: see Westmoreland County Deeds and Wills Book IV, p. 229.

to take this problem in her stride. She refused to obey the order on the grounds that most of the papers pertained to personal matters. The Council or General Court then issued several other orders, the last of which was as follows:

"the 17th day of Jan'ry 1689 it was ordered that Mrs. Spencer should permit Col. Richard Lee and Col. Isaac Allerton to have the perusall of all the pap'rs belonging to Mr. Secretary Spencer, de'd, and to take into their care all such as should concern the Government, . . . if the said Spencer or Scrimgeour shall refuse, it is ord'r'd that she or he . . . do appear at James City before the Rt. Hono'ble their Majesties Lt. Gov'r and Council on the 5th day of the next Gener'll Court, . . ."[42]

In the middle of this personal debacle for the Rector of Cople Parish, William and Mary were proclaimed King and Queen, and The Bishop of London commissioned "James Blair, our Commissary in and throughout all of Virginia" on the 15th of December, 1689.[43]

As soon as Blair received his commission, he called a convention of the clergy of the colony to be held at Jamestown on July 23, 1690. Two important matters were acted upon: first, the resolution for help in establishment of a College in Virginia, (William and Mary); second, the organization of an ecclesiastical jurisdiction and the establishment of a series of ecclesiastical courts for the trial of both clerical and lay offenders against the moral law.[44] Cople Parish played a prominent part in this, especially Nomini Church. At the close of the convention, The Rev. Blair announced:

"I have nominated and appointed the persons following, ministers of the gospel in the several precincts hereafter mentioned, my substitutes and surrogates viz:

(Several clergy are named to take care of the areas from the James on the south side, York, Matapony and Rappahannock . . . then)

as also the Rev. Mr. John Farinfold (minister in Northumberland County), my substitut and surrogat in and through all that part of the Colony lying and being betwixt the Rivers of Rappahannock on the South and Potomock on the North . . . and for this end, with the consent and advice of the Clergy at the General Meeting aforesd, I do require that the said substitutes assisted with the minister of their several precincts or the major part of them, to hold a meeting *twice a* year at the times and places hereafter mentions:"

42. Ibid.
43. *Virginia's Mother Church*, p. 279.
44. Ibid, p. 280.

"Nominy, in Cople Parish, would be host to these meetings on the fourth Wednesday in April and the fourth Wednesday in August. *Divine service was to be devoutly read, and a sermon preached, explaining some of the articles of our Holy Faith of the main duties of a Christian life. Or against the prevailing sins of time and place."*[45] The tavern at Nomini Ferry, run by Lewis Markham (great-grand-father of Chief Justice John Marshall*), must have been a pretty lively place after one of these sessions.

As a brief summary of this proclamation, it may be said that the new Commissary, with the approval of the clergy of the Colony supporting him, announced "he *intended to revive and put in execution* the ecclesiastical laws against all cursers, swearers and blasphemers; all whoremongers, fornicators and adulterers; all drunkards, ranters, profaners of the Lord's day and contemners of the sacraments; and all other scandalous persons whether of the clergy or laity within the Colony and Dominion of Virginia."[45a]

This paints a rather sorry picture of the morals of the day. We do not have the records of the service held in Cople Parish at Nomini, but to this day the Diocese of Virginia is divided into "Regions" and meetings are held Spring and Fall.

Another kind of "wild life was abroad" in the Parish at this time. The Westmoreland Court House records report a petition to the Governor and Council of state in 1691:

"Wolves harbored in great forest and swamps of this County if not by some tymely and effectual means prevented will tend to utter ruine of the destruction of our stocks of young cattle, sheep and hoggs. Permission to trap, hunt and otherwise to catch and destroy these ravenous creatures is begged."[46]

Nomini Church was apparently used often for meetings other than church services. In October 1691, "Colonel William Peirce, Captain Thomas Youell, Mr. Henry Rosse and Mr. John Jordan are requested to meet Captain Hardidge on Wednesday next at Nominy Church and treat with him about purchasing the lands appointed to be laid out for a town for this County."[47]

Before a town was "laid out," Mr. Scrimgeour passed to his reward in November 1691. We have to assume Mr. Farinfold, from Chicacoan Parish, the Surrogate for the area to represent Commissary Blair, held the burial

---

45. Ibid, pp. 282–284.
*Elizabeth Markham married Thomas Marshall of Washington Parish.
45a. Ibid, p. 285.
46. Westmoreland County Record Book 1691–1699, p. 14.
47. Westmoreland County Order Book, 1690–1698, p. 49.

service. There is no record of where Mr. Scrimgeour was buried, but he left a large estate consisting of "ready money, plate, tobacco, securities for moneys and tobaccoes, slaves, servants, sheep houses, cattle and hoggs, wearing apparell and other personalities. His personal property was appraised at 61,303 pounds of tobacco. This included the appraisal of a library valued at 10,000 pounds of tobacco."[48]

Almost immediately upon the death of The Rev. Mr. Scrimgeour, John Bolton appeared as minister of the Parish and by November 30, 1693, had married Frances, the widow of Colonel Nicholas Spencer.[49]

The controversy over the government papers had hardly quieted down when Frances Spencer, now Mrs. Bolton, was again the object of the Court's displeasure, and had again involved Cople's rector in the dispute.

Frances took possession of the property of the deceased Mr. Scrimgeour and would not recognize that the estate had been granted to William Scrimgeour, brother of the former rector. Mr. William Scrimgeour had come to the colonies from Scotland to claim his inheritance. He accused Mrs. Bolton of taking possession of the personal property of his brother.[50] Mr. Bolton justified his part in the scheme by stating that the former minister had bequeathed all his property to Mrs. Bolton's first husband, and since he was Col. Spencer's successor, he was just "exercising his right" to control the property. Mrs. Bolton claimed that when the "devisee had died before the devisor (Scrimgeour), by a non-cupative will had left all of his property to her." Mrs. Spencer Bolton had witnesses to this "will" give the following depositions to the Court.

"Deposition of Hannah Clayton, aged 47 years or thereabouts, that being with Mr. John Scrimgeour at the house of Madam Frances Spencer the day before he died, being sick and the sickness wherewith he died, said to Hannah Clayton take notice that I give all that I have to Madam Spencer and to her son Nicholas.

Hannah Clayton"

"Deposition of John Carryer, aged 15 years and thereabouts, saith that Mr. John Scrimgeour, being sick at Madam Spencer's house the same day he died, heard the said John Scrimgeour say to Madam Frances Spencer that all he had he did give to her and wished he had more for her sake.

John Corrier"[51]

These depositions were given November 29, 1691.

---

48. Ibid, p. 189.
49. Ibid, p. 122.
50. Ibid, p. 5, p. 62.
51. Westmoreland County Record Book (Nov. 29, 1691.)

The Court Records are full of appearances in Court by Frances and John Bolton or their lawyers intermittently for several years. Finally they could no longer hold the ill-acquired effects of the deceased cleric when the Court ordered in very straight forward language to have the "Sheriff take John Bolton and Frances, his wife, (lately called Frances Spencer) and bring their bodies before his Majesties' court to answer charges of Wm. Scrimgeour."

The suit against the Boltons was finally settled by the Court when they were ordered to "pay William Scrimgeour the appraised value of the Rev. John Scrimgeour's personal property."[52]

The poor second Rector of Cople Parish spent a great deal of time defending himself against accusations ranging from disorderly conduct to stealing, which all proved to be false. All were "dismissed. No proof."[53] However, it seems his marriage was in trouble also. Madam Spencer-Bolton used her influence to try to discredit his claim to being an English Cleric. The records state: "Mr. John Bolton and his wife, 'being at variance,' evidence was used with some of the shippe officers to swear him an Irishman and that they knew him and his relations in Ireland." (This would indicate, if true, that Mr. Bolton was using false credentials as a minister of the Church of England.) The Court decided the charges "to be malicious forgery, contrived for the ruin of the said Bolton." The Sheriff was ordered to take the accusors "at once into his custody and take them to a common whipping post and give them thirty lashes or stripes on their bare backs, *well laid on*, and then to discharge them." This same sentence was pronounced for Margaret Fitzgerald for "bearing false witness" against Mr. Bolton."[54] So much for gossips!

Apparently the whipping post wasn't very effective, for we find in the records the following:

"May 26, 1697, By order of the Court, Ducking stools will be forthwith provided and fixed in each Parish of this County as soon as conveniently may be. One in Washington Parish at Capt. Lawrence Washington's Mill Dam and one to be at Col. Issac Allerton's Mill Dam in Copely Parish. Capt. Willoughby Allerton requested and impowered by the Court to procure the same and bee well and substantially done." Also "this court will reimburse the charge and satisfie for trouble in Next County Court."[55]

---

52. Ibid, p. 182.
53. Ibid, p. 158a, Nov. 28, 1694.
54. Ibid, 1690–98, p. 144a.
55. Ibid, p. 242.

In spite of the rector's problems, the services of the Parish were held regularly at Nomini. We know this because of the following Court order:

"Captain Thomas Youell is appointed for one whole year to keep the Ferry at Nominy and to give speedy passage to horse and foot every working day for all passengers betwixt sunrise and sunset, and in time from break of day so long as day is on the skies, and *on Sundays only for* persons going to and from Church and no other, and he be paid five thousand pounds of Tobo."[56]

Thomas Youell, who had been a Justice since 1673 of the County and member of the House of Burgesses died May 29, 1695. He named in his will his grandsons, Youell English, Youell Watts and Thomas Spence and his granddaughters, Ann Watts, Winifred English and daughter Spence as well as John Atwill. His burial service was probably read by Mr. Bolton. Mr. Youell was buried on the top of the east back of Nomini Creek, overlooking the ferry landing, where Nomini Church stands today.[57]

Mr. Bolton died in the spring of 1697. Even though he died in debt, there were several disputes over his estate.[58] Because of this we have the only records of what happened to him and also something about the state of the Parish.[59]

"on Dec. 3, 1697, Gawen Corbin, Gent. of Pecatone, obtained an attachment against John Bolton's (Clerk) Estate, for 10 lbs. sterling. Which being delivered to Mr. John Minor, then Deputy Sheriff, made return Dec. 3 then inhand what Estate may appear to have due. Several persons objected, they having also attachments against Estate and since apparently there were insufficient funds to cover the amount. The Estate attached was part of Bolton's salary allowed him by the Vestry for performing ministerial functions in the County and was put in the hands of Sam'l Thompson, Gent., High Sheriff to collect"[59a]

The "ministerial functions" referred to attest to the fact that Mr. Bolton was trying to attend to the Parish needs during these trying times in his personal life. Perhaps he was buried near Mr. Youell on the bank at Nomini. There is no record.

At the time of Mr. Bolton's death, there must have been an outbreak of some disease in the Parish. At least twelve heads of households died and their

---

56. Westmoreland County Order Book 1690–98, Oct. 1, p. 40.
57. Ibid, Book 3, p. 168.
58. Westmoreland County Record Book, May 26.
59. Westmoreland County Deeds and Wills, 1698, Feb. 3.
59a. Westmoreland County Order Book.

wills were probated in the following twelve months.[60] At Court held in April 1698, it is recorded:

"It is ordered that Thomas White bee constable for that precinct of Copeley Parish where *Henry Kirk* late served. It was also ordered that John Dowsett bee sworn his deputy."

"It is ordered that the Clark due on behalf of the Court signifie to His Excellency the Governor of the *great mortality* which has befallen us in this county with the loss of severall of our commissioners and to recommend to him Nicholas Spencer, Esq. (son of the late Col.), Capt. Willoughby Allerton, Mr. John Sturman, Mr. John Scott, Mr. Lewis Markham, Mr. James Taylor, and Mr. Charles Ashton to bee added to the Commission, and also in answer to his Excellency's letter of 28 of Feb. 1697/ 98 to return that there is not any pitch or tarr usually made in this County and very little flax or hemp or other navall stores and but very small probability of improvement."[61]

Wills on record for this period have some very interesting bequests.

June 22, 1698–Aug. 31, 1698:* Joseph Hardwick's will left his Bible to his friend Temperance Blanchflower, her husband Benjamin named as Executor.

Jan. 31, 1697–Feb. 23, 1697: William Payne of Cople leaves "My daughter Anne, by a Former venture, 6 cows, 6 ewes, furniture etc. and after my death to go to Col. Lee's house"

Feb. 7, 1698–March 30, 1698: James Hardwick left to his son Joseph "My silver hilted sword and belt given me by Capt. Wm. Hardwick." Along with other bequests he leaves "a caudle cup and the ladle to daughter Lydia Hardwick."

Feb. 5, 1697–April 27, 1698: Original Brown includes in his will a bequest to his son William, "horses, pistols and bayonets."

Feb. 1, 1696/7–May 26, 1696: Robert Middleton leaves John and Nathaniel Garland, sons of Nathaniel Garland, "1 crown to by gloves."

May 9, 1698–April 27, 1699: Thomas Jones "leaves to Frances Thorn, widow, a man servant named Richard Coggin having 5 years to serve;" he also gives "to John Maurning, Cooper, 1 hat; William Horton 3 yards of serge; Thomas Landford 2 buck skins. Frances Thorn, Executor."

April 3, 1698–April 27, 1698: John Miller leaves to "his friends Richard Cradunck 1 horse, Philip Camose 1 horse, and Elizabeth Booth 1 horse."

Jan. 26, 1696–Feb. 24, 1696: John Rice, "of Nomini," among other bequests leaves to his "son Zorabable, 1 cow."

March 30, 1698–April 27, 1698: George Tunbridge left to Mary Brown, daughter of Original Brown and Jane his wife all my estate; latter to be Exx. said Mary under age."

Jan. 14, 1697–April 27, 1698: Arthur Harris left his wife "50 acres of land and houses to wife Ellenor for life; sons Arthur and William all my Cooper's tools and 50 acres of land. Daughter Anne Harris 1 heifer. Wife Exx."

---

60. Westmoreland County Deeds and Wills, 1696–1698.
61. Westmoreland County Order Book, 1698, p. 263.
*These dates represent first, the date the will was made; second when it was probated.

Jan. 2, 1698–Oct. 26, 1698: John Davis left "son John all my carpenter's tools and mare; son Elias mare and colt; wife Ann exx and residue of estate."

Dec. 8, 1697–Feb. 23, 1698: Stephen Bailey, "to son John 50 acres; son William home plantation; dau. Anne Smith one iron pot, one mare and one shilling; Anne Bailey, dau of Stephen Bailey deceased, one heifer; Mary, daughter of William Walker, deceased, one heifer."[62]

During the early life of Cople Parish, the leaders of the community were not only intensely interested in establishing churches, good relations with neighbors, productive farms and comfortable housing, they were also anxious to see their children educated. When Richard Sturman died in 1669, he left instructions in his will for his friends "Col. Nicholas Spencer and Lt. Col. John Washington to aid my wife and children to return to England where they will receive an education."[63] Sons were sent back "Home" if their fathers could afford the expense. Ministers and Clerks taught in some of the homes. Tutors from England and Scotland were hired to prepare the sons for university.

There were free schools in the Colony in the 17th Century. Philip Alexander Bruce, in his *Institutional History of Virginia*, quotes from Beverley's *History of Virginia:* "Tracts of land, houses and other things were granted to free schools for the education of children in many parts of the country; and some of these are so large that of themselves they are a handsome maintenance to the master; but the additional allowance which gentlemen give with their sons to render them comfortable subsistence. These schools have been founded by the legacies of well inclined gentlemen. In all other places, where such endowments have not been already made, the people join and build schools for their children where they may learn on very easy terms."[64] So far as we know, this type of school did not exist in Cople Parish. Because of its agricultural nature and distance of homes from one another, it was not practical.

Those who could not afford private tutors apprenticed their sons to masons, blacksmiths, carpenters, coopers and the like to learn valuable trades. These apprenticeships were made a matter of record, i.e.: "Richard Sutton, with the consent of his father late of the Parish of Copeley is bound apprentice to Griffin Humphreys to live for the term of 4 years from this day. Griffin doth oblige himself to teach and instruct Richard in the arts and mysteries of a Tanner and Shoemaker, (which he now useth) after the best manner that he may."[65]

---

62. *Wills of Westmoreland County, Virginia*, Augusta B. Fothergill, Appeals Press, 1925.
63. Ibid, p. 10.
64. *Institutional History of Virginia*, Vol. 1, Phillip A. Bruce, p. 359.
65. Westmoreland County Order Book, 1696–1697, p. 282.

In the late 1600's prominent members of Cople Parish were educated men. As already noted, Isaac Allerton, Jr. was graduated from Harvard, John Lee received a B.A. degree from Queen's College in England and afterward obtained a diploma of Doctor of Physic. His brother, Richard II, was also educated in England "and acquired such scholarship that, in later life he was in the habit of writing marginal notes in his books indiscriminately in Latin, Greek and Hebrew."[66] Books were valued highly and were ordered from London for private libraries. In 1690 Commissary Blair put into motion the plan to have every county invited to subscribe their pledges for gifts for the establishment of the College of William and Mary.[67] Vestrymen of Cople Parish were members of the House of Burgesses and were interested in the welfare of all the people of the Colony, so we can be reasonably sure members of the Parish subscribed to the plan for higher education. After much work on the part of Commissary Blair and the Board of Visitors appointed by the General Assembly, and "after the letting of contracts, the cornerstone of the college building was laid with great ceremony and wide rejoicing on August 8, 1695."

There was indeed a need for education in Cople Parish. On November 1, 1694, during Mr. Bolton's tenure as rector, several members of Cople Parish were embroiled in a court case which showed plainly a need for enlightenment. One William Hale had accused Phillis Mony, wife of Hugh Mony, of witchcraft. She, according to Hale, "had bewitched Henry Dunkin's horse and made him start and tear the said Henry Dunkin's legg, and also that she had teached daughter (John Dunkin's wife) to bee a witch, who had also teached her said husband to bee a wizard." Phillis and her husband brought William Hale into court to answer these charges saying "Phillis is a good, true, faithful and loyal subject of our sovereign Lord and Lady, the King and Queen, and the feare of God always have before her eyes and from all manner of witchery, sorcery, witchcraft or any such like wicked and base crime free has kept, yet William Hale being not ignorant of the premises, but envying the happy estate of Phillis, and, not only entending to deprive Phillis of her good name and bring her to bee brought into the evil opinion of all her neighbors, but also to cause her to be brought into the danger of forfeiting and losing her life, in January 1693 at the house of Henry Dunkin in the County aforesaid did malitiously declare these false words . . ." Phillis and Hugh stated that they were "dampnified" and had received "damage to the

---

66. *The Lees of Virginia*, Edwards Jennings Lee, p. 69.
67. *Virginia's Mother Church*, Vol. II, p. 90.

value of 20,000 lbs of Tobacco." Willoughby Allerton, attorney for William
Hale, pleads him not guilty of this scandalous accusation "supposed by him
to be spoken" and the jury found for the defendant that "hee is not guilty."
A nonsuit was granted him."[68]

This case was possibly a distant echo of the Salem witchcraft trials taking
place in the Massachusetts Bay Colony in the 1690's . . . remember some of
the settlers in Cople Parish had come down from New England.

Meanwhile, at the Yeocomico Race Track on August 15, 1694, a well
documented race took place between Rodman Kenner's horse, Smoaker, and
John Hartley's horse, Cammell. It seems the two brothers, Richard and
Rodman Kenner, had been less than honest in running the race. The
agreement was between Capt. Kenner and John Hartley to "run the quarter
and half of a mile for 20 shillings sterling a piece and 577 pounds of tobacco
to be paid by the loser to him that should come first to the end of the race
after fair starting and running."[68a] According to Mr. Hartley's testimony, by
his attorney Robert Brent, one Kenner brother went to the far end of the
track and sat on the rail and waved his hat to frighten Mr. Hartley's horse
and prevented Cammell from winning the race. Therefore Mr. Hartley denies
that Capt. Kenner's horse won the race because he cheated, and so he refused
to pay the agreed upon amount.

The jury sided with the Kenners and John Hartley was ordered to pay the
20 shillings sterling and 1154 pounds of tobacco.[68b]

Cople was thirty-six years old and well established as the Seventeenth
Century drew to a close.

In 1700 the parishioners were settling into a routine of life fashioned after
the English country system most of them had left behind. Since Mr. Bolton's
death in 1697, services had been read by James Breechlin, Clerk.

Mr. Breechlin, according to H. Ragland Eubank's WPA record, conducted
a school in the Parish in 1701.[69] Tutors from Scotland and England were hired
by certain families to teach their children and very often these teachers were
employed as Clerks for the Parish.

1702 proved to be a very important year in the life of the Parish as well as
the Colony of Virginia and England. Queen Anne ascended the throne; Mr.
Breechlin sailed for England to receive Holy Orders;[69a] Mr. Robert Hore is

---

68. Westmoreland County Order Book, Nov. 1, 1694.
68a. Ibid, August 29, 1694, p. 154a.
68b. Ibid, Oct. 31, 1694, p. 154a.
69. Helen Crabbe Tayloe Research notes, Westmoreland County Records 1698–1705, p. 174b.
69a. Ibid.

now "Clerk of Cople Parish Church;"[69b] Colonel Isaac Allerton died in December and left in his will a gift to "Cople Parish Church of 10 lbs. sterling for ornament for the said Church,"[70] and The Rev. Samuel Gray became the third rector of the Parish.

The parishes in Virginia "had the right to select the ministers whom they desired to serve as rectors of their parishes;"[71] therefore, in 1702 Cople vestry selected The Rev. Samuel Gray, late of Christ Church, Middlesex County. He was recommended for the position by his former vestrymen and justices of Middlesex County. A petition to His Excellency Francis Nicholson, Esq. from Cople Vestry meeting held March 17, 1702/3 read as follows:

"We the Subscribers Vestrymen of Copley Parish in the County of Westmoreland being destitute of a Minister and having the bearer Samuel Gray, Clerk, well recommended to us by many worthy Gent. of the County where he has lived several years, are willing with your Excellency's leave to entertain him as our minister for the ensuing year as hath been usual ever since we were a parish.

> Your Excys most humble servants: Jno. Gerrard, James Westcomb,
> Michell Willington
> Gerard Hutt, Jno. Bushwood (rod?), W. Allerton, Robert Barrett
> Richard Lee, Fra. Wright, Jno. Sturman

At a vestry held in & for the sd parish March ye 17th. 1702/3[72]

Thus did Samuel Gray become the third rector of Cople Parish. During his rectorship the Parish was very active. Both the second Nomini Church and the second Yeocomico Church were erected.

When Mr. Gray arrived he found Nomini Church on the west bank of Nomini Creek now over forty years old and in much need of repair. Yeocomico Church built circa 1655 was in the same condition. Quite a stir was caused by the Vestry when they were presented a gift of one acre of land on the east bank of Nomini Creek from Youell Watkins on which to build a new church. The original Chapel of Ease would be replaced by a new structure which would be erected on the right cliff above the ferry landing. Mr. Watkins stipulated that it be built over the graves of his ancestors and grandfather, Thomas Youell.[73] There was some opposition to moving the church site. Henry Ashton, a member of the Vestry at this time, and his

---

69b. Westmoreland County Order Book 1690–1698, p. 40.
70. Westmoreland County Deed Book 3, p. 115.
71. *Virginia's Mother Church*, p. 517
72. *Virginia Magazine of History and Biography*, Vol. 24, p. 151, from original Council papers 1698–1702 "regard to the Rev. Samuel Gray."
73. Westmoreland County Will Book 3, pp. 168–169.

brother Charles, were opposed to the plan. They lived at Nomini Plantation on the west side of Nomini River. Both Henry and Charles were Burgesses from Westmoreland County, and on April 10, 1702/3, they presented the following petition to the House of Burgesses and Council of Colonial Virginia:

"The petition from the parish of Copeley in the County of Westmoreland being read, Resolved, That a Church for ye parish of Copeley in ye County of Westmoreland ought to be kept and maintained on the West side Nomini River in the same place where it hath stood for the space of about fourty years past.

Resolved that the proceeding of the Vestry in ye Parish of Copeley in the County of Westmoreland in order to the building a Church on ye East side of Nomini River in a place where no Church was ever before built, are illegal and void. Ordered that the said petition with ye Resolves of ye House thereon ordered be carried back to ye Council by the Burgesses of the said County of Westmoreland.

A message from the Council by Mr. Robertson

By ye Council"

Present
His Excellency, Edm. Jennings, Matthew Page, Benj. Harrison, James Blair, Philip Ludwell, Wm. Bassett and Henry Duke, Esq. Ordered:
That the Clk of Gen. Assembly carry the following message to the house of Burgesses:
By the Council
Mr. Speaker & Gent. of the House of Burgesses:
A message to the Council by Mr. Charles Ashton & Mr. Henry Ashton who brought the Resolves of the house of Burgesses on the petition of the inhabitants of Cople Parish to which they desired their Hon. Concurrence.
And the Resolves were read & assented to by the Council.
Ordered
That the Clk of ye Ge. Assembly carry the said Resolves to the House of Burg. & acq (sic) them that ye Council have assented thereto.
A message from the Burg.[esses] to the Council by Mr. Miles Cary & others who brought the following Resolves in answer to their hon. message of this day
By the House of Burgesses"[74]

However, on August 25, 1703, Henry Ashton and James Westcomb, Churchwarden of Cople Parish, accepted the gift on behalf of the parishioners of the Parish and as a result, and, in spite of the controversy, the second Nomini Church was erected on the eastern side of the river and the Cople parishioners have worshiped at this site for almost 300 years.

In this period at the "other" end of the Parish, *Henings Statutes* tells us that

---

74. Journal of the House of Burgesses 1702–1712, ed. H. R. McIlwaine, p. 34.

Nomini Episcopal Church.

in 1706 Kinsale town was founded by Act of Association."[75] It has remained the only town in a predominately rural community.

At Tucker Hill, meanwhile, masons were putting the finishing touches on the new Yeocomico Church, signed with their initials molded into the brick work under the round east window. The date 1706, also molded in brick just under the roof line and to the right of the small door leading to the chancel on the southeast side, leaves no question as to when the brickwork was completed. Above the entrance to the quaint porch on the southwest side, there is an ornamental thistle flanked by an "S" on the left and an "m" on the right and topped by a "G". Many have conjectured regarding the representation of these symbols. The truth is that one story is as good as another. We do know for a fact that the Wicket Gate in the door leading from the porch to the main entrance of the Church was a door used in the earlier building and is said to be the only original one of its kind in the country.

For a technical description of the construction of Yeocomico Church one can find several scholarly articles. Harden deV. Pratt, in Vol. IV and V of

The Northern Neck Historical Magazine,[76] gives a detailed account, as does the late Harry Lee Arnest III, a member of Cople Parish all of his short life and a graduate of the University of Virginia School of Historical Architecture, and Alice Preston Moore, his wife, in their research entitled "A Survey of Period Architecture."[77]

Not only were the parishioners building churches and organizing towns in 1706, they were opening and clearing the highways throughout the area. The Courts were ordered by the General Assembly to name surveyors for the several precincts in each parish, and through the records in the court house, we have a clear picture of the boundaries of the Parish at that date. They show that the following men were appointed for the precincts in Cople Parish November 27, 1706:

John Chilton named surveyor of highways beginning at Washington's Run down to Nomini Ferry and back from thence by Mr. John Sturman's up the Court House road and all other usual roads within that precinct.

William Haslergigg to be surveyor for the roads leading from Nomini Ferry

Yeocomico Church built 1706.

76. *Northern Neck of Virginia Historical Magazine,* Vol. IV, pp. 299–230 and Vol. V, pp. 407–408.
77. *Westmoreland County, Virginia,* 1653–1983, ed. W. B. Norris, pp. 302–305.

to the white oak and Mill Cross road to Nomini Mill and usual roads within that precinct.

John Wright Smith is appointed for that precinct of Cople Parish from Jacob Ranyes Run down the main road by the two mills so far as the white oak with the crossroad striking out of the main road beyond John Gladdin's toward Yeocomico Church together with Nomini forest and river.

William Chandler was named for the precinct leading from Sandy Valley by Nomini and Machodoc Necks and all the usual roads within the said necks.

Thomas Newton for the precinct leading from the white oak by Col. Lee's down to Tucker's Run, and also from the said white oak down the county to Flint's Mill and all usual roads within the precinct.

Mr. Vincent Cox was appointed for the precinct beginning at Tucker's Run leading into Yeocomico Neck and all the usual roads within the said neck leading from thence into the main road down to Flint's Mill and all other accustomed roads within the precinct.

Thomas Walker Wheelwright was appointed from Yeocomico Forest precinct to the main road leading from Mr. John Middleton, dec. toward Rappahannock Ferry so far as the bounds of the County extends and all the usual and necessary roads in the said precinct.[78]

During this period it was the duty of the Court, according to Eubank's notes, to appoint annually a Constable for each precinct in the County of Westmoreland. In 1706 "Thomas Baker was appointed for that precinct of Copely Parish, lately served by William Chandler. James Thomas was appointed for that precinct of Copley Parish where Charnock Cox lately officiated."[79] The newly appointed Constables were then directed to "forthwith repair to some of her Majesties justices . . . hereby required to administer the oath appointed by law for the due execution of his said office."[80]

On May 28, 1707, the Court, in accordance with the act of the General Assembly, appointed to take the "list of tythables for the present year" the following justices: Henry Ashton, gent. for Cople Parish upper precinct; George Eskridge, gent. for the lower precinct of Cople Parish.[81]

Another member of Cople Parish was named to an important county job at this time. The Court House was in need of much attention and on "March 28, 1707, the Justices of the County agreed with John Garner of the Parish of Cople to build, or cause to be built, a good substantial English frame house,

78. Westmoreland County Order Book 1705–1721, p. 42. Researched by Mrs. Helen Crabbe Tayloe.
79. Ibid, p. 42.
80. Ibid.
81. Westmoreland County Order Book 1705–1721, p. 56.

the wall to be of brick twelve feet high from the floor to the plat with brick gable ended and brick porch, etc."[82] Is it possible John Garner was involved in the building of Yeocomico Church and his reputation noticed by her Majesties Justices?

In 1708 Cople Parish was once again without a rector. Mr. Gray notified the parishioners that he and his wife were leaving for England and he wished to "outcry" his estate for sale April 4, 1708.[83] He died in St. Peter's Parish, New Kent, in 1709.[84] Mr. Gray will always be remembered as the leader of the Parish when the second Nomini Church and second Yeocomico Church were built. Mr. Gray may also have had a severe illness while in the Parish, for on Feb. 1, 1704, Dr. Alexander Spence of Spence's Point in Cople Parish declared against him for one thousand, five hundred pounds of "Tobo. due for physick visits and attendance."[84a] There is also a record of Daniel McCarty being empowered as Mr. Gray's Attorney.

The fourth rector of Cople, The Rev. James Breechlin, was no stranger to the Parish, having acted as Clerk from 1699 to 1702. In 1704 he returned from England where he had been ordained and was rector of St. Paul's Parish, New Kent County (Hanover County after 1702) and, according to Mr. Eubank's notes, came to Cople from Sittenbourne Parish in 1709.

Mr. Breechlin was very popular among his parishioners during his second stay in the Parish and was associated with Col. Thomas Lee in several property transactions on the upper Potomac and upper Rappahannock. Col. Lee was agent for the proprietors of the Northern Neck. He was living at "Machodoc" at this time and encouraged Mr. Breechlin to take up land in the unsettled piedmont sections of the proprietary. Many land deals are recorded in the County records in which Mr. Breechlin was either the seller or purchaser. He lived at The Glebe with his second wife, Sarah, sister of Thomas Sorrell, who was Clerk of the County Court. There is no record of his first wife. Francis Spencer of Secretary's Point, son of Colonel Nicholas Spencer, dec., left in his will "two suits of clothes to my neighbor, the Rev. James Breechlin."[85]

Another gift to the Parish was recorded in the Court Records. "At a Court held for the County the 28th day of Sept. 1709, William Harper's last will and testament was proved by oath of John Baker and Elizabeth Rice, two of the witnesses thereto and probate granted executors therein named. Thomas

82. *Westmoreland County History*, p. 116. Research of Mrs. Virginia Sherman.
83. Westmoreland County Order Book 1705–1721, p. 113.
84. St. Peter's Parish Register and Vestry Book, New Kent County, May 19, 1709.
84a. Westmoreland County Order Book, 1698–1705, p. 251, 254.
85. Westmoreland County Wills and Deeds Book 8, p. 210.

Sorrell, Clerk of the Court." A codicil to the will states "I desire that a pulpit cloth and cup be sent for to England & bestored on Yeocomico Church by my Executors."[86]

On the same page of this Record Book under the recording of Mr. Brent's will, is the indenture made the 20th day of August, 1709, between Nicholas Spencer (son of the Secretary) "of Cople in the County of Bedford in the Kingdom of England," and "Robert Carter of Rappahannock River."[87] This transaction is interesting because it records the date when Robert Carter purchased the land which was to become famous as Nominy Hall.

In 1714 Cople Parish was fifty years old. There are now 1,543 tithables in Westmoreland County. Willoughby Allerton is Justice of the Peace. John Bushrod and George Eskridge are Coroners, Willoughby Allerton and George Eskridge are Burgesses for the County and also the Tobacco Agents. Francis Wright is Sheriff. Church Wardens and Vestrymen for the years 1705 and 1714:[88] John Bushrod, Willoughby Allerton, John Chilton, Francis Wright, Henry Ashton, Willoughby Newton, John Wright, Daniel Tebbs, George Eskridge.

The second generation had taken over and the Parish was in good hands.

BIBLIOGRAPHY

Brydon, G. Maclaren, D. D. *Virginia's Mother Church and the Political Conditions Under Which it Grew.* Philadelphia: Church Historical Society, 1952.

Eaton, David W. *Historical Atlas of Westmoreland County, Virginia.* Richmond: Dietz Press, 1942.

Fothergill, Augusta B. *Wills of Westmoreland County, Virginia 1654–1800.* Appeals Press, 1925.

Hawks, Francis L. *Contributions to the Ecclesiastical History of the United States of America.* New York: Harper and Brothers, 1836.

Hening, William Waller. *The Statutes at Large:* being a collection of all the Laws of Virginia from the First Session of the Legislature in the year 1619. Richmond: Franklin Press, 1820.

Institutional History of Virginia in the 17th Century. New York: G. P. Putnam's Sons, 1910.

Journal of the House of Burgesses of Virginia 1702–1712. Edited by H. R. McIlwaine, Richmond, 1912.

---

86. Ibid, p. 228, 1709.
87. Ibid, p. 231.
88. Westmoreland County Order Book, 1705–1721, p. 203.

Lee, Edward Jennings. *The Lees of Virginia: 1642–1892*. Baltimore: Baltimore Genealogical Publishing Co., 1983.

Legislative Journals of the Council of Colonial Virginia. Edited by H. R. McIlwaine. Richmond, 1918.

Northern Neck of Virginia Historical Magazine 1951–1989. Richmond: Dietz Press.

Northumberland County Order Book, Courthouse, Heathsville.

Northumberland County Patent Book. Courthouse, Heathsville.

Tayloe, Helen Crabbe. Unpublished research for H. Ragland Eubank with W.P.A. Writers Project 1935–41. Northern Neck Museum Library, Montross.

Virginia Magazine of History and Biography. Richmond: Virginia Historical Society.

Westmoreland County, Virginia 1653–1983. Edited by W. B. Norris, Jr. Montross: 1983.

Westmoreland County Deeds and Patent Books. Courthouse, Montross.

Westmoreland County Order Books. Courthouse, Montross.

Westmoreland County Records. Abstracted and Compiled by J. F. Dorman. Washington, D.C.: Westmoreland County Records 1973.

Westmoreland County Records, Wills and Deeds. Courthouse, Montross.

William and Mary Quarterly Historical Magazine, Vol. XVI. Richmond: Whittet & Shepperson, 1908.

Yeocomico Church

Edward White Photographs
Kinsale-Va. 1999

THE LIFE OF COPLE PARISH, 1709–1764

by BERTHA LAWRENCE NEWTON DAVISON*

1709–1722

The first fifty years of Cople Parish were explored in the 1990 Vol. of the Northern Neck Historical Magazine which leads to the following article on the next fifty years 1714–1764. However, we will begin with 1709.

Westmoreland County Court Records abound in material concerning Cople Parish which is fortunate since all the Church records of the Parish from 1664 to 1849 were lost in the fire which burned the rectory in 1913. Wills, inventories and other legal documents help unfold the story and also keep the record straight.

The fourth rector of Cople Parish, the Reverend James Breechin, was no stranger to the area having as previously noted, lived here and acted as clerk and tutor from 1699 to 1702 before going to England to receive his ordination to the Priesthood. When he returned in 1704 he was rector of St. Paul's Parish, New Kent County and came to Cople in 1709 from Sittenbourn Parish, in Essex County.[1] He had a long and interesting ministry according to the records relating to him and the parish which are found in the Westmoreland County Clerk's office, Montross, Virginia.

Mr. Breechin seems to have been very popular with his parishioners during his second stay and was closely associated with Col. Thomas Lee. In 1715 he patented a 795 acre tract of land at the falls of the Potomac in what is now Fairfax County.[2] Apparently he was a good businessman.

Mr. Breechin was married to Sarah Sorrel, sister to Thomas Sorrel, Clerk of the Westmoreland County Court. She was his second wife. There seems to be no record of his first wife except to note in his will her name "Ann". There were two sons, William and James, and two daughters, Anna and Jane, all by his second wife.[3]

Queen Anne was on the throne of England when Mr. Breechin came to Cople Parish. After a happy relationship with her subjects, in regard to church affairs,* she died in 1712 and George I succeeded her.

---

*This is the second in a series of articles about this historic parish. See Vol. XL, p. 4578–4612.
1. Research papers of H. Ragland Eubank and Mrs. Helen Tayloe, Westmoreland County Museum, Montross, Virginia.
2. Ibid.
3. Will of James Breechin, *Extracts of Wills of Westmoreland County, Virginia*, Augusta B. Forthergill, Appeals Press 1925 taken from West. Co. Wills Vol. 11 Oct. 1721. Pro. 6 April 1722.
*Queen Anne's gifts of Silver Plate to Churches of Colony.

During this period when church attendance was compulsory, services were read from the Book of Common Prayer which included the recital of the ten Commandments prominently displayed on the walls of the church beside the Holy Table, just in case you did not have your own Prayer Book or did not know these basic tenets of the Christian Religion. Also, there were readings from both the Old and New Testaments each Sunday. Prayers for the whole state of Christ's Church were recited, and one would wonder why this did not have more influence on the inhabitants of Cople Parish; but human nature being what it is, all the problems connected with society flourished in this seemingly quiet part of the world. It is amazing how easily the early parishioners settled into the old country ways. The only difference was that one did not have to be born to high office; if you were clever, alert, responsible, honest and in the right place you were recognized and could aspire to any office. Indentured servants, slaves, and women were naturally excluded.

June 30, 1709, "Daniel Tebbs is appointed Surveyor of the highway in that precinct where Thomas Newton lately served and also for the road that leads from the white oak by Robert Hores to the swamp commonly called Turks swamp and it is ordered he immediately cause all roads aforesaid to be well and sufficiently repaired and amended according to Law."[4]

It seems there was a great deal of activity around the parish churches both inside and out that kept the sheriff and wardens busy. There were several instances of arrests for swearing in the churchyard which were dismissed. Many interesting items appear in the county court records in regard to church attendance, or lack of it, and punishment for nonconformity to the accepted practice of worshiping the "Lord every Sunday in His church." To the vestry of Cople Parish this meant either Nomini or Yeocomico. In 1712 one such item in the county clerk's office states: "Jan. 28, 1712, Robert Ball* being presented by the grand jury for not going to his parish church according to law, his attn. appeared who alleged that the said Ball was a Quaker and to his knowledge did frequent meetings. Whereupon the said presentment was dismissed".[4a]

In 1717 nine persons were presented to the Westmoreland County Court on the charge of "convening under the pretence of divine worship with divers

---

4. *WCR Orders*, 1705–1721, page 126.
*Robert Ball lived at Water View, according to *Eubank's Guide* it was "just above Sandy Point in Yeocomico Neck. It was washed away in the storm of 1933.
4a. *West. Co. Orders*, Jan. 1712, page 282. Please read Chap. 17. *Virginia's Mother Church* by G. Maclaren Brydon D.D. Vol. 1., Copyright 1947, Virginia Historical Society, printed in U.S.A. Whittet & Shepperson, Richmond, Virginia.

others in concenticles contrary and repugnant to law". They were presented at Yeocomico Church on next Lord's Day to acknowledge their wrong doing at the divine service in the following words, "I do acknowledge and confess before God and in the presence of this congregation that I have been guilty of convening and meeting in unlawful assemblies, and and I do so humbly ask God and this congregation's forgiveness of my offense therein, and do also promise never to commit the like again".[5]

It had taken a while for the powers that be to carry out the intent of the Act of Toleration in the remote areas of the colony. Dr. Brydon explains in his chapter, "The Effects of the Toleration Acts in Virginia," what happened in Cople Parish after this ordeal took place:

"Three years later members of the same group were again presented upon the same charge by the grand jury, but, when the case came to trial, appeal was made to the General Court, (in Williamsburg) and no further record of it appeared in the Westmoreland Court. One might also hazard a guess that the action of the court of the remote county of Westmoreland in 1717, in punishing a group of non-conformists contrary to the established policy of the colonial government, occurred without the knowledge of the authorities in Williamsburg. When appeal was made to the council upon the event of the second presentment, somebody in authority read the riot act to the honorable justices of the Peace of Westmoreland."[5a]

The Great Awakening came into being at this period. A very wonderful account of this spiritual renewal within the Christian Church was written by Dr. Brydon, and should be read by all who want to have a clear and Christian approach to just what did take place within the colonies in the name of religion*. Praise the Lord for the understanding and fellowship which exists between the different denominations in Cople Parish today!

It is sad to read the many lists of court cases in the Westmoreland County Records of that time in history detailing the many cases of "Base Born" Children and their mothers, the majority of whom were indentured servants. The church wardens were responsible for the care and support of these children if their rightful parents did not assume this responsibility. The courts were busy trying to collect fines from those who were responsible and the money was used for the support of the children. Stiff sentences were given in many cases; however, this did not seem to stop the offense of bearing unwanted babies and did as much good then as it does now.

---

5. Ibid: Page 257.
5a. Ibid.

"On July 27, 1715, William Perry was bound over to the Court to appear and answer for his misbehavior in Cople Parish Church at Nomini. He alleged that he had acted 'nothing for which he ought to be accused . . .' and thereupon they dismissed the case".[6]

The rector lived at the Glebe and the Spencers lived at Secretary Point. The Ashtons still lived at Nominy Plantation and all were active in the parish. John Bushrod lived at Bushfield. The Wrights still owned Cabin Point. Richard Lee II died in 1715, and his sons inherited the Machodoc property. When Richard Lee III died in 1718, Thomas and Henry became the owners of these acres. Henry lived at Lee Hall which was built about 1720, and Thomas and his family lived at "Machodoc" on upper Machodoc Greek where his father had lived . . . Col Thomas Lee's Land Office was close by on Lee Creek, a branch of Machodoc Creek where the Customs House was located. Col. Lee had succeeded his father as naval officer and collector of customs.[7]

A beautiful tribute to Col. Richard Lee II is quoted by Gov. Spotswood, July 26, 1712: "I shall only desire leave to joine with the Collo. Quary in a letter I have seen of his in behalf of Collo. Richard Lee, sometimes Collector of North Potomack, He is a Gentleman of as fair character as any in the County for his exact justice, honesty and unexceptionable Loyalty in all the Stations wherein he has served in this Government, he has behaved himself with great integrity and sufficiency, and when his advanced age would no longer permit him to execute to his own satisfaction the duty of Naval Officer to the same District, I thought I could not better reward his merit than by bestowing that employment on his son."[7a]

The Hague neighborhood was a busy center of activity. The Kings Highway wound its way up the ridge of the Northern Neck and little hamlets began to develop along this road which pushed its way through the forest paths to make way for the carriages of "King" Carter's agents as they inspected the Fairfax holdings. It was about this time Col. Thomas Lee purchased a tract of land from Nathaniel Pope called the "Cliffs" about 20 miles up the Potomac from Machodoc.

The Eskridge family acquired Wilton plantation in 1717. Elba was the home of the Cox family. Wilmington, near Tucker Hill was the home of Mrs. Rose Tucker Gerrard Newton, widow of John Newton. When she died in 1712 she left her property to her son Thomas Newton who was Sheriff of Westmoreland. Willoughby Allerton lived on his plantation, The Narrows,

---

6. *Westmoreland County Orders* 1705–1722.
7. *Eubank's Historic Northern Neck of Virginia.*
7a. *Letter's of Governor Spotswood*, July 26, 1712. Collection of Virginia Historical Society.

on the east side of Machodoc Creek. The Bailey family lived at Kinsale in the Great House.[8]

John Bushrod died in 1719 and was buried in the garden at Bushfield. The grave stone is still there with several other grave stones which have been cared for carefully through the years.

The Wright family burial ground at Cabin Point was protected by law on the books in Westmoreland County Clerk's office according to Charles Hoppin. He states "Under the laws of Virginia this burial ground of the Wright family could not be sold by any Wright when selling land surrounding it."[9] This grave yard has not survived.

It is interesting to discover the name Dorothy was very popular for daughters in this period. Charles Hoppin made an exhaustive search to locate the identity of John Wright's wife, Dorothy, because he says "this was due to the prevalence in the Northern Neck of Virginia of women named Dorothy. Seventeen Dorothys of marriageable age appear in the records (circa 1705). The surnames of these Dorothys were Randsom, Gatewood, Smith, Gouldman, Armstrong, Henry, Riply, Dudley, Baughan, Durham, Strother, McClanan, Abbot and Awbrey. The last name, Dorothy Awbrey, by process of elimination, proves to be the wife of John Wright". It seems the Awbreys lived on the Machodoc River not far from the Wrights, and both families moved to what is now Prince William County in 1723.[9a] However the name Dorothy was not as prominent as Elizabeth and Mary which occur most often in the record books along with a few Sarah's, Anne's, Frances, Jane's and others. The most unusual girls name at this period was John Bushrod's daughter, Apphia, named in his will March 1720. She was Mrs. Fauntleroy.[10]

In the Will Books of the County are listed many families who were parishioners of Mr. Breechin. Some of them are as follows:

John Garner made his will in 1712 and it was probated in 1713. He left land in Ragged Point and Horn Harbor to his son Abraham and other bequest are made to his sons Joseph, John and Jeremiah. He also refers to his "old Mill at Blice's".

John Wright, blacksmith, of Cople Parish (not the "Cabin Point" Wright), left in his will, Jan. 1713, the best of "my smith's tools and largest anvil to son John" He names Anna, daughter of Elizabeth and Thomas Sorrell, in his list of bequests. He must have been closely associated with Mr. Breechin since his wife was a Sorrell.

8. *Westmoreland County, Virginia*, page 17.
9. Charles Arthur Hoppin. *Ancestors of George Washington Vol. 1* page 368. E. F. Grover Co. 1923.
9a. Ibid.
10. *Wills of Westmoreland County, Virginia* 1654–1800 by Fothergill, Appeals Press 1925.

Thomas Bonum died Jan. 1717. In his will he leaves a horse to Capt. Eskridge. His late wife's jewelry to Sarah Baker, consisting of a pearl necklace, an amber necklace and locket.

Roger Wiggington wrote his will Mar. 3, 1717, and it was probated 14 of Aug. 1718. Willoughby Allerton is named Executor. (Can we assume they were close neighbors?) He left his shoe buckles to son Roger; to son William "my watch"; daughters Elizabeth and Ann Wiggington 1 negro each; son Henry 1 negro, feather bed and furniture, to sons William and Roger, 1 negro each.

Richard Kennor's will was dated Jan. 1719. He left to son Winder Kenner "land where I live to the land where Mr. William Chandler now lives."

John Bushrod's will was dated 1719 and probated on Mar. 30. 1720. He left his wife Hannah the Plantation "whereon I now live" and other bequests referred to previously.

Osman Crabb's will was dated 1719. He left land in Nominy to sons Osman and Gerrard.

Francis Spencer of "Cople, gent." left 10,000 lbs of tobacco to "my bro. John's daughter Frances Spencer; to Rev. James Breechin 2 suits of clothes; friend Daniel McCarty residue of estate after 1 negro Sam to George Eskridge Jr.[11]

The will of Patrick Spence of Copeley (Cople) Parish, Westmoreland County, Virginia, who had moved to "Arlington," Dorset, England was proved in England May 4, 1710, by Daniel Gundry. "Debts to be paid and to be buried at the discretion of loving friend Daniel Gundry of Arlington, merchant. To my cousin Patrick Spence, son of my late uncle Patrick Spence, my practice of law in the forest near Westmoreland County Court House in Virginia, and my two slaves called Aggedy and Bess and my gold seal ring to my sister Mary Spence; all my land lying near Potomac River in Westmoreland County to my cousin Rose Neele, daughter of my late sister Dorcas Neele, 50 lbs, to be paid when she is 16 or married. To my cousin Robert Mason, son of my late sister Elizabeth Mason, 50 lbs, when he is 16, To my cousin Thomas Spence, son of my late uncle Patrick Spence, 10,000 lbs. of tobacco. My slave mulatto Tom to be freed. To Daniel Gundry all my clothes and things at Arlington, my best horse or 10 lbs. in lieu. To Captain George Eskridge of Virginia all my law books and my silver watch which he now has.

11. Ibid.

Residue of my real and personal estate in Britain and Virginia to my sister Mary Spence."[11a]

Legend says Alexander Spence befriended George Eskridge when he came to the colonies as a young boy. When he was old enough, he sent him to England to school and to study law. The faith in the ability of the young fellow was not misplaced for it is on record Eskridge became a leading citizen, an able lawyer, and served as vestryman and churchwarden many years.

In 1714 George Eskridge and Willoughby Allerton represented Westmoreland County in the House of Burgesses. Daniel McCarty and Willoughby Allerton seem to trade the positions of Sheriff and Burgess back and forth. Justices from Cople Parish at this time in the County were Henry Ashton, John Bushrod, George Eskridge, Daniel McCarty, Thomas Bonum, John Chilton, James Bayley (Bailey?) and Willoughby Allerton. George Eskridge and Willoughby Allerton also served as Coroner and Tobacco Inspector. Henry Ashton served often as Sheriff and Burgess. Daniel McCarty was the Speaker of the House of Burgesses 1715–1718. In 1720 Thomas Lee is listed as a member of the House of Burgesses and Henry Lee was Sheriff. A list of members of Cople Parish Vestry and Church Wardens for this period can be found in Westmoreland County, Virginia History.[12]

George Eskridge served as Governor of the Potomac District Tobacco Agents in 1714, as Queen's Attorney, then King's Attorney, during Mr. Breechin's rectorship and was well known and respected throughout the Colony.[12a]

The Journal of John Fontaine sheds a good light on the life in Cople Parish in 1715–1717. He tells of setting sail from Cork, Ireland, November 1714 to buy land for his family in Virginia. He took four indentured servants "for in Virginia such servants sold well and he could claim 50 acres of land for each person he imported, including himself". On board the *Dove of Bideford*, he took linens, frieze cloth, shoes, ironwork, stationery, Bibles and prayer books. This craft, captained by William Shipley, was a one-hundred-ton, square-

---

11a. *Genealogical Gleanings in England,* by Peter Wilson Coldham, page 209, National Genealogical Society Quarterly, Sept. 1974. Mr. George H. S. King, F.A.S.G. late of Fredericksburg added the following note: "An only son, Patrick, was aged 19 in 1704 when his father Captain Alexander Spence died testate in Westmoreland County. Papers in the subsequent suite allege that he was incapable to bequeath his landed estate. The husbands of Patrick's three sisters passed the entire matter over to Hon. Richard Carter for arbitration in 1712 at which time Patrick had only one sister living, Mary Spence a minor, and two sisters dead: Elizabeth, wife of Matthew Mason of Maryland, and Dorcas, wife of Richard Neale. Mason and Neale were allotted portions for their children by their Spence wives. Soon afterwards Mary Spence married Charles Lee of Cobbs Hall, Northumberland County, Virginia, where the entire business was to be recorded in Northumberland County Record Book 5 (1718–1713) 319".

12. *Westmoreland County History,* pages 675–680.

12a. *Northern Neck of Virginia Historical Society,* Vol. XVI, p. 1451–1467.

stern vessel, that carried four guns. It had been built in Virginia though she was registered in Bideford, England, and was in the habit of shuttling back and forth "between Potomac and Bideford" carrying tobacco one way and mixed cargoes of textiles, iron, and other needed supplies back to the colonies. There were close commercial connections between Bideford and Barnstable, England, with Maryland and Virginia.[13] Fontaine had quite an eventful beginning. A dreadful storm damaged the ship so badly it had to return to Bideford January 23, 1715. After making repairs, the second journey was begun on February 28, 1715, and on May 26, three months later, Mr. Fontaine came safely to the Virginia Capes. The *Dove* sailed up the Chesapeake Bay to the Potomac River, I will quote the diary:

"May 28, 1715. Saturday.

"In morning about 10 of the clock I landed in Virginia and walked about four miles to the collector, one Mr. McCartney (Daniel McCarty), to land my things which cost me an English crown. I enquired if my men would do well there, but found no encouragement. A guinea passes for 26 shillings and all foreign coins go by weight. An ounce of silver passes for 6/3; and four pennyweight gold for 20 shillings.

"May 29, 1715. Sunday. About 8 of the clock we came ashore and went to church which is about four miles from the place we landed. The day was very hot and roads dusty. We got to church, but came a little late. We had part of the sermon. The people seemed to me very pale and yellow.* After the minister had made an end, every one of the men pulled out their pipes and smoked a pipe of tobacco. I informed myself further about my own business, but found that Williamsburg was the only place for my design. I was invited to dinner by one Mrs. Hughes.† She lent me a horse and the master of the ship another and we went to her house where we dined, after which we went on board. I am resolved to hire a sloop and go to Williamsburg.

"May 30, 1715. Monday. In the morning I went to one Captain Eskridge and bargained with him for a shallop to go to Williamsburg. I am to give him 5 lbs. for the hire of her and to maintain my people. I went with the sloop on board and loaded my goods on her and made all things ready for this second voyage. I lay on board the ship where we had several planters that got drunk that night.

"May 31, 1715. Tuesday. Virginia. This morning Captain Eskridge came

---

13. Extracts from "The Journal of John Fontaine" 1710–1719, page 10. Edited by Edward Porter Alexander for the Colonial Williamsburg Foundation.
*Malaria was rampant at the time in Cople Parish due to the climate.
†Is it possible the "Mrs. Hughes" referred to was Mrs. "Hewes," the mother of Mary Ball? Mrs. Hewes was living in the area across Hampton Hall Creek at Cherry Point, Northumberland County.

on board our ship and I agreed to pay him his 5 lbs. in goods at 50 pr.cent. I gave him:

1 piece of linen containing 20 yards	L3	6	8
Eight pair shoes at 4/ a pair	1	12	0
One pair gloves I gave him	0	1	4
	L5	0	0"[14]

M r. Fontaine then set sail for Williamsburg "via Chesapeake Bay up York River and Queen's Creek."

The next record we have of Mr. Fontaine visiting Cople Parish tells us: "I received a letter from Mr. Matthew Maury that he was at Captain Eskridge's house with his goods where he would wait for me". He then describes his uncomfortable trip overland. He reached "Bowler's, his ferry" on the Rappahannock March 29, 1718. He crossed the river and at seven came to Capt. Eskridge's house to find Mr. Maury had left. Because he was very sick he remained with Eskridges for three days getting his strength back for the arduous journey home. "On April 11 I mounted my horse and this day came as far as Mr. Naylor's house where I lay". April 2 he crossed the river in a small boat and "was in danger of being drowned" and spent the night at Mr. Baylor's. The next day he went home* and noted in his diary "I made going and coming 135 miles".[16]

There is a "Blackbeard Pond" near the Potomac River west of "Ragged Point". So named, the legend goes, because Edward Teach, the dreaded pirate "Blackbeard", came up the Potomac wreaking havoc on the shipping in the area and buried a treasure along our banks. This fascinating tale is just a story teller's yarn according to those who have investigated this bit of Virginiana thoroughly.[17] Too bad! However it is certainly true Blackbeard was making raids on shipping and vessels off the Virginia Capes at this time. No doubt sailing from the York, up the Bay, and into the Potomac to Yeocomico River and Sandy Point would have been hazardous. I suggest this is the reason Mr. Fontaine risked the tortuous journey via land from Williamsburg across the several peninsulas that separate the Northern Neck from south side, rather then have a meeting with Teach.

---

14. Ibid page 81.
15. Ibid page 82.
*"Home" was between Williamsburg and West Point as far as I have been able to determine.
16. Ibid. page 124. Farewell to Virginia.
17. *Westmoreland County History*, page 58.

In 1720 an addition was built on the Glebe house to accommodate Mr. and Mrs. Breechin's growing family, one would suspect.[18]

There have been references in several places of a marriage said to have been performed by The Rev. Mr. James "Brichen" (Breechin?) at Yeocomico Church in 1720 and said to have been recorded in the Northumberland County Clerk's Office in Heathsville, Virginia.[19] So far I have not been able to find the record Book referred to. But if this marriage actually took place, then one can imagine several of the guests at this wedding might have stopped to check the time on the sundial which stands on the side of the walk leading to the entrance of the church. The inscription on the sundial is "Philip Smith 1717." So far I have not been able to unlock the mystery of the sundial or of a Philip Smith having been associated with the parish circa 1717.

When Parishioners gathered outside after services at Yeocomico during Mr. Breechin's rectorship, they probably read the inscription on the old stone with the names of Peter Moon and John Cogger, which legend says was placed here as a memorial to the builders of the church and is still standing, although very worn with age, just to the right and a little south of the right hand corner of the church.[20]

At the General Assembly held in the Capital in Williamsburg, Nov. 2, 1720, there was passed an "Act for settling new ferries on the Pamunky, Mattapony, and Potomack rivers and for ascertaining the rates of Ferriage for Wheel-Carriages." Hening reports:

" I. Whereas a good regulation of ferries within this his Majesty's colony and dominion of Virginia, hath been found very beneficial and useful for the dispatch of public affairs and for the ease and benefit of travellers, and men in business; but by reason of the increase of settlements, and otherwise, the ferries already appointed by law, are not sufficient to answer the ends aforesaid: For remedy whereof, and for the better transportation of goods and merchandize.
II. Be it enacted buy the Lieutenant-Governor, Council, and Burgesses, of this present General Assembly and it is hereby enacted by authority of the same, that ferries be constantly kept at the places hereafter named; and that the rates for passing the said ferries, and transportation of the said goods and merchandize be as follow, that is to say:
        "On Potowmack River,
From Colonel Rice Hoe's, to Cedar Point, in Maryland, the price for a man, two shillings, for a horse, two shillings".[21]

---

18. *Eubank's The Authentic Guide Book of Historic Northern Neck of Virginia*, page 47.
19. Eubank's papers and research of Mrs. Helen C. Tayloe.
20. "Sketch of Yeocomico Church" by Wat Tyler Mayo, Walter Randolph Crabb and S. Downing Cox, Committee of the Congregation. 1906—C. F. Sudworth, Printers, Washington, D. C.
21. William Waller Henning *Statues.*

The Act also deals with the licences and regulations of the times, etc. It is also stated that ferry keepers (within this Colony) are encouraged to provide "convenient boats, for transportation or coaches, carts and wagons."[21a] Daniel McCarty and George Eskridge were members of the House of Burgesses at this time.

In February 1722 Col. Henry Ashton's first wife died at Nominy Plantation which lies to the west of Nominy Creek in Currioman Neck and was at this time in part of Cople Parish. Mrs. Ashton's tomb has been protected by the several owners of this land over the past 269 years. The epitaph reads:

"Beneath this stone is laid the body of Elizabeth, the wife of Col. Henry Ashton and daughter of Capt. William Hardidge by Frances his wife, who for her piety to God, faithfulness, love and obedience to her husband, tenderness to her children, carefulness of her family, and charity to the poor was equalled by few, excelled by none. She had by her said husband four children, Frances, Elizabeth, Annie and Grace. The two latter only survived her. After finishing her most neighborly and Christian life, with joy she resigned her soul to God (in faith) on Monday the 25th of February in the year of our Lord, 1722, and in the 43rd year of her age. Her death was lamented by all who knew her".[22]

It would be interesting to know if Mr. Breechin read the burial office at Mrs. Ashton's funeral. He himself died in early 1722 and his will was probated April 6, 1722.[23] There is no record of where he is buried, perhaps at the Glebe; thus this is another of the many mysteries of Cople Parish.

1723–1733

"The fifth rector of Cople Parish was a Welchman, The Rev. Walter Jones, son of Hector of Llanellyn County, Carnarvon. Pleb. Jesus College, Oxford. Matriculated April 8, 1717, age 18. K.B., N. Carolina, Dec. 17, 1724".[24]

Mr. Jones was the third rector of Cople Parish to find a wife among his flock. Before August 26, 1727, he and Behethland Newton were married.[25] She was the daughter of Capt. Thomas Newton and Elizabeth Storke. It would be nice if we knew just where the parson and his bride pledged their vows, probably at her parents' home, "Wilmington," a typical colonial farm house near Tucker Hill.[26] It is logical to assume the happy pair lived at the

---

21a. Ibid.
22. *Eubank's The Authentic Guide Book of the Historic Northern Neck*, page 47.
23. *Wills and Deeds of Westmoreland County*, D.B.V11 Fothergill, page 77.
24. Research of H. Ragland Eubank and Mrs. Helen Crabb Tayloe.
25. Will of Thomas Newton, West. Co. Wills 1727, page 89.
26. Wilmington. *West. Co. Wills 1712*, page 48.

Glebe. The Jones family did not live extravagantly, judging by the inventory of Mr. Jones possessions made by order of the court to value and appraise his estate and then filed in the courthouse after his death. Among the items listed were:

Four beds, bolsters, sheets, quilts and blankets, one bed with valence curtain with sheets and quilt, "and other good furniture", one dozen flagged chairs, six leather chairs, one sofa, one oval table, two large oval tables, child's cradle and a small chair, trunk, small looking glass, old rug, one warming pan, eleven pieces of earthenware, another entry with nine pieces of earthenware, four knives and forks, four silver spoons, a spinning wheel, eleven bushels and a half of salt, one iron pot rack and three small hooks, one iron spit, eleven glass bottles, pair of fire tongs, one gridiron, two washing tubs and pail, one piggin, frying pan, brass skimmer 'and other things'. Ten good books and twenty-nine old books, two table 'cloughts' and six napkins, nine drinking glasses, a tin of candles, two glass salts, small bowl and a box with buttons. There was also listed one servant women, one girl, three negro men named Lark, Pompey, and Dink, and one negro women. On the farm land were four cows and yearlings, one cow with calf, a sow, six pigs and eight shoats, three two-year old horses, one roan horse, one black horse and one white horse, saddle and bridle, parcel of old lumber, twenty-two pieces of cherry plank, axes, spades, one set of wedges, two pounds of gun powder, a gun, one boat, an "old canoe," and cart and wheels.[27]

There is no record to tell us how large a family with which the Joneses were blessed. The fact they had a cradle and several beds indicates there were several children in the home.

Mrs. Jones had plenty to do to keep things running smoothly at the Glebe. Even with servants to help care for the house, the meat house, the garden, and the animals, the life of a housewife was not easy. One is not to forget that sewing was done by hand as well as the weaving of cloth and spinning of wool for clothes worn by everyone in the family, including the servants, black and white. Even the stockings had to be knitted. Milk had to be put in the spring to keep cool, butter had to be churned, and the many other everyday household chores.

In season the jams and jellies, pickles and preserves must be made to keep the pantry stocked. A knowledge of nursing the sick was another skill the 18th century "lady of the house" was expected to possess, and the job of caring for all the members of the plantation family during sickness fell to her

---

27. Inventory of Jones estate. *West. Inventory Books 1733, 1734–1735 Vol. I,* page 139.

lot. The herb garden was a must as medical ointments were made from many of these plants. Treating various and sundry ailments, when living in an isolated area with no doctor near, was expected of "The Mistress," and Mrs. Jones no doubt lived this type of life on the Glebe lands. There were ducks and geese in the winter and plenty of seafood for the table all year long. The deer and quail were plentiful. The rector and his family had a very pleasant place to live. We assume they traveled a great deal by boat since the Glebe lands were almost surrounded by water with the Potomac on the north and Machodoc Creek on the east. Mr. Jones very likely rode horseback as he made his rounds visiting his flock in the area. There is no mention of a coach in the inventory.

Daniel McCarty, one of the leaders of the parish and a burgess, died in 1724 and was buried in a tomb of Yeocomico Church* His extensive will tells several stories, including the fact that his son Daniel was in England receiving an education at this time under the care of Mr. John Gilpin of Whitehaven. When he returned home he was to have "all my law and gospel books". Colonel McCarty lived very near Yeocomico Church on the property he acquired by marriage. His wife, Anna, was connected to the Payne and Corbin families. He left his wife "Anna 12 slaves, use of plantation and personal property for life and use of her children". The home plantation went to Daniel at death of his mother.[28]

Thomas Sorrell was Clerk of the Court when Mr. Jones came to the parish.[29] He died in January 1726 and was succeeded in the Clerkship by another resident of Cople Parish, George Tuberville of Hickory Hill.[30] In his will Sorrell left "son James land; son John land devised me by my father-in-law Daniel Ocanny and land on Nominy where I formerly lived; son John land in James City County bequeathed me by my father, John Sorrell, deceased; nephew Thomas Sorrell land; my bro. John Sorrell of James City County deceased; said nephew and his sisters, Elizabeth and Frances, a ring each; daus. Anna and Winifred; wife Elizabeth her horse, saddle, bridle, rings, clothing, three slaves and use of my plantation for life; Geo. Turberbille and William Sturman Exrs."[31] Apparently the Sorrells came from Jamestown to the Northern Neck. It is touching to note Mr. Sorrell names his brother John even though he predeceased him. I wonder what would have happened

---

*The remains of the tomb are still there under the east window of the church.
28. *Wills of Westmoreland County, Virginia 1654–1800 by Fathergill*, page 79.
29. *Eaton's Atlas*, page 8, Clerk's Office.
30. Ibid.
31. *Wills of Westmoreland Co., Virginia by Fathergill,*, page 85.

to Mrs. Sorrell's clothes if he had not left them to her! We learn a great deal about the customs of Cople Parish in reading these old wills.

"John King's will, dated 3 December 1726, names son James and grandson John Spence; my bro's. daughter Mary; son-in-law John Spence 1 gun; Daniel son of Major George Eskridge, 1 gun; wife Margaret rest of estate." He undoubtedly lived near Sandy Point and Kings Pond which was named for him.[32]

Elias Morrice's will, dated 10, August 1726, states he is to be buried in Nominy Church yard. He leaves "wife Bridget 20 head of cattle and household furniture; godchildren Jeremiah and Elizabeth Nash; James son of Jeremiah Nash; my countryman David Williams; Exrs. my wife and Nathaniel Nash."[33] Mr. Jones probably read the burial office. We have no other record of Mr. Morrice.

Lettice Fitzhugh Turberville, second wife of Major George Turberville, a large landowner in the Northern Neck, died at "Hickory Hill" in 1732. Her husband honored her with an epitaph on her tombstone, which according to Mary Newton Stanard," was evidently the model of her sex and time." It read:

"From a child she knew the scriptures which made her wise unto Salvation: From her Infancy she Learned to walk in the Paths of Virtue. She was Beautiful But not Vain: witty But not Talkative: Her Religion was pure Fervent and of the Church of England: Her Virtue Steadfast, Easy, Natural: Her Mind had that mixture of Nobleness and Gentleness As Made Her Lovely in the Eyes of All People. She Was Marryed to Capt. George Turberville, May 16, 1727. The best of Wives Made him the Happiest of Husbands. She died the 10th of Feb. 1732, in the 25th year if her Age and 6th of her marryage. Who can express the grief. Soon Did She finish her Course of Life. Early was she Exempted from the Miseries of Human Life By God's particular Grace. Thus Doth He Deal With his perticuler Favorites.

> All that was good in women kind
> A Beauteous Form More Lovely Mind
> Lies buryed under Neath this stone
> Who Living was excelled by None."[33a]

This epitaph gives us a splendid impression, not only of the lovely young women it memorialized, but an insight into the ideals which were most

---

32. Ibid. page 86.
33. Ibid. page 86.
33a. Mary Newton Stanard, *Colonial Virginia, Its People and Customs*, Page 350. J. B. Lippncott Company, Philadelphia, Pennsylvania, 1917.

admired in that day and age. It also tells a good deal about the character of the people of Cople Parish. The graveyard at "Hickory Hill" is still well kept, but this stone has disappeared.

A Spirit of Toleration statement by Lt. Gov. Gooch in his inaugural address February 1, 1727, leads us to believe the new governor had heard rumors that all was not "peaches and cream" in the religious life of the colony. He made it his business to point out just what would be "tolerated" and what would not be acceptable. He said:

"Concerning any dissenters among you with conscience, truly scrupulous, they shall be given indulgence which is so constant with the genius of Christian Religion that it can never be inconsistent with the interest of the Church of England."[34]

On January 29, 1729, a fire burned the home of Thomas and Hannah Lee at "Machodoc." The Lees were already in the process of building a great mansion on the Clifts property purchased in 1718. When the Lees moved from the Hague area is not a matter of record; but, in the process of moving, Mrs. Lee's handsome round top wooden Chest was left behind to spend the next two hundred years in the vicinity of Hague. In the 1900's it was used as a wood box by Dr. William Fairfax's family at "La Grange." The chest is now at Stratford Hall in excellent condition.* The chest probably came to Cople Parish when Hannah Ludwell Lee arrived as a bride in 1722. In 1729, at the time of the fire, Colonel Lee was listed as Justice of the Peace and a member of the House of Burgesses and a vestryman. The old house site has been called "Burnt House Field" ever since the fire.

Col. Henry Ashton's will, dated 26 February 1730, left his large estate as follows: "to wife and daughter Grace 2200 acres of land; also land to granddaus. Elizabeth and Anne Aylett, daus. of Capt. William Aylett and Anne his wife who was my dau. deceased, 400 acres of land; granddau. Elizabeth Turbeville 800 acres of land; son Henry my pistols, sword and holster; son John; dau. Elizabeth Ashton 1000 acres of land in Stafford; Cousin Burdett Ashton 1000 acres of land in Stafford; Godson John, son of Charles Ashton decd., land in back woods on Broad Run, Stafford Co., and the other part of same tract to my sons Henry and John which lies near Col. Carter's copper mines; sister Mrs. Sarah Macgill; exrs. in trust Capt. George Turbeville, Capt. Burdett Ashton, Mr. Andrew Munroe, Mr. Richard Watts".[35]

---

34. *Journal of the House of Burgess*, Feb. 1, 1727.
*The chest is marked with the initials H.L.
35. *Wills of Westmoreland County*, page 93.

Ashton was buried on his estate Nominy Plantation by his first wife's tomb which has the Hardige coat of arms. His tomb is emblazoned with the Ashton coat of arms as is the third tomb of his daughter Frances. After 260 years these tombs stand as monuments to a faithful family of Cople parish and to the respectful way the several owners of the land have cared for these interesting relics of the seventeenth century through the ages.

The daughters of the Ashtons were Frances, who married George Turbeville of Hickory Hill; Grace, who married Richard Lee, nephew of Col. Thomas Lee; Anne, who married Col. William Aylett, whose daughter Anne married George Washington's half brother Augustine Washington, and the other daughter Elizabeth, who married Col. William Booth. Booth, after the death of Col. Aylett, became master of Nominy Plantation. This is the reason the Plantation is called "Booths" in many instances. After the death of his first wife, Col. Aylett married Elizabeth, daughter of Col. George Eskridge of Sandy Point.[36] The Cople families were all related one way or the other it seems, and were a closely knit group. Even if you were not related by blood or marriage it was the practice to be good neighbors and help whenever needed. The wills attest to this fact. Neighbors named as Executors was a common practice.

During this time Mary Ball was living in Cople Parish "under the tutelage and government" of Col. George Eskridge which was stipulated in her mother's, Mary Ball Hewes, will.[37] Mrs. Hewes died in 1721 when Mary Ball was 12 years old; therefore, the young girl must have attended services at Yeocomico and Nomini often with her guardian. She must have ridden the little grey dapple horse, left to her by her brother-in-law Samuel Bonum, all over Yeocomico Neck and was quite a pretty sight on the "good silk plush riding saddle" her mother's will had directed her executor buy for her.[37a] Perhaps she collected shells as she played along the beach at Sandy Point. Romance blossomed when a friend of her guardian came visiting from Washington Parish in the quest of a wife to help him care for his three children. (His first wife had died November 1729.) Augustine Washington was pleased with the "healthy orphan of moderate height, rounded figure and pleasant voice" of Mary Ball aged 23.[38]

Thus independent Mary Ball was married to the tall, handsome, planter and vestryman of Washington Parish the sixth day of March 1731, and went

36. *Eubank's The Authentic Guide Book of Historic Northern Neck of Virginia*, pages 47–48.
37. *George Washington, Vol. I*, Douglas Southall Freeman, Scribners, New York 1948, pages 42–46.
37a. Ibid.
38. Ibid.

to live on beautiful Pope's Creek with a life style much like the comfortable, simple one she left behind at Sandy Point.[39] There is no account of just where they were united in marriage, but it is a safe bet that Mr. Jones tied the knot. This would be the highlight of his ministry in Cople Parish as who is not aware of the importance of this match in history? In the following winter, Mary Ball was delivered of her first child February 22, 1732, and named him George in honor, it is said, of her childhood friend and guardian. There is no truth that the father of his county was baptized at Yeocomico, but family ties being what they were, Mary Ball would have certainly made a trip to Sandy Point to show off her little boy.

It was about this time Robert "King" Carter built Nomini Hall for his son Robert whose wife was Priscilla Bladen. He died in 1734 and was succeeded by his son Robert III who grew up to be the famous Councillor Robert Carter. This magnificent mansion was built on a bluff at the head of Nomini Creek.

By February 25, 1733, Mr. Jones had died and his wife was settling his estate with the help of her brother, Willoughby Newton. Poor Behethland, referred to as "relic" of the Reverend Walter Jones in his inventory, had to see all of her household goods put up for sale in order to pay the parson's debts.[40] The accounts were settled to the satisfaction of the court and recorded in the Westmoreland Court House by October 6, 1735.[41] Mr. Jones did not leave a will. He was rector of Cople Parish for ten years. Willoughby Newton married Sarah, the daughter of George Eskridge and Rebecca Bonum. Because of the family responsibility involved, Mrs. Jones probably moved into her brother's home and was welcomed as long as she needed their help. In the 17th century widows did not stay unmarried very long and Mrs. Jones was no exception. Her second husband was Samuel Oldham.[42]

1733–1740

Dr. Edward Lewis Goodwin's "History of the Church in Virginia" lists Charles Green as rector of Cople Parish in 1734[43] and suggests he was rector for a time between 1733 and 1740.[44] Several other publications have made this same mistake.* After extensive research on the subject, Captain William

---

39. Ibid.
40. *Westmoreland County Records Inventory Book 1*, page 139.
41. Ibid.
42. *Old Churches and Families of Virginia*. Meade Vol. II page 172.
43. *Brydon's Addendum to Goodwin's Colonial Churches in Virginia*. Published in 1933 by Dr. G. Maclaren Brydon.
44. *Goodwin's Colonial Church in Virginia*, page 102.
Northern Neck Historical Magazine Dec. 1970, page 2053.

King[45] has discovered there appears to be doubt about who was minister, or if there was one for the Parish in 1733 to 1740.

Captain King says the first known reference to Charles Green, Westmoreland County, Virginia, was as a witness to James Coleman's will dated 28th. December, 1735[46]. Order Book 1731–39 records a number of court cases recorded for Charles Green.[47] Also recorded on the same date is the following: "Patrick Creeses a servant boy, belonging to Doctor Charles Green, is adjudged seven years old which is ordered to be recorded"[48] Mr. Green is not referred to as minister or rector in any of these instances. However, in a 1743 West. Order Book 1739–1743, a court suit refers to "The Reverend Charles Green, Clk."[49]

Here are the "facts" of the Charles Green History according to Goodwin:

"Charles Green M.D.: son of Moor Green of Monmouth town (pleb). Matriculated March 15, 1727–28, age 18. B.A. 1731. M.A., January 15, 1735–36. Ordained for Truro Parish, 1737. Minister of Truro Parish [in present day Fairfax County] from 1737 to 1764. Died 1764".[50]

All this considered, just what role did Mr. Green play in the life of Cople Parish?

Here is the summary of Captain King's conclusion to this question: "It would appear Charles Green finished his academic endeavors January 15, 1735–36, received his licence to practice medicine at that time or shortly thereafter. He probably arrived in the colonies about the middle of 1735, set up primary residence in Westmoreland County and conducted his medical practice. He may have been Col. George Eskridge's physician during his final days and perhaps provided other services for Eskridge such as a personal secretary.

"In Westmoreland Records it is noted Col. Eskridge's estate paid Dr. Charles Green 30.13.5. monies[50a], and the payment appears to have been made in 1740. (This would have been a sizable payment for those days). Dr. Green may have traveled to Prince William County during this period. By mid 1736, it would appear he had decided to make his residence in Prince William County, and thus he filed suit in Westmoreland County to recover from those he had provided services for that which was due him. He followed

---

45. Captain William King, Retired United States Coast Guard and active member of Cople Parish. Treasurer of Parish since 1990.
46. *Wills and Deeds Book 18 Part 11*, page 280.
47. *Order Book 1731–39, Part 11*, page 201.
48. Ibid page 220.
49. Ibid page 208.
50. *Goodwin's Colonial Churches In Virginia*, page 274.
50a. *West. and Inventories book 1723–46*, page 296.

these suits in Westmoreland County until he was satisfied while he was a resident in Prince William County about the middle of 1736. He very likely was ordained by the Bishop of London sometime during the early to middle part of 1737.[51] In regard to his being the rector or minister of Cople Parish,[52] he could not have acted in that capacity prior to arriving in Westmoreland County; he should not have been during his residency in Westmoreland (1735–36) because he was not ordained and could not have acted legally in that capacity. From the time he was ordained, he was minister and rector of Truro Parish, and thus could not have been rector in two locations".

Captain King continues: "Obviously, from the beginning, Charles Green showed some interest in doing ministry. With his close ties to Col. Eskridge, who was a stalwart supporter of Cople Parish, one can easily assume that Charles Green was involved with the Parish. (One should remember Col. Eskridge was the guardian of Mary Ball, the second wife of Augustine Washington, which may explain the relationship which brought about the recommendation by Washington of Charles Green for minister of Truro Parish)[53]. Very likely Charles Green, when in Cople Parish (1735–1736), provided lay ministry services. He also probably provided services to the Parish after he was ordained and was rector of Truro Parish. However, nothing can be found to support the position that Charles Green was ever rector or minister here. Also, there is no evidence to support any other person as rector or minister of Cople Parish for the years 1733–1740".

The Rev. Hugh Jones in a pamphlet called "the present state of Virginia"[54] deals with the problem of the parishes in the case of the ministers death or absence. This is a great help in understanding just who may have conducted the services after Mr. Jones's death and the arrival of the Reverend Charles Rose circa 1740. Mr. Jones said: "The Clerk in Case of the Minister's death or absence has great Business and is a kind of Curate, performing frequently all the Offices of the Church, except the two Sacraments and Matrimony: In some places they read the lessons, whether, or if, the minister be sick or infirm, if the Clerk can read tolerably well. Likewise, might they be allowed to bury when a Minister cannot possibly be had before the corpse would

51. Research of Mrs. Helen C. Tayloe. West. Museum.
52. Ibid.
53. Truro Parish Vestry Minutes, 19 August 1736.
54. Dr. Brydon Vol. 1: pages 395–396–397
Excerpts from "of the state of the church and clergy of Virginia", an account written by the Reverend Hugh Jones who was master of the grammar school of William and Mary College 1716, and professor of history and mathematics in 1717. On a return trip to England in 1722 he wrote his report of conditions in Virginia and published it in 1724. Dr. Brydon says it is a well-balanced and fair statement of conditions both civil and ecclesiastical as he found them.

corrupt in hot weather; but little more should be granted them, since some Places long accustomed to hear only their Clerk read Prayers and Sermons at Church, have no right Notions of the Office, Respect, and Dignity of a Clergyman. For registering Births and Burials, there is a small Allowance which is generally given to the Clerk, who takes that Trouble off the Minister's hands".[55]

Neighboring Ministers performed service in the vacant parishes. Since the Rev. Mr. Rodrick MacCullock was the rector in Washington Parish, we believe he must have read the burial office for his brother clergyman. Who read the burial office for all the good folk of the Parish who died from 1733 to 1740? Probably someone appointed as Clerk. There were a great number of burials then. Several prominent people passed away and were no doubt treated with the customary respect reserved for men and women who had served, lived, and died in the Parish. Mr. Jones tells us: "It is customary to bury in Gardens or Orchards, where whole Families lye interred together, in a Spot generally handsomely enclosed, planted with Evergreens, and the Graves kept decently: Hence, likewise arises the Occasion of preaching Funeral Sermons in Houses, where at Funerals are assembled a great Congregation of Neighbors and Friends"[55a]. During the time Cople was without a rector, several members of the Parish died:

Elizabeth Middleton 1733, Frances Wigginton 1733, William Rice 1733, William Walker 1733, John Self 1733, William Butler 1734, Elizabeth Hardwick, 1734, John Cooper 1734, Colonel George Eskridge 1735, John Bailey 1736, James Coleman 1735, Edmund Jeffress 1736, William Shaw 1736, Mary Chilton 1747, Gerrard Ball 1737, James Hardwick 1737, Thomas Sturman 1737, Daniel Crabb 1739, Hannah Cooper 1739, Elizabeth Rowbothan 1739, Isaac Allerton 1739, John Footman 1739. It is interesting to read the wills with names still familiar in the Parish and to see how interwoven the families were and with what care they left their estates, large or small.[56]

Churchwardens during this period were: George Eskridge and Robert Carter, Henry Lee and William Sturman, John Footman and Wharton Ransdell, William Aylett and Willoughby Newton, Patrick Spence and Thomas Bennett

Vestrymen: Thomas Lee,* Robert Carter, William Aylett, Thomas Bennet,

---

55. Ibid.
55a. Ibid.
56. *Wills of Westmoreland County, Virginia.* Fothergill.
*Note: Thomas Lee served on the Vestry but not as Churchwarden according to this list. The Lee family had moved to their new home Stratford Hall and Col. Lee was very involved in affairs of state in Williamsburg.

George Lee, Samuel Eskridge, Thomas Chilton, Willoughby Newton, George Turberville, Patrick Spence, Nicholas Minor, John Bushrod, Wharton Ransdell and Henry Lee.[57]

1740–1761

The Rev. Charles Rose K.B.* Va. March 1736–37[58] came to Cople Parish as rector, circa 1738–40. He was rector until his death in 1761. Mrs. Rose, the former Catherine Tarent of Essex County, Virginia, the sister-in-law of the Rev. Robert Rose of St. Anne's Parish in Essex Co., Virginia, older brother of Charles Rose.[59] The new rector and his wife lived at the Glebe.[60]

This was a busy time in the life of the Parish. In August 1739 the court "ordered and directed that the Churchwardens of Cople parish & the Church-wardens of Washington parish in this county do within ten days after the receipt of this order Cause a Vestry to be called and to meet and divide the said Parishes into so many precincts as they shall think convenient."[61] This order was for the processioning of the bounds of each land owner in the parish. After the processioners completed their tasks, they had to bring a report to the County court for filing. These records give a true account of where members of the parish lived in relationship to one another.[62]

George Turberville, member of the parish, Clerk of the Westmoreland County Court, and former Churchwarden, died in 1742. He stated in his will "I give twenty pounds sterling to be sent for to Great Britain in course goods to be distributed here to the poor of Cople Parish. Item: I give and bequeath to the use of Nomony Church in Cople Parish ten pounds sterling to buy ornaments such as the Lord's Prayer, The Creed and Ten Commandments which I desire my Ex't's may send for to Great Brittian as soon as conveniently can after my decease at the charge of my estate."[63]. At this time there must have been discussions in the vestry meetings concerning building a new church of brick at Nomini.

The Rev. James Blair, Commissary of the Bishop of London in the Colony for 54 years, died in 1743 and was mourned throughout the colony. He had established the College of William and Mary and was a strong supporter of

---

57. *Westmoreland County Virginia 1653–1983.*
*K.B means "King's Bounty". Ordained and sent by the King.
58. *Old Churches and Families*, Meade II, page 147.
59. "Diary of Robert Rose," page XIV–XV.
60. Ibid. page 24.
61. *WCR Order Book*, Aug. 29, 1739–1743—Page 12b.
62. Ibid. April 29, 1740.
63. *Westmoreland Co. Records Orders Deed and Wills*, Book 9, page 200.

education. He was a scholar and encouraged the clergy to promote schools in the parishes. However, there were no schools in Cople Parish during this period on record. It was the Churchwardens responsibility, with the help of the rector as tutor, to educate the parishioners. Even though there is no record of schools in Cople Parish at this period, there were regular classes for instruction in private homes which seem to satisfy the demands of the people. Trades were still taught by apprenticeship. The yeoman class did not think it necessary to read and write if you had a trade. Education was then left to the whims of parents. "This family responsibilities for the education of its children was reflected in the requirement which was usually, if not invariably, written into the agreement by which churchwardens bound out orphaned children as apprentices, or gave the charge of such children to masters and mistresses who would care for them. This provision was that the child should be taught to write, to cipher, and to read the Bible."[64]

Judging by private libraries on record, many Cople landowners were well educated, enlightened and concerned with education.[65] The *Virginia Gazette*, first printed in Williamsburg in 1736, was circulating with news of the day which kept parishioners informed about the world in current events and literature. 'The Other Side of the Question", a document written in opposition to the Whig (Non Royalist) position of the Duchess of Marlborough, was being read and discussed by the clergy and members of the parish.[66]

In January 1747, Parson Rose of St. Anne's Parish visited his brother at the Glebe and seemed to enjoy going around the parish. Jan. 2nd. He "visited Mr. Bushrode and dined" (I assume this meant he visited Bushfield.) Jan. 3. Went to Church, Mr. Dickson preached". Jan. 4. Spent day at Major George Lee's. (Mount Pleasant) Next day "went surveying with Major Lee and spent the evening with Mrs. Mary Lee". (Cabin Point)" Jan. 6th. went and spent the day at Mr. Gawen Corbin's," (Pecatone) returned to Col. Fitzhugh's about eleven at night". On the next day, Mr. Rose went with Col. Lee and his son to his house at Stratford. Mr. Rose stayed for two days with the Lees, "talking and reading." On the 9th. he was "detained by the rain at Stratford", but on the 10th. he started the return journey home via the ferry "at Leeds."[67]

This diary of Mr. Rose's brother gives us a pleasant view of the hospitality which the members of the parish extended visitors. Cople Parish was a land of gracious living.

64. *Virginia's Mother Church*, Brydon, Vol. 1, page 390.
65. *Northern Neck Historical Magazine Vol. XIV*, Eskridge Inventory, pages 1313–1315.
66. "Diary of Robert Rose," page 24.
67. Ibid. page 24–25.

I wish Mr. Rose had made notes about just how he traveled. Apparently he was accompanied from Essex by a young minister, Dr. Dickson,* who was invited to preach by the rector. There is no mention of which church they attended. The trip to Leedstown to "catch" the ferry must have been something after the rain of the previous day. His not referring to, what must have been, a rough and muddy road says a great deal about the character of these eighteenth century parsons. They were rugged.

In October 1748 Henry Lee's will was probated. He was the brother to Col. Thomas Lee and lived at Lee Hall.

He left his land at King Copsico to son John. To son Richard he left Lee Hall. To son Henry he left 3500 acres in Fairfax County. To daughter Lettice, wife of William Ball gent. of Lancaster County, 40 lbs. and furniture. His widow, Mary Bland Lee, was to live at Lee Hall for life.[68]

Thomas Lee was a county justice, burgess and member of the Council. He became acting governor of the colony when the crown-appointed Governor Gooch went to England and was absent from his post. Thus in 1749 Thomas Lee became President of the Council of State. Before this Col. Lee had been consumed with the business of making a peaceful settlement with the frontier Indians and paving the way for the success of the Ohio Company. Lee was the first president of the famous company. "Its first move was to secure the Forks of the Ohio—at the junction of the Allegheny and Monongahela rivers— at the site of what became Fort Pitt, later Pittsburg, during the French and Indian War."[69]

Meanwhile back in Cople Parish, the beginning of a small revolution was taking place. We learn from the Journals of the House of Burgess, April 14, 1749, "that a petition of the Freeholders and Housekeepers of the Parish of Cople, in the County of Westmoreland, living above Nominy Ferry, had been read in Council and was by them referred to the consideration of this House; and the said Petition was read, ordered that the said Petition be referred to the consideration of the Committee of Propositions and Grievances; and that they do examine into the Matter thereof and report the same with their opinion thereupon to the House."[70]

This effort to form another parish was rejected by the House of Burgesses a week later April 21, 1749: "Resolved, that it is the opinion of this Committee, That the Petition of the Freeholders and House-keepers of Cople, in the

---

*Mr. Dickson was a young clergyman visiting in the area and looking for a parish. He settled in Lynnhaven Parish, Princess Anne County, Virginia, 1748. Rose notes, 844.

68. *WRC Will Book*, Nov. 22, 1755.

69. *Westmoreland County History*, Walter B. Norris, Jr. Editor, pages 180–181.

70. *Journals of House of Burgess 1742–1749*, page 363.

County of Westmoreland, living above Nomini Ferry, for dividing the said county into three Parishes; be rejected."[71] Three days earlier, April 18, 1749, The House of Burgesses received this document: "A petition of the inhabitants of the Parish of Cople . . . was read, setting forth that, contrary to Law there has been, for several Years past, an acting vestryman of that parish who is not an inhabitant thereof; that the said Vestryman has a great influence in the said vestry and has often been the occasion of many Grievances to the Inhabitants of the said Parish; that one of the Churchwardens of the said Parish did attempt to corrupt a Freeholder and bribe his vote, at the last election of Burgesses for that county, by offering to resign his Place in the said vestry to the said Freeholder, in consideration of the said Freeholders voting as he should desire; and praying that the vestry of the said parish may be dissolved, or that the Petitioners grievances may be otherwise redressed as this House shall think fit.

"Ordered, That the said petition be referred to the consideration of the Committee of Privileges and elections; that they do examine into the allegation thereof and report the same as it shall appear to them, with their opinion thereupon to the House".[72] May 6, 1749, two weeks later, the following took place in the House of Burgesses:

"Mr. Ludwell, from the committee of Privileges & Elections, reported, that the committee had under their consideration the petition of the inhabitants of the Parish of Cople, and County of Westmoreland . . . and had examined a witness as to the matter of the said petition, and heard as well the petitioners for, as Mr. Richard Lee against, the petition; whereupon it appeared to the committee that on the Day of the last Election of Burgesses to serve this present General assembly for the County of Westmoreland, the said Richard Lee applied to one Robert Middleton, a Free-holder of the said County, at the Court-house, before he had polled and offered to him, that if he would give his vote at the said Election for Mr. George Lee, a member of this house, the Hon. Thomas Lee, Esq'r, a member of the Vestry of the said parishioner would resign his Place in the said vestry, and the said Robert Middleton might succeed him; to which the said Robert Middleton answered, that if he could not come in at the fore door, he would not come in at the back Door; but that it does not appear to this committee that the sitting member, or any other Person, desired the said Richard Lee to apply to the said Robert Middleton and ask him to vote for the sitting member or was

---

71. Ibid. 1742–49., Page 373.
72. Ibid., Page 367.

privy to it; upon which the committee had come to a resolution, which they had directed him to report to the House; and he read same in his Place, and then delivered the Report in at the Table, when it was again read, and agreed to by the House as follows:

"Resolved, that the said Richard Lee, in offering the said Robert Middleton and if he would give his vote at the Election of Burgesses to serve in this present General Assembly for the County of Westmoreland, for Mr. George Lee, the sitting member, the Hon. Thomas Lee, Esq'r. would resign his Place in the vestry of the said Parish, and the said Robert Middleton might succeed him, is guilty of a Breach of the Privileges of this house.

"Ordered, that the said Richard Lee be taken into custody of the Sergeant at Arms."

Next page of the Journal of the House of Burgesses has the following report:

"A petition of Richard Lee, in custody of the Sergeant at Arms, was presented to the house and read, setting forth, That he is under the deepest Concern for having been guilty of a breach of the privileges of this House; that his offence was the effect of his Ignorance and that for the future he would be careful to avoid every Thing of the like Sort; and praying to be discharged."

"Ordered, that he be discharged out of custody, paying a fee."[72a] This settled the matter for the time being.

It was in 1750 the vestry made a bargain with Robert Vaulx, Contractor of Washington Parish, to rebuild the church at Nomini. At that time Robert Vaulx "had agreed to have this done according to the Tenure of his Bond entered into for that purpose, payable to Thomas Chilton and James Steptoe, Gent. (both members of Cople Vestry at this time) and to their successors, etc., and bearing date the Seventh day of February 1750.[73] County Records record on May 31, 1753 : "William Pevice, Bricklayer, ag. Robert Vaulx: By consent of the Parties, It is Ordered that John Aries and Thos. Sanford do view the work done by the Petitioner on the new Church in Cople Parish, and it is also ordered that William Craighill do view the work done by the Petitioner on the Church in Washington Parish; and make report of the same therein to next Court to be held for this County."[73a] It looks as if Mr. Pevice was bringing suit against Mr. Vaulx. The next mention of Mr. Pevice was at

---

72a. Ibid., page 394.
73. *WCR. Orders 1752–1755*, page 288 b. Copied from Tayloe Research papers of Aug. 1938 in Westmoreland County Museum, Montross, Virginia.
73a. Ibid. page 104.

Court March 29, 1754, the petition brought by William Pevice, bricklayer, against Robert Vaulx, Gent. is agreed and dismissed."[73b]

Mrs. Thomas Lee died and was brought back to Cople for burial in Burnt House Field in early 1750. The Colonel died Nov. 14, 1750. His wish was to be buried at Burnt House Field between his mother and his beloved Hannah. His wishes were honored and the graves are looked after until this day by the Society of the Lees of Virginia. Philip Ludwell Lee and Richard Henry Lee lived at Stratford. Philip Ludwell was a member of Washington Parish but Richard Henry stayed a member of Cople Parish. His cousin Richard Lee lived at *Lee Hall* and cousin George Lee lived at *Mount Pleasant*.

On Nov. 28, 1751, Daniel Tebbs asked permission to build a mill over Tucker's Run above Yeocomico Church.* Daniel Tebbs was a member of the Vestry and also one of the Inspectors at Yeocomico and Rust's warehouse. At this time Edward Ransdell, also a vestryman, was one of the Inspectors at Nominy. These jobs were very important. Tobacco was the chief crop and was being raised without regard to the terrible toll it was taking on the soil. The draught in the late 1738 was forgotten when good weather in 1739–1740 caused large yields of tobacco. Since the slave trade was a normal part of life at this time, negroes were unloaded from ships moored at these warehouses and sent to market for sale to planters who needed manpower to harvest the crops. Then hogsheads of tobacco would be rolled on the ships waiting at the wharf to receive the next shipments bound for Great Britain. The Inspectors' job was very exacting. They were picked for these posts with care.

The tobacco crop failed in 1755, according to history, and the salaries of the clergy could not be paid in tobacco as the law provided; therefore, the legislature passed an act to enable the inhabitants of the colony to pay their debts in money for the present year".[74] This began the controversy between the clergy and the government and many of the varieties over what was known as The Two-Penny Act.[74a]

One wonders what was happening to the warehouses in Cople Parish during this period. Actually quite a bit.

August 25, 1755, "Daniel Tebbs, Fleet Cox, Benedict Middleton, and John Crabb are by the Court nominated and recommended to the Hon'ble Robert Dinwiddie, Esq., Governor and Commander in Chief of this Colony, for him to choose and appoint two of them to execute the Office of Inspectors at

---

73b. Ibid. page 161b.
*Daniel Tebbs was appointed Lieutenant in Captain John Newton's Troop Company 29th. day of July, 1755. WRC. Order Book 1752–1755, page 288. Tayloe Research.
74. *Hawks Ecclesiastical History*, pages 118–122.
74a. *N.N. Of Va. Historical Magazine*, Vol. XXIII, page 2450.

Yeocomico and Rust's warehouse." On the same date "Edward Ransdell, William Previce, Thomas Spence and Foxhall Sturman are nominated to the office of Inspector at Nominy warehouse."[75] On November 27, 1753, "Edward Ransdell and William Pevise, Inspectors at Nomini Warehouse, presented into Court an account of two thousand five hundred and eighty-eight pounds of transfer tobacco in their hands." The same day "Daniel Tebbs and Fleet Cox Inspectors at Yeocomico and Rust's Warehouse presented into Court an Account of Three thousand five hundred and eighty pounds of transfer Tobacco in their hands."[76]

At the same time that the inspectors were presenting the above records to the Court, the names of Samuel Oldham and Augustine Washington were considered by the Court for recommendation to the "Honorable Robert Dinwiddie, Esq., His Majestie's Lieutenant-Governor and Commander in Chief of this Colony," for him to appoint them Coroners in the County of Westmoreland. Samuel Oldham for Cople Parish and Augustine Washington for Washington Parish.[77]

Twenty years before the Revolution, there was a rumbling of discontent in the Parish, not with the British government but with each other. Many petitions are on record about this beginning as far back as October and November 30, 1748, when "Mr. Carter reported that his committee had prepared a bill for dissolving and electing a new vestry."[78] In May 1755, five years later, the House of Burgess came to this conclusion:

"Whereas it is represented to this Assembly that several persons for many years past have acted, and still continue to act, as vestrymen of the parish of Cople, in the county of Westmoreland, who are not duly elected for that office; for remedy whereof, Be it enacted. That the vestry or pretended vestry of the said parish of Cople is hereby *dissolved*, and that all and every act and acts, thing and things, which at any time or times hereafter, shall or may be performed, suffered or done by them as a vestry or pretended vestry of the said parish shall be, and are hereby declared to be utterly void to all intents and purposes whatsoever.

"Provided always, That all and every levy and levies heretofore laid, and all and every other act and acts, thing and things, by the said vestry or pretended vestry done or suffered, shall be good, valid, and effectual, in as full and ample a manner, as the same would have been, if the said vestry had been duly elected.

---

75. *WRC Order Book 1752–1755*, page 119, Tayloe Research. 1938.
76. Ibid. page 12.
77. Ibid. page 41.
78. *House of Burgesses Journals 1748–*, page 310.

"And be it further enacted . . . That the freeholders and housekeepers of the said parish of Cople shall meet at some convenient time and place, to be appointed and publicly advertised at least twenty days before, by the sheriff of the said county of Westmoreland, and before the twentieth day of July next, and then and there, elect twelve of the most able and discreet persons of their parish, to be vestrymen of the said parish; which said vestrymen so having taken the oaths appointed by law, and subscribed to be conformable to the doctrine and discipline of the church of England, shall to all intents and purposes, be deemed and taken to be the vestrymen of the said parish."[79]

In Westmoreland County at Court held 29th of July, Anno Domini, 1755, were present John Bushrod, Richard Jackson, James Steptoe and Richard Henry Lee, Gentlemen Justices. This was the day chosen to carry out the orders of the House of Burgess and so:

"On July 29, 1755
John Bushrod, Daniel Tebbs, Richard Lee, Benedict Middleton, Willoughby Newton, Robert Middleton, George Lee, John Newton, Samuel Oldham, Robert Carter, Fleet Cox, and James Steptoe gent. on being elected Vestrymen of Cople Parish, took oaths to the Government and subscribed the test."[80]

Because of the controversy concerning the vestry, the problem of the Nomini church contractors in 1754 had been left unfinished. It was the first order of business for the new vestry.

The next order of business in the Courthouse on the same day as the election was the matter of completing the new Nomini Church which had been contracted for in 1750[81]. It appears that Mr. Robert Vaulx had died in March 1755 leaving the church unfinished. Gawen Corbin and Richard Lee, Churchwardens of Cople Plts. brought suit against "John Bushrod and Augustine Washington acting Executors of Robert Vaulx Gent. deceased" who did not deny that the estate of Mr. Vaulx owes the said Plaintiffs one thousand and two hundred pounds current money,* "therefore it is considered that the said Plts. do recover against the said Debts. (out of the estate of the said Dec'd Robert,) in their hand the said One Thousand Two hundred pounds current money, together with their costs by them in their behalf expended and the said Plts. may have thereof Executed Ec.

"But the said Judgment (except the costs) is to be discharged by the

79. *Hening's Statutes Vol. 6*, page 517.
80. *WCR Orders 1752–1755* page 288.
81. Ibid, page 288b.
*Money advanced to Robert Vaulx by Vestry for purchase of building materials.

payment of whatever sum or sums of money the Churchwardens of Cople Parish shall agree with workmen for to complete and finish the new Church at Nomini in the same manner as Robert Vaulx had agreed to have done according to the Tenure of his Bond entered into for that purpose, payable to Thomas Chilton and James Steptoe Gent. and to the successors Etc. and bearing date the seventh day of Feb. 1750".[82]

These court records restablish the fact Nomini was refurbished and bricked over circa 1755. Also that the men of Cople Parish were good and careful managers of the Parish affairs.

It had long been the practice of Churchwardens to see that orphans were cared for and sometimes, although the parents had named a guardian for their children in wills, this did not prevent them from becoming wards of the court. This happened to the orphans of Samuel Eskridge:

Jan. 29, 1754 "Upon the motion of Peter Rust, Guardian to Richard Eskridge, Burdet Eskridge and Rebekah Eskridge infants Orphans of Samuel Eskridge deceased, and informing the court that their estates are insufficient to maintain them, It is therefore ordered that the Churchwardens of Cople parish do bind them out Apprentices According to Law."[83] Records show that "Rebekah was bound out to Richard Bernard until she arrives to the age of eighteen years".[84] The court records tell us that a year later Rust is in trouble himself. "June 24, 1755, having presented Peter Rust overseer of the roads from Yeocomico warehouse to Coleman's bridge, for not keeping the same in repair according to Law, who have been summoned to answer the same, but (altho duly required) came not nor did he say any thing in his own defence, He is therefore fined according to Law fifteen shillings current money which he is hereby ordered to pay to the Churchwardens of Cople Parish for use of the poor thereof."[84a] This I think was poetic justice.

"The court being informed that Vincent Rust had just before swore two profane oaths in the Court yard. It is considered by the Court that he be fined ten shillings according to the law for that offence which he is hereby ordered to pay the Churchwardens of Cople Parish for the use of the poor thereof and costs"[85]. There are many court records of this nature which tell a good deal about the problems the churchwardens faced because of the laws dealing with personal behavior.

82. *WCR Orders 1752–1755*, page 288 b. Copied from Tayloe 1938 research, This page is not in Record Book now. These books were repaired in the 40's and 50's. This page may have been lost.
83. Ibid. page 135b.
84. Ibid, Page 138.
84a. *WCR Order 1752–1755*, page 274.
85. *WCR Order Book 1758–1761*, page 4 B.

On May 31, 1757, Richard Henry Lee, Gent. was ordered by the court to take list of Tithables for the Upper precinct of Cople Parish and John Newton, Gent. Tithables for the lower[86]. At the same court Gawen Corbin, Gent., having been elected to the vestry of Cople Parish, took the oaths to the government and subscribed the test".[86a]

May 30, 1758, the Court "Ordered that Richard Jackson, gent. take the list of Tithables for the lower Precinct of Cople Parish" Richard Lee, Gent would take them for the Upper Precinct of the parish.[86b]

Mr. Gawen Corbin died at Pecatone in 1760. His will was probated July 29, 1760, and caused quite a problem in the affairs of his widow, Hannah Corbin, sister of Richard Henry Lee.[87]

After 21 years in Cople Parish as rector, The Rev. Mr. Rose died in 1761. His will "was presented on June 30, 1761, to the court by his relict Catherine Rose and Executrix therein named who made oath thereto and the same being proved by Francis Lajon, John Self and Alexander Rose witness hereto and ordered to be recorded". According to his will he had three sons, Robert, John, and Alexander, and two daughters, Catherine and Molly. He left each of his children 1 negro. His brother Alexander and nephew John Rose were named as the Executors.[88] The language of this will, very plain and forthright, was in sharp contrast to the will of Sarah Callis which was probated November 1755 and witnessed by Mr Rose. For example the first part of the will begins:

"In the name of God amen. I, Sarah Callis of Cople Parish in County of Westmoreland, being very sick and weak but of perfect mind and memory thanks be to God for it and calling to mind the *uncertainty of this transitory life* do make this my last will and testament in manner and form as follows. First I bequeath my soul to God that gave it to me and my body to the earth *in certain and sure hope of the joyful resurrection of the last day.*"[89] The wording shows Mrs. Callis was a devout christian and was very familiar with the Biblical references in the Book of Common Prayer. She left her large Bible to her son Robert. Two sons William and Francis were her executors. Eliza Atwill, Charles Rose and Richard Callis were witnesses to the will.

The Rev. Mr. Rose probably felt no need to give such a witness in his will. A great deal took place in the Parish during his rectorship but we know very

---

86. *WCR Orders 1755–1758*, page 150b.
86a. Ibid.
86b. Ibid. *Orders 1755–1758*, page 213-B.
87. *Wills of Westmoreland County*, Fothergill, page 144.
88. *WCR Orders 1761–1764*, page 2.
89. Ibid. 1752–1755 July 29, 1755 page 288.

little about him. His name appears as witness to several wills which attests to the fact he visited the sick and dying. Judging by the history of the parish during the 1750's, Mr. Rose was confronted with many problems which he managed to have resolved peaceably. It has been believed he was buried at the Glebe, but we have no records to prove this. We do know for a fact he died in the spring of 1761.

1761–1764

There are several referances to The Rev. Augustine Smith during the period 1761–1764 as "minister of Cople Parish",[90] but verification has not been possible.

As the Parish began its 100th year in 1764, the Rev. Thomas Smith took over as rector and stayed to guide the people through a most turbulent period.

Mr. Smith came as rector in 1764 and served a long and interesting twenty-five years until his death in 1789.

I would like to thank the many people who have helped me in with this project, especially J. Paul Hudson, Historian, who encouraged me to begin this task and has continued to give me his support; the staff at the Westmoreland County Clerk's Office; Westmoreland County Museum and Northern Neck Historical Library at Montross; Mrs. Oswald Anderson for her help in preparing the first manuscript for publication; Mrs. Lynn Norris for taking the pictures of Yeocomico and Nomini Churches which appeared in the 1990 article, and Dr. V. Perdue Davis of the Bishop's Library at Mayo Memorial House at 110 W. Franklin St., Richmond, Virginia.

---

90. Meade, Vol. II, page 147.

St. James Episcopal Church
Tidwells, Virginia

Edward White Photographer
Russell Va. 1999

COPLE PARISH 1764–1814

by BERTHA NEWTON DAVISON*

The following article by Bertha Newton Davison is the third installment of a history of Cople Parish to be published in the Northern Neck of Virginia Historical Magazine. It is being compiled from the research of many historians, from excerpts of diaries and by using the records in the Westmoreland County Court House and the Westmoreland Museum and Library. This is by no means an "original" document as the complier has drawn heavily upon all the sources available in order to put the history of Cople Parish in chronological order. Cople has an interesting story and it needs to be told! The author greatly appreciated the patient assistance of the magazine editor, Mrs. J. Dall Brown, Jr.

The first hundred years of Cople Parish, 1664–1764, were outstanding, productive, and remarkable for the role its people played in the affairs of the Colony of Virginia. The busy trade in tobacco shipped to England from the many warehouses along the creeks and rivers helped to create the comfortable life styles the families enjoyed, and the attention given to education and responsibility was shown in the care of their fellowmen.

The next fifty years were filled with excitement and turmoil. There were wars, rumors of wars, and the dissolution of the established Colonial Church which made difficult and dangerous times for Cople and her people.

Churchwardens, as the Parish celebrated its centennial, were Willoughby Newton and John Augustine Washington.[1] The boundary of the Parish, at this time in the mid 1700's between Cople and Washington Parishes, was Cold Harbor Creek on a line connecting its head with Cat Point Creek and then to the Richmond County line.[2]

In 1764 Cople Parish was a beautiful place to live. Most of the homes at that time were built near the water with marvelous views. However, "Lawfield," the home of Judge Richard Parker was built on a high point of land not too far from Montross the county seat; "Chantilly," close to Stratford Hall, was the home of Richard Henry Lee and his wife Anne Aylett who was born at "Harmony Hall" near Sandy Point; "Nominy Plantation" on Currio-

*Bertha Newton Davison was born in Cople Parish and has been a life-long resident of Westmoreland County.

1. *Westmoreland County, Virginia 1653–1983*. Edited by Walter Norris Jr., published for the Westmoreland Commission of History and Archaeology by Walsworth Publishing Co. Marcline, Missouri, 1983.

2. "The Authentic Guide Book of Historic Northern Neck of Virginia," H. Ragland Eubank, Printed by Whittit and Shepperson, Richmond, Virginia, 1934. pp. 45–62.

man Bay, the seat of the Ashton family where Col. William Booth lived with his wife, another Anne Aylett, granddaughter of Col. Henry Ashton; "Nomini Hall", situated at the head of Nomini Creek, was the home of Councillor Robert Carter and his young family: "Bushfield," home of Gen. George Washington's brother, John Augustine Washington and his wife Hannah Bushrod, daughter of John Bushrod and Mildred Corbin Bushrod, daughter of John and Mildred Corbin of King and Queen County. The John Augustine Washingtons moved to "Bushfield" from "Mount Vernon" (when George Washington married and brought his bride to Mount Vernon which he had shared with his brother John until that time). John and Hannah are buried in the garden at "Bushfield" overlooking Nomini River and the Potomac; "Hickory Hill" on the "Ridge," was home for the Turbervilles; "Peckatone," was the home of Hannah Lee Corbin and her daughter Martha Corbin who married George Turberville in 1769 and lived there after her marriage; "Lee Hall" at Hague, was the home of "Squire" Lee; "Wilton" was home of the Jackson family; "Ayrfield" was named by John Ballentine of Ayr, Scotland, whose daughter married John Murphy in 1787; the Baileys lived at "The Great House" on the Yeocomico River at Kinsale. The two Churches of the Parish were Nomini and Yeocomico.

The Reverend Thomas Smith, the first Virginia born rector of Cople Parish, came in 1765. Mr. Smith, the son of Gregory Smith and Lucy Cooke Smith, was born in King and Queen County in 1740. He was sent to England to be educated, graduated from Trinity College, Cambridge, and was ordained at age 25 by Bishop Porteus, Bishop of London. He was married December 7, 1765, to Mary Smith, unrelated daughter of John Smith, Esq. of Middlesex County, Virginia. The Smiths, of course, lived at the Glebe where their six children were born. Only three lived to maturity.[3]

The hated Stamp Act was very much the topic of the area when Mr. Smith came to the Parish. The Act of the British Parliament in 1765 would demand "a stamp duty on all papers used for legal documents, liquor licenses, academic degrees, newspapers, pamphlets and almanacs."[4] This act was a direct tax without representation and was met with opposition throughout the colonies. The residents of Cople Parish answered the call of Thomas Ludwell Lee for planters to assemble at Leeds Town and make plans to stop any one complying with this act. Richard Henry Lee, vestryman of Cople

---

3. "Memorials of a Southern Planter" by Susan Dabney Smedes, Published by Cushing and Bailey in Baltimore, Maryland, 1888.
4. *Westmoreland County, Virginia*, page 616, paragraph 4.

Parish, drafted the resolutions on February 27, 1766, which were signed by one hundred and fifteen patriots.[5] Richard Henry Lee, George Turberville, John Ballantine, Jr., Thomas Chilton, Jos. Peirce, Rich'd Lee, Daniel Tebbs, John Newton, Peter Rust and John Augustine Washington were all of Cople Parish. The Virginia Assembly declared the act was unjust and illegal because of the protest of the colonies, spurred on by the outrage displayed and bravery of the men who gathered at Leeds Town to sign "The Leedstown Resolutions." The Stamp Act Congress met in New York in October 1766 and declared the Stamp Act taxes could not be collected without the peoples consent. This resistance by the Americans forced the British Parliament to repeal the Stamp Act in 1766.

In 1764 Churchwardens of Cople Parish were ordered by the court to "Bind out the orphan of William Rice dec'd to John Ariss to learn the trade of carpenter & House Joiner, according to the Law."[7] Legend says John Ariss was the architect when Nomini Church was renovated in the 1750's.

The mistress of "Lee Hall" and mother of "Squire" Lee, whose maiden name was Mary Bland, died in 1764.[8] Because of her marriage to Henry Lee many members of Cople Parish trace their ancestry to the Randolphs and Blands of "Turkey Island" and "Flowerdew Hundred," Prince George County, Virginia.

In his will probated in 1766, Presley Cox left to his son Fleet Cox, a vestryman in Cople Parish, a Bible and a looking glass among other bequests.[8a] In 1767 two more of the vestrymen of the Parish died. John Newton's will was probated Jan. 8, 1767, and his father's, Willoughby Newton, on May 26, 1767. John left a wife and son, Willoughby II. They lived at "Wilmington," near Tucker Hill.[8b] Willoughby I and his wife lived at "The Oaks," also near Tucker Hill.

In 1768 Anne Aylett Lee, first wife of Richard Henry Lee, died. She was buried at "Burnt House Field," the Lee graveyard near Mount Pleasant near Hague. A beautiful tribute was erected to her memory by her grieving husband in Nomini Church.

"Sacred to the memory of Mrs. Anne Lee, wife of Col. Richard H. Lee. This monument was erected by her afflicted husband, in year 1769.

---

5. *Ibid.* Paragraph 5. Quoted from *Hennings Statutes.*
7. *Westmoreland County Records—1761–1764*, page 101 B.
8. *Wills of Westmoreland County, Virginia, 1654–1800*, by Augusta B. Fothergill. Appeals Press, 1925, page 155.
8a. *Ibid.*, page 157.
8b. *Ibid.*, page 158.

Reflect dear readers on the uncertainty of human life, since neither esteemed temperament nor the most amiable goodness could save this excellent lady from death in the bloom of life. She left behind her four children, two sons and two daughters". Obit 12 Dec. 1768, A E T.P. 30

Was then so precious a flower but given us to behold it waste, the short lived blossom of an hour, too nice, too fair, too sweet to last."[8c]

In Diaries of George Washington he records attending church at Nomini on May 22, 1768, "Went to church at Nominy and returned to Mr. Booth's to dinner. Mr. Smith, the Parson, dined with us." Another entry on the 23 of May states: "At Mr. Booth's all day with Rev'd Mr. Smith." General Washington also visited "Bushfield" on numerous occasions in May 1768.[9]

Cople Parish was a very social society during the 1760's and early 1770's. Families visited back and forth, attended foxhunts, horse races, had fishing parties on the creeks and rivers, and cock fights. Large dinners were served at 3 PM and in the evening there was dancing to the music supplied by the neighborhood fiddler. And, of course, there was service at one of the two churches in Cople every Sunday. Holy Communion was usually celebrated three times a year: at Easter, Whitsunday, and Christmas. The service was held in the chancel in the east end of the church. The usual Sunday services were conducted from the pulpit and the minister wore the surplice while conducting the service, and then changed to the black scholastic gown before preaching the sermon. The pulpits were usually three decker structures where the minister read the service from the middle desk and went up to the top desk to preach."* There was no provision in the Churches for heat or artificial light because the law of the Colony forbade meetings at night. Because the life in Colonial Virginia was almost entirely agricultural and there were very few towns, the churches were always the meeting places of the people. The church with its regular weekly services occupied a large place in the social life of the community. A time was set during the service for official notices such as the Governor's proclamations, new laws to be brought quickly to the people, and other matters of importance. It has been truly said that, in the difficult years just before the Revolution, resistance to Great Britain was begun and fomented in the vestry-meetings of the various parishes. From these meetings it spread to the churchyards where the people assembled at the hours of the service."[10]

8c. Nomini Church Plaque.
9. *Diaries of G. Washington Vol. 1*, page 268, Fitzpatrick Editor(John C) 1925- Houghton Mifflin - Boston
*Yeocomico had such a pulpit at one time before 1814.
10. *The Colonial Churches in Virginia*, prepared by Dr. G. Maclaren Brydon, Histographer of the Diocese of Virginia and Miss Mary A. Goodwin, Histographer of the Diocese of Southern Virginia.

Bishop Meade states work was done on Yeocomico Church in 1773. "I have in my possession a contract with the vestry for the repairs of this church (Yeocomico) in 1773, at a cost of one hundred pounds, (or five hundred dollars). In the agreement, various repairs within and without the house in the walls around the yard are specified but nothing said about a new roof."[10a] (This was a goodly sum, I would think, for those days.)

Phillip Fithian, a student from the Presbyterian Seminary at Princeton, N.J., gives a wonderful account in his famous *Journal* of life in Cople Parish beginning in 1773 to 1774. He was the tutor of the Carter children at "Nomini Hall." A Nov. 7, 1773, entry says, "Rode to Yeocomico Church—8 miles— heard Parson Smith. He showed us the uncertainty of riches, and their insufficiency to make us happy—Dined at Captain Walker's; with Parson Smith; his wife; her sister, a young lady."[11] (Could this Captain Walker have been the owner of Poplar Plain?)

In another entry in Fithian's *Journal*, "Sunday, September 18, 1774." The Colonel gave me at breakfast the offer of a seat in his boat to Church. The morning was fine, Nomini River alive with boats and Canoes some going to Church, some fishing, & some Sporting—Mr. Smith gave us a very practical Sermon against the common vices here in particular against the practice of abusing slaves.

The report concerning Boston is much talked of & still confirmed! We all dined at Mr. Turberville's; Miss Corbin looks fresh & plump as ever. Towards evening arose a pretty furious Thunder-Gust, which we hardly escaped on our way home. I observed that several, but in special Mr. Carter, is not pleased with Mr. Smith's Sentiments of Slavery."[11a]

The following Sunday service was held at Yeocomico Church. Mr. Fithian's account is very interesting. "I rode to Ucomico (sic) Church: I was surprised when the Psalm began, to hear a large Collection of voices singing at the same time, from a Gallery, entirely contrary to what I have seen before for it is seldom in the fullest Congregation's, that more sing than the Clerk, & about two others! I am told that a singing Master of good abilities has been among this society lately & put them on a respectable Method which they, at present, pursue."[12]

In spite of a good choir, the church was having problems. Dissenters were

10a. *Old Churches and Families of Virginia*, by Bishop Meade, Vol. 11. Published by J. B. Lippincott, Philadelphia, Pa., page 149.
11. *Journal and Letters of Philip Vickers Fithian*, Colonial Williamsburg, Inc. Sales Agents: The Dietz Press, Richmond, Virginia. 1945. page 28.
11a. *Ibid.*, Page 252.
12. *Ibid.*, Page 256.

beginning to make converts in the Northern Neck. Their preachers were zealous. They minced no words about what they thought were the evils of the Established Church and blamed the Church for the laws requiring every dissenting minister to register in the County Court and record his preaching places. They were arrested and charged with disturbing the peace.* This did not deter them as they were inspired to preach what they considered God had called them to preach, the Gospel as they understood it, to a people who were "the dupes of a devilish ecclesiastical monster."[13]

Col. Robert Carter was appointed to the Vestry of the parish and accepted the Communion vessals and linen for safe keeping.[14] On March 2, 1775, Mr. Carter wrote a letter to Capt. John Turberville explaining why he could not attend a Vestry meeting at Appleby.[14a] On the 5th of October, 1776 Robert Carter wrote to the Clerk of the Vestry, Mr. Reubin Jordon, and resigned because as he explained, "due to leaving home and will not return shortly," he could not attend the meeting of the Vestry called for the following Friday. He asked that someone be appointed in his place.[15]

The Methodists had been in Virginia since 1772 as a Society within the Established Church and were quietly holding meetings throughout the Colonies.

Parson Smith, as he was referred to by General Washington, held services regularly at Nomini and Yeocomico, alternating Sundays, except when the weather was too stormy. If the weather was severely cold, Mr. Smith read the service from the prayerbook and would not preach a sermon. The Tutor, Fithian, seems to have thoroughly approved of this arrangement. Fithian also reports on Parson Smith and his wife's social life. They attended the famous ball held at Lee Hall by Squire Richard Lee in Jan. 1774. Fithian notes "Parson Smith's and Parson Giberne's wives danced but I saw neither of the Clergymen either dance or game." At the "four day ball" some of the guests who were not dancing were toasting the Sons of America and singing Liberty songs, others were playing cards. Apparently Col. Carter did not attend but had instructed his sons to go and stay all night and to bring him an account of all the company at the ball. The first day of the Ball was on Sunday. Mr. Smith sent his compliments to the tutor who had neglected to attend Church services with the Carter boys in the morning. That afternoon it is reported

---

*Read Chapter IX *Vol. II Virginia's Mother Church*, "The Awakening Within the Church," especially page 200, the third paragraph.

13. *Virginia's Mother Church*, page 183, Vol. II.

14. *Northern Neck Historical Magazine*, Vol. XVI, page 1508.

14a. *Ibid.*, page 1510–1511.

15. *Ibid.*, page 1514.

the Parson went skating on Hickory Hill Mill Pond with a group of gentlemen before they attended the Ball.[16]

Apparently Mr. Smith was popular with his parishioners. He had been rector of the parish for nine years. Four children were born at the Glebe by 1773.[16a] If he had any bad habits I am sure Mr. Fithian would have noted the facts in his diary. On Sunday February 1773 the Tutor notes the Rev. Mr. Giberne, minister from Richmond County, preached at Yeocomico. His topic was Felix trembling at Paul's sermon. Mr. and Mrs. Giberne are often mentioned in the Journal. Mrs. Giberne was the daughter of Moore Fauntleroy and was the widow of Charles Beale of Richmond County when she married Mr. Giberne. Mr. Giberne had a reputation for being an especially sociable and convivial man. It may have been his actions that gave the clergy such a bad name during this period.[16b]

On April 1, 1774, Good Friday services were held at Yeocomico Church. Mr. Smith is reported to have given a long sermon "and well chosen." April 3 was Easter Sunday. Mr. Fithian seemed pleased with the service. "All the Parish met together, High, Low, Black, White, all came out. After the Sermon the Sacrament was administered, but none are admitted except communicants to see how the matter is conducted."[17]

Col. Carter subscribed to a variety of periodicals including *The Williamsburg Gazette*, and *The Pennsylvania Gazette*, (which published the news that Dr. Walter Jones, a popular physician in the Northern Neck, was made a member of the American Philosophical Society in 1774), and *The Monthly Review*, which published remarks on the poetry and writings of "that ingenuous African Phillis Wheatly" of Boston which, according to Fithian, "astonished Bob Carter when I read them to him".[18]

Col. and Mrs. Carter were very well read, as were other members of the Parish, and were well aware of what was happening in Massachusetts. It came as no surprise when

"At a respectable Meeting of the Free-holders and other Inhabitants of the county of Westmoreland assembled on due notice, at the Court House of the said County on Wednesday, the 22nd. of June, 1774, to put in writing their opposition to the

16. *Philip Vickers Fithian Journal*, pages 74 to 77.
16a. *Jamestown to Charlestown*, Published by Mary Rutherford Hughes Tayloe, 1985, page 130.
16b. *Journal of Philip Fithian*. Page 25.
17. *Ibid.*, page 119.
18. Ibid., page 96. "Phillis Wheatley had been brought from Africa to Boston as a slave in 1761. She was educated by the daughters of her owner, John Wheatley. She manifested remarkable acquisitive powers and soon attracted attention by the excellent character of her verse. Her first bound volume, *Poems on Various Subjects, Religious and Moral*, was published in 1773.

proceedings of the 'late House of Burgesses of this Colony' and to state their alarm and fear that 'ruin is threatened to the ancient constitutional rights of North America' "[19]. (In the 9th paragraph it was noted: "We do appoint Richard Henry Lee and Richard Lee, Esquires, the late representatives of this county, to attend the general meeting of Deputies from all the counties; and we desire that they do exert their best abilities to get these our earnest desires, for the security of public liberty, assented to."[19a] Parson Smith, Rector of Cople Parish, was elected chairman.

The First Continental Congress met on Sept. 5, 1774. Leaders of the Congress included Richard Henry Lee of Cople Parish. The second Congress met in Philadelphia May 10, 1775. George Washington was selected to become Commander-in-Chief of the army and the rest is history! Cople Parish had nurtured two of the foremost leaders of the Revolution.

On May 23, 1775, The Committee of Safety of Westmoreland County met at the Court House with the Rev. Thomas Smith, Chairman, and fifteen other members of the said Committee and put into writing the five resolves called The Westmoreland County Resolves. The fifth resolve states:

"That the thanks of this Committee are justly due to the Delegates of the late Continental Congress, and to the Delegates from this Colony particularly, for their prudent, wise, and active conduct, in asserting the liberties of America; and that design of government which, in some instances, we are informed, has already been carried into execution, to deprive them of all offices, civil and military, tends manifestly to disturb the minds of the people in general; and that we consider every person advising such a measure, or who shall accept of any office or preferment, of which any of the noble asserters of American liberty have been deprived, as an enemy to this country.

Ordered, that the Clerk transmit a copy of the foregoing Resolutions to the Printer as soon as conveniently may be published in the *Gazette*. James Davenport, Clerk."[21]

On February 27, 1775, another baby girl, Sara, had been born to the Smiths at the Glebe. This was a happy event. A welcome sister for their seven year old daughter Mary, and for four year old Gregory.[22] Life was going on in spite of the changes brought about by the fight for liberty from British rule.

Dr. William Flood, a much beloved physician and prominent land owner,

---

19. H. Ragland Eubank papers, Westmoreland County Museum Library.
19a. Ibid.
21. H. Ragland Eubank Papers. Resolutions of Westmoreland County Committee of Safety.
22. *Jamestown to Charlestown*, page 130.

died in 1775 and left his land called "Kinsail" (sic) to his son William and also his seal and coat of arms. He also left a son Nicholas, and two daughters, Elizabeth and Alice (who became Mrs. Walter Jones).[23]

Reference is made in *Memorials of a Southern Planter* to the death of the Smith's son Gregory in 1776. He was buried in the garden at the Glebe. There was very little medicine for childhood diseases except for loving care of families who kept watch over their sick children. The doctor had few remedies to help. It is also recorded that Daniel Tebbs died in 1776. He was a prominent man in Cople Parish, who had signed the Leedstown Resolutions and was active in the Parish in several capacities. He left three sons, William, Fouchee, and Daniel and two daughters, Elizabeth and Martha.[24]

Turbulent years were ahead for the "Established" Church but the Parish managed to stay active in spite of the upheaval. The vestry was still functioning with Richard Henry Lee, Thomas Chilton, Joseph Pierce, John Augustine Washington and Joseph Lane, Gent. listed as members in 1777.[25]

On April 29, 1777, Kinsale became the location of a hospital to care for Small Pox victims. "Ordered that Doctor Walter Jones and Doctor George Steptoe have leave to inoculate for the small pox at Kinsale, which is appointed a Hospital for that purpose, and that they appoint four Persons as Guards for the purpose of preventing the said small pox."[26]

The 16th Article of the Bill of Rights of the new Commonwealth of Virginia on June 12, 1776, dealt with changes in repeal of all existing laws against Non-Conformers and Dissenters. They were completely exempt from all levies, taxes and impositions whatever toward maintaining and supporting the church as it now is or "hereafter may be established and its ministers." The law that provided for the support of the Clergy was suspended even as it applied to members of the established Church. No dissenters from the Church could be forced to support it. The last action they took was to amend the Prayer Book of the Established Church by erasing the prayers for the King and royal family from every service and inserting in the collects for Morning and Evening Prayer a "prayer for the Magistrates of the Commonwealth." In 1778 it was decreed "All vestries be relieved from the care of the poor, all other Civil functions had been removed and Vestries were chosen from and by members of the Episcopal Church."[27]

In 1778, the Assembly ordered the appointment of Overseers of the Poor

23. *Wills of Westmoreland County, Virginia* by Augusta B. Fothergill, page 172.
24. Ibid., page 172.
25. *Westmoreland County Order Book 1776–1786*, page 16.
26. Ibid., page 40.
27. *Colonial Church In Virginia.* The Reverend Edward Lewis Goodwin, pages 206–213.

to act in place of Vestrymen or Church Wardens who had attended to the poor of the Parish until the dissolution of the Established Church. Now they would be sworn in for the County. This was the point in time when the authority of the Parish passed to the County Government; the Separation of Church and State. On November 24, 1781, Alexander Sparks and George Fairfax Lee, two of the vestryman of Cople Parish, took the oath and qualified.[28] Also on November 30, 1784, Samuel Templeman and Catesby Jones, gent. took the oath and qualified.[28a] Samuel Templeman became a leader in the Nomini Baptist Church at Templemans.

In 1779, the Court "Ordered that the Churchwardens of Cople Parish bind out John Davis to James Kelly, according to law." On March 30, of that same year the order was to "bind out George Barnwell Shannon and John Short to George Cary, Joiner."[29] It would take a long while to untangle the strings which bound the Church and the State but it was done, if very slowly.

About this time Col. Robert Carter wrote to Mr. Francis Christian to inform him that his daughters would not attend his dancing classes any more. He and his wife "are of the opinion that dancing is not a Christian qualification; that if there be no evils in the act of dancing it is often productive of a revel, and it is admitted by every denomination of Christians that there is no reveling in the New Jerusalem."[30]

Col. Carter kept copies of all his correspondence which gives us a wonderful insight into the life in Cople Parish during and right after the War for Independence.

The Reverend Mr. Smith's family tells a story handed down through the generations which relates that during the war, life at the Glebe went along as usual until one day an alarm was given that the British were coming up the Potomac River. The account, by Mr. Smith's granddaughter, states that the Rector ordered everything which could be collected in a hurry be put in a wagon and driven to a safe place. As the servants were loading the wagon, the oxen shifted their weight and one of the wagon wheels was pushed against a plank on which a line of bee hives were standing, This upset the bee hives, and bees began swarming all over the place and were stinging everything in their path. The family and servants fled into the house, where key holes were stuffed with cotton to keep the infuriated bees out. The poor oxen ran away and the fowls which were in coops on the wagon were stung to death. The

28. *Westmoreland County Orders 1776–1786*, page 116.
28a. Ibid., page 254. Helen C. Tayloe Research.
29. *Westmoreland County Orders—1776–1786*, pp. 71–72. Helen C. Tayloe Research.
30. *Northern Neck Of Virginia Historical Magazine.* "Robert Carter of Nomini Hall." pp 1508–1539. Dr. J. Motley Booker.

"alarm" turned out to be false, and no British ship came near Glebe creek at that time![31]

The Professorship of Divinity at the College of William and Mary was abolished in 1779. The reason given for this was simple and in keeping with the mood of the times: "the Institution had been established for the purpose of preparing clergy for the Church of England and there was no longer need for it since the new order is not in favor of any particular sect . . . this would be incompatible with Freedom of a Republic."[32]

In 1779 the Act for support of the Clergy was repealed. This meant that Mr. Smith would have to support his growing family without benefits accorded the clergy under the Established Church; however, he could stay at the Glebe and continue to cultivate the land. We have no record of Mr. Smith doing this, but several ministers supported themselves by teaching. This was a time of hardship for everyone. The stoppage of shipments of tobacco, the main crop at that time, was being felt throughout the area. Members of the Parish were making their own clothing, no fine imports from abroad at this time, no ships bringing treasures from "home," no silks or children's toys. (This was when American craftsmen began to come into their own.). Spinning wheels were busy on each plantation and weaving was a daily occupation for housewives, and they learned they could do without many luxuries which had been ordered from England before the revolution. I wonder if the Coffee Tree bean was roasted and ground as a substitute for the coffee denied the victims of the blockade?. Col. Carter at Nomini Hall was smelting iron for use in making utensils, such as hoes and plows, which he bartered to his neighbors for corn, wheat, and beans.[33]

Victory at last! October 19, 1781! The War was at an end! In an excerpt from a letter from John Turberville to his brother George of "Pecatone" dated "Hickory Hill, December 21, 1781" we have this wonderful picture of the reaction of a member of the Parish to this momentous occasion!

"Cornwallis was taken last Thursday. The American Flag flying in York on that day. The militia of this County will be up today. Great rejoicing below. I am just going to the (word illegible) to hear further about it as I expect the whole proceedings and the amt. of stories, etc. will be humerus"[34] It took awhile for the good news to reach Cople Parish.

---

31. "Memorials of a Southern Planter"; Susan Dabney Smedes, page 15.
32. Brydon's *Virginia's Mother Church*, page 431-432.
33. *Northern Neck of Virginia Historical Magazine*, Vol. XVI. "Robert Carter of Nomini Hall"—Abstracts of Letters 1784—by J. Motley Booker, page 1520.
34. Papers of H. Ragland Eubank. Letter the late Mrs. Robert Beale (nee Louise Murphy) of Hague, Virginia, aunt of Mrs. Charles Y. Griffith, great-great granddaughter of George Turberville and his wife

In 1782 it didn't take long, I'm sure, for the good news of the birth of a son to Parson and Mrs. Smith to reach members of the parish. He was named John Augustine Smith and was destined to become President of The College of William and Mary.[35]

In 1784 Peter Mullin died and his will was probated May 25. This information should be very interesting to Cople Parish residents today. Apparently Mr. Mullin was concerned about the education of the children of the Parish. In his will he gives to "wife Elizabeth land and at her death to be sold and money used to school 12 poor children who live within 3 miles of Yeocomico Church for 2 years, then 12 more and so on until all money spent save, 5 pound which is for care of the graveyard."[36] What a wonderful way to be remembered!

Dr. George Steptoe also died in 1784. His will was probated on May 27. He left to "his wife Elizabeth land called 'Windsor' near the Court House; a child unborn; son Edward residue of estate; bros. James and William Exrs."[37]

In December 1784, the church leaders now turned their minds to "Rescue and Restore" the Anglican church and took steps to organize the Episcopal Church out of what had been called The Church of England in the Colony of Virginia. Ever since the settlement at Jamestown, the church had been established, supported, and governed under the laws of the mother country of the Colony until June 1776 when The State Constitution was adopted. The General Assembly granted the request from a large group of clergyman to disestablish the old church entirely, and thus the parishioners would be free to govern themselves. The General Assembly also passed an act to incorporate the parishes, ministers, and people of the old church under the new name, The Protestant Episcopal Church of Virginia. It was also enacted that in every parish in the Commonwealth, the members of the Anglican Communion should meet on Easter week 1785 and elect 12 men as the vestry of their Parish, and these men should meet and elect two representatives to attend a meeting of all delegates from all Parishes to form a Diocesan Organization and to elect a Bishop. This was a big step. The church had not had a Bishop in this country since the beginning. Every candidate for ordination had to go to England for his holy orders. Now they would organize a Standing committee which would give the church National Standing and

Martha Corbin of "Pecatone". This letter was copied by Mr. Eubank in the early thirties. Mrs Beale's home was destroyed by fire and all her valuable papers were lost. We owe Mr. Eubank a debt of gratitude for saving these bits of history.

35. *Jamestown to Charlestown*, by Mary Rutherford Hughes Tayloe, Page 130.
36. *Wills of Westmoreland County, Virginia*, Page 178.
37. Ibid., page 178.

enable them to demand that the Order of Bishops be granted to them. And so it was that the first annual convention of the Protestant Episcopal Church of Virginia met May 18, 1785, at the State Capitol in Richmond.[38]

When the Methodists formed themselves into a distinct and separate denomination from the Episcopal Church, a large blow was struck Cople Parish. The Methodist had been a missionary society within the Established Church, and it was hoped they would join with the Protestant Episcopal Church but this was not to be. The Methodist organized into a separate denomination in 1784.[38a]

The Vestry lost one of its loyal members in September 1785 when Benedict Middleton died. His father, Robert Middleton, had also served on the vestry.[39]

At a second diocesan convention held in May 1786, the Rev. David Griffith, rector of Fairfax Parish, was elected for consecration as Bishop of Virginia. Sad to tell he was never able to go to England for consecration. The Church was too poor to send him and his health was failing, so after three years he resigned his election.[39a] In 1790 The Rev. James Madison, President of the College of William and Mary, was elected Bishop of Virginia. After the United States government had been organized in 1789 and "an establishment of a stable currency," the financial conditions in Virginia were such that the Bishop elect could go to England and be consecrated. On Sept. 20, 1790, in the archiepiscopal palace at Lambeth, The Rev. James Madison was consecrated by the Archbishop of Canterbury, the Bishop of London and Bishop of Rochester. At long last Virginia finally had a bishop![40]

While all the solemn affairs of state and church were being attended to, a young lady, Miss Lucinda Lee, was visiting her relatives in Cople Parish in 1787 and keeping a Journal.[41] Her visits to Chantilly, Thompson's Hill (at Nominy Ferry), Bushfield, Lee Hall, and Pecatone, with side excursions to The Ballentines at Ayrfield to see the preparations for Anne Ballentine's

---

38. *Highlights Along The Road.* The Rev. Maclaren Brydon D.D. Va. Diocesan Library, 1957, page 28. and Brydon's *Virginia Mother Church*, page 567.

38a. *The Colonial Churches of Virginia*, Rev. Edward Lewis Goodwin, D.D. Published by Morehouse Publishing Company, Milwaukee, Wis. 1905, page 105, and "Early Days of the Diocese of Virginia," An address by G. Maclaren Brydon, 1935, in pamphlet form in Virginia Diocesan Library. 110 W. Franklin Street, Richmond, Virginia.

39. *Wills of Westmoreland County Virginia*, page 183.

39a. The Rev. David Griffith has many descendants in Cople Parish today.

40. "Highlights Along The Road," pamphlet by G. McClaren Brydon, Diocese of Virginia, 1957. *Ecclesiastical History of the United States*, by Francis L. Hawks, Rector of St. Thomas' Church, New York, Published by Harper and Brothers, N.Y., 1836, Chapter X, page 210.

41. Ludwell Lee Montague in *Northern Neck Historical Magazine*, Vol. XVII, page 1825. corrects the date from 1782 to 1787. "The Journal of a Young Lady of Virginia" gives the research to prove the change. The error was made when the booklet was published in 1871.

wedding to Mr. Murphy (which took place November 8, 1787) are all recorded in great detail. While staying at Chantilly she tells of "collecting in the Chamber on Sunday morning reading the lessons of the day." (Richard Henry Lee was a vestry man of Cople Parish. It is assumed he read the lessons from the Book of Common Prayer.) The following Sunday she attends service at Nominy but does not mention the sermon or Parson Smith. (Her journalism ran more to descriptions of flirtations with young men who seemed to spend a lot of time visiting around, looking over the crop of eligible mates, the ladies gowns, and who was present at whatever function, which was perfectly normal for a sixteen year old). However, on her trip back to Chantilly on Sunday 28 of October, her thoughts are turned to more serious matters, as she describes a baptism in Nominy creek:

"We dine at Dr. Thompson's in the evening. At Doctor Thompson's we heard, close by, there were six people dipt. (sic) We had curiosity to see them, and according went. I assure you it is a very Solemn Sight." In the next sentence she writes, "We brought two Beaux home with us, Mr. Beale, and Mr. Stark". Her thoughts never rested long away from fun and frolic![42] It was no doubt refreshing to have this gay spirit around and we are fortunate to have this account to answer any questions about the Social life of Cople Parish and the "leading lights" of the period.

Because of the following research information just recently completed by Camille Wells for Mr. and Mrs. John Morrow, it is safe to say the Garner family lived at "Kirnon" and were members of Cople Parish and had been for some years. At this time, on the eleventh day of July 1787, an item appears in the Westestmoreland County Records which states:

"James Garner to George Garner, both of Cople Parish. For 100 pounds, a tract of 100 acres, one lot or tenement of land whereon I now live,. Bounded by the lands of George Garner, John Ballantine, Fleet Cox and the main road to Richard Lee's and John Turberville's land."[43] An interesting item appeared in print a year after this, stating that Mr. George Garner was the Coroner for the County.

From Calendar of Virginia State Papers: "Inquisition, 28, Nov. by George Garner, Gent., Coroner . . upon view of body of Capt. John Rochester, late Sheriff of the County, found on the main road leading from Westmoreland Courthouse to Nominy, and there lying dead. (names of several men), good and lawful men of the Parish of Cople to enquire how and in what manner

42. "Journal of a Young Lady of Virginia." Northern Neck of Virginia Historical Magazine, NNVHM Vol. XVII pages 1589–1680.
43. *Westmoreland County Deed & Will Book 21*, page 346.

the said John Rochester, Gentleman, came by his death, upon their oaths do say that 'he was accidentally killed by a fall from his horse'. Signed James Bland. C.W.C.".*

Mr. Smith attended the Council forming the Protestant Episcopal Church, and the Parish was represented in The General Assembly by able men such as Richard Henry Lee. Mr. Smith had "weathered the storm" and was still holding services in 1787.[44] He had attended the first convention, but it is not likely he attended the 1786 council because that year his 13 year old daughter, Ann, so the Smith family legend says, was sorting over some blackberries she had picked as she stood in the pantry of "The Glebe." A storm came up and lightening came in the window and killed her. Parson Smith called for the Parish Clerk to come and read the burial service over her. It is remembered that Mr. Smith "disapproved of eulogies or funeral sermons," as they are called. He had great reverence for everything sacred and his children were reared to follow such a beautiful example—for instance the children were taught never to sing a hymn as they would a song. He considered it an insult to be offered remuneration for administering the sacraments of the Church, for Baptism, administering the communion (to the sick of course), and for reading the Burial service over the dead."[45]

In 1788 Yeocomico Church had been built eighty two years when The gentleman of the surrounding estates were assessed to repair the roof. This was before Parson Smith died.[46]

Mr. Smith died in October 1789 after an illness of about two years. He was buried in the garden at the Glebe with his children who had predeceased him. Mrs. Smith was left with three children. Sara was fourteen and John Augustine seven. Mary was twenty and married to Philip Lee of Leeville[47]. Since we have no Parish records to help us, we do not know just when the Smiths moved from the Glebe. But ties with the parish were not broken because when John Augustine grew up, he returned and claimed Letitia Lee of "Lee Hall" as his bride.

At the General Convention of the Church in October 1789, The Book of Common Prayer of the Protestant Episcopal Church was finally adopted.[48]

---

*This piece of information pertaining to Cople was sent by J. Paul Hudson, histographer with the National Park Service, retired. He found it in a Calendar of Virginia State Papers, Vol. 7, p. 378.

44. *Virginia's Mother Church*, Dr. G. Maclaren Brydon list of Clergy for 1774 and actively involved in the War for Independence, pp. 434–612

45. Ellen M. Bagby: "John Augustine Smith": in *William & Mary Quarterly*. Vol. 12, pp. 10–11. Research of H. Ryland Eubank.

46. *Old Churches and Families of Virginia*, letter from William Rogers in 1857 to Bishop Meade, page 157.

47. *Wills of Westmoreland County, Virginia*, by Augusta B. Fothergill, page 189–190.

48. Dr. Brydon's *Virginia's Mother Church*, page 464.

The next and last rector of Cople Parish was James Elliot. We have no record of his birth, but it has been published that he was ordained September 23, 1787, by Bishop White of Pennsylvania. He was rector of Petsworth Parish in Gloucester County, Virginia 1788–1790; came to Cople in 1792 and stayed until 1802; was in Washington Parish in 1805 and moved to Kentucky.[49] He was married to Elizabeth Brockenbrough, daughter of Col. Austin Brockenbrough[49a] He attended the convention of the Episcopal Church in 1799,[49b] He did not leave a very good reputation in any of his parishes. It is on record that "out of one hundred clergymen who came into Virginia parishes after the Revolution between 1785–1814, sixteen were notoriously bad." This probably accounts for the "falling away" suffered by Cople at this time. This is a hard fact but true, "parishes which could stand adversity and denominational hatred could not stand the disgrace and shame of an immoral pastor."[49c] "One rotten apple spoils the barrel" as the saying goes, and the dissenting denominations were really making inroads into the Parish flock. They were ordaining their chosen members and, since The Episcopal Church had no minister in residence, or one the members respected, to perform the rites of the church, it was only natural the people would call on the ministers of the new congregations. Thus these papers were recorded:

June 25, 1793, "Steward Redman, Gentleman, hath this day produced to the Court his credentials of his ordination as a minister of the Methodist Church and received from the Senior Majistrate certificate to celebrate the rites of matrimony."[50]

February 25, 1794, "Samuel Templeman produced to this Court the credentials of his ordination as a member of the Baptist Church and received from the Senior Majistrate a certificate to celebrate the rites of matrimony."[51]

August 1, 1791, Colonel Robert Carter, one of the wealthiest men in Virginia, filed a "Deed of emancipation" setting free the more than 500 "negroes & mulatto slaves" who were his absolute property. "I have for sometime past been convinced that to retain them in slavery is contrary to the true principles of Religion & Justice & therefore it is my 'duty to manumit them.' This did not secure freedom for all 500 slaves at once. Instead, he

---

49. Brydon's pamphlet, "Early Days of the Diocese of Virginia," page 19. Clergy Ordained After Revolution in Virginia 1785–1814.
49a. November 20, 1792. The Marriage Took Place Source: *Virginia History Magazine*. Brockenbough family. Vol. 5., page 448.
49b. "Journal of the Convention of the Diocese of Virginia in Richmond May 7, 1799." *Ecclesiastical History of the United States of America*, by Francis L. Hawks, Rector of St. Thomas Church, New York. Vol. 1 Harper & Brothers, 1836, p. 72.
49c. Dr. Brydon's *Virginia Mother Church*, page 506.
50. *Westmoreland County Record Book, No. 7, 1790–1798*, p. 170.
51. Ibid., page 122.

established a schedule by which 15 slaves, starting with the oldest would be set free each January 1, over a period of 21 years. This was in keeping with Virginia law which at the time banned the freeing of underage slaves. Carter owned 60,000 acres on 18 plantations. There are ninety names on the list in the Court House Record of this deed page 213, 244, 291–292.[52] Mrs. Inez Johnson has written a Black History of Westmoreland which covers the subject of slavery in Cople Parish very well.

Now came the sad news that the Glebe lands belonging to the parishes of The Episcopal Church in Virginia had been declared property of the State. This was a big blow. The Acts of the General Assembly of Virginia for the years 1784, 1785, 1788, 1799, and 1801 told the story and are the best way to learn just what really happened. A good account, and as unbiased as you can find, is in Dr. H. J. Eckenrode's *Separation of Church and State.*[53] The funds realized from the sale of this church property were meant to be used for the care of the poor, for education, and for poor houses.

During the 1790's the Parish not only suffered from the problems of the Church property debacle, but several of the influential members of the Parish had become charter members of Nomini Baptist church which was formed in 1786. Col. Robert Carter, Samuel Templeman, and Capt. Joseph Pierce, all members of the Vestry of Cople, headed the list.[54] John Augustine Washington died at Bushfield in 1787.[55] General George Washington noted in his Diary, written at Mount Vernon, January 10, 1787:

"Just before dinner Mr. Brindley, manager of the Susquehanna works, and his son-in-law came in on their way to South Carolina. About the same time I recd. by ex-press the account of the sudden death (by a fit of the Gout in the head) of my beloved Brother, Colo. Jno. Ague. Washington. At Home all day." On Jan. 12th. Gen. Washington, in his Leger B, writes he has sent 'by Majr. G. A. Washington to buy mourning ring for me £16.16.0,' and January 12th. in his diary he says, "Home all day writing letters and doing other matters previous to Majr. Geo Washington setting out for New Kent."[55a]

In the 1790's the Parish lost by death some of her most faithful and able members: 1791 Fleet Cox, William Middleton, Elias Davis, of Cople Parish;* 1793 George Turberville of Pecatone, Cople Parish;* 1794 Churchman and

---

52. *Robert Carter of Nomini Hall, Westmoreland County, Virginia*, page 543.
53. *Journals of The House of Delegates 1784–1786–1799–1801.* H. J. Eckenrode *Separation of Church and State in Virginia.* State Library, 1910.
54. "History of Nomini Baptist Church" by Elton Healy. *Northern Neck Historical Magazine Vol. XIX*, page 1855.
55. *Will's of Westmoreland County*, Augusta Fothergill, page 188.
55a. *Diaries of George Washington.* Donald Jackson, Editor, Dorothy Twohig Associate Editor. University Press, of Virginia, Charlottesville, Virginia, 1976, page 160 and Footnote.

Patriot Richard Henry Lee; 1795. John Massey of Cople Parish,* Colonel Richard Lee, member of the Virginia Legislature; 1799 Bruce Omohundro of Cople Parish,* Solomon Robinson of Cople Parish,* Samuel Rust of Cople Parish,* John Crabb of Cople Parish,* John Hutt, merchant of Nominy ferry with Gerrard Hutt, and John Turberville of "Cople Parish, Hickory Hill,"*.[56]

We will assume The Rector at this time was The Rev. James Elloit because in the Court House in Montross it was recorded the widow of Col. Richard Lee, Sarah Bland Poythress Lee and Willoughy Newton II were married May 23, 1796, "by The Reverend James Elloit of Ye Protestant Episcopal Church".[57] Col. Lee and Willoughby Newton had been members of the house of Delegates of Virginia 1793–1794. Whether they served on the vestry at that time we do not know because of no Church records for this period. No member of Cople Parish served in the House of Delegates after 1796 until George Garner was elected in 1799 and served until 1803 when Stephen Bailey was elected. Stephen Bailey stayed on until 1816. Peter Cox represented Westmoreland from 1809–1810. Richard Parker. from 1807–1810.[57a]

"November 23, 1801, Thomas Spence and Charles Sanford qualified as Overseers of the Poor in Cople Parish. William Porter is appointed Overseer of the Poor in Cople Parish in room [place] of John Murphy who refused to act. Nathaniel Mothershead is appointed Overseer of the Poor in Cople Parish"[58]

At the General Association in 1802, the Legislature passed a law forbidding the taking of Glebe lands for sale as long as there was an incumbent Minister or was sold at minister's request. Cople was without a minister in 1805 when Mr. Elliot is listed as Rector of Washington Parish. Therefore, the Glebe lands were seized by the Overseers of the Poor in compliance with the law; however, the Glebe lands were not sold until 1812. In the Court House Records is the following:

"June 12. Deed of land called "The Glebe," from Overseers of the Poor of Westmoreland County to John Chandler, is this day acknowledged by Henry Lee and John Neale, other subscribing Overseers to the s'd deed.[59]

"October 1812. A deed for the sale of the Glebe land of Cople having been previously proved to John Chandler from the Overseers of the Poor of this

---

56. *Wills of Westmoreland County, Virginia.* Augusta Fothergill, Vol. XVIII Vol. XIX, Vol. XX.
*Denotes the phrase "of Cople Parish," written in the Will right after the deceased name, to declare loyalty to Parish.
57. Westmoreland County Records.
57a. *Westmoreland County, Virginia History,* Edited by Walter B. Norris, page 692.
58. *Westmoreland County Orders 1801–1804,* page 190–191.
59. *W. C.R. Deeds and Wills Book* No. 22, page 275. Research of Mrs. Helen C. Tayloe for Writers Project. In Museum Library in Montross.

county John Neale and Henry Lee, Jr. two of the remaining overseers of the Poor of this day acknowledged the same in open Court and it is ordered to be recorded."[60]

This was indeed a difficult time in Cople Parish as well as other Parishes of Virginia. The church buildings were falling into desrepair. There was no minister to hold regular services and no hope of getting one without the Glebe lands to help support them. To top this off, the war of 1812 began and again all shipping was at a virtual standstill because of the British blockade and Cople parishioners felt the hardship of war once again.

Thomas Brown, son of William and Margaret Templeman Brown, was born in 1785 on a farm adjoining "Walnut Farm," on Nomini Creek, the home of Corbin Washington, (son of John Agustine Washington,) and close by Bushfield. In his, memoirs written when he was 78 and had become the Governor of Florida, he told of his grandmother taking care of his family after the death of his mother. "She was a strict member of the Episcopal Church and complied with all the forms. She regularly had morning and evening service and read the prayers herself which she did with great dignity."[61] This is one example of how the Book of Common Prayer kept the Episcopal church alive. The services for each Sunday were read at home and morning and evening prayer during the week. The children were taught the Creed and the Catechism, the Collects and the Commandments. No doubt, members of the Parish attended the Nomini Baptist Church and the Methodist Meeting, too, yet still hoping their churches would be revived and the Church buildings reopened.

During the war of 1812, Cople Parish began to really suffer in the summer of 1813 when the British ships of war came up the Potomac River. Richard Parker was Commander of Westmoreland's 111th Militia Regiment. On July 15, 1813, Major John Turberville of "Pecatone" sent word to headquarters that sixteen British Ships of war were seen from a place near Yeocomico River, (which is a branch of the Potomac River) pass up the Potomac on the 14th with crowded sail and supposed to be in pursuit of the "Scorpion," a U.S. Sloop of War flying before them. Enemy barges entered Yeocomico River and fired on the armed schooner "Asp" of the gun boat Squadron as they lay at anchor in Kinsale harbor just off the point of the Baileys' property. The schooner was captured and boarded by the enemy, hand-to-hand combat ensued, and Midshipman James B. Sigourney of the U.S. Navy was killed.

---

60. Ibid.
61. "Extracts from a Manuscript of Thomas Brown" *Northern Neck of Virginia Historical Society*, Vol. XVIII, pp 1816-1817.

The Bailey family buried him in their family graveyard at the "Great House."[62]

Just before the war in 1807, the Westmoreland County Order Books showed "Henry Tapscott is appointed overseer of the road leading from Sandy Point over Courtney's run by Yeocomico Church to Tucker's Run and to the beginning in the room [place] of John Critcher."[63] Little did these gentlemen know the road would be used in a few years to carry a detachment of United States Infantry from Sandy Point to Yeocomico Church yard!

According to the record, this detachment of soldiers was sent in the fall of 1813 from the 36th Regiment of U.S. Infantry at Washington to "watch the movements of the British, by order of General Bloomsfield."[64] Because of this, we can thank the mosquitoes for chasing these soldiers to "seek out encampment in what is called there the "Forest or high ground." "The officer in charge of this detachment was Lt. William Luttrell Rogers of Princeton, New Jersey, and he proved to be a blessing to Cople Parish after the war was over. Here is his story of the encampment:

"Among other places recommended to us by the late General Alexander Parker,* we visited the ruins of Yeocomico Church".

After a description of the broken brick wall and the vines and overgrown trees in the yard, Mr. Rogers goes on to say:

"With some difficulty I entered the porch which was built of brick, and formed the upper part of the cross, spacious and on a level with the ground, its massive double doorway quite open, presenting within as hopeless a ruin as its exterior, the roof rotted away at its angles, one of the galleries partly down, the girders rotted off and fallen upon the pews and the wall in two places mouldered away by years of saturation from rain and snow. The remains of a large Bible still lay upon the desk. The font was gone, which I was told was of marble and now used for 'convivial purposes.' The chancel, in the eastern arm of the cross, to the right of the pulpit, surmounted by a large Gothic window, much broken, was still in tolerable preservation. In it was the Communion table, its frame antique covered with a heavy walnut slab, sound, but rough and soiled from exposure. Large frames, once covered with canvas exhibiting

---

62. *Westmoreland County, Virginia History*, page 354.

63. *Westmoreland County Records*. Orders 1804–1807, page 497. Research of Mrs. Helen C. Tayloe for Writers Project. In Museum Library, Montross, Virginia.

64. *Old Churches and Families of Virginia* by Meade, Vol. II, pages 154–157. Letter of Mr. W. L. Rogers to Bishop Meade.

*General Alexander Parker lived at "Springfield" on the Yeocomico River. His step-daughter, Betsy Simpson, was married to Thomas Brown whose brother, Richard Brown, built "Windsor" near Montross in 1811.

in distinct characters The Lord's Prayer, The Ten Commandments, and other texts of Scripture, hung upon the walls, now much defaced, mouldered, and torn. The aisles were paved with bricks, covered with abundant evidence of its being the resort of sheep and cattle running at large, and to complete the evidence of its abandonment, the ceiling, which was of boards, was tenanted by squirrels, snakes and scorpions. In contemplating the scene before me, I felt a mysterious attachment to this relic of piety and early faith of our fathers, not dreaming (being a stranger and wanderer) at some future day I should be honored and favoured by the commission to restore this temple, now in the dust, to the service of my creator and redeemer". Mr. Rogers goes on to say that the soldiers pitched their tents outside the wall, they cleaned up the yard, removed the tree which lay across the roof, cleaned the church and repaired what they could in order to use the building to store their equipment. Mr. Rogers assured Bishop Meade they did not deface the church, but left it in much better condition than they found it. Mr. Rogers also tells of "Mr. Murphy who lived at Ayrfield, half a mile from Yeocomico Church whose estate of some thousand of acres surrounded the church and burial ground on all sides. He was a gentleman of intellectual culture, an honored magistrate and a Presbyterian of the 'Covenant school; whose residence was the seat of hospitality, the home of the clergy, with a welcome to all who proclaimed the glad tidings."[64a]

In the late spring of 1814, Mr. Roger's detachment was ordered to Maryland, and the old church was abandoned once again. (Mr. Rogers did not forget Yeocomico Church nor the hospitality of the Murphys, and in 1816 he married Anne Ballentine Murphy, the granddaughter of Mr. Murphy of Ayrfield.)[64b]

Beginning again in July 1814, the British were out in full force. 1500 troops were reported on their way to the Court House in Montross. Then on July 22, Lt. Col. Peyton of the 45th Regiment of Stafford County reports to the Governor that 1500 British are in possession of the Westmoreland Court House. Colonel Parker had his hands full with rumors and some reports that unfortunately were true.[65]

Brig. General John P. Hungerford reported to the governor on July 27th: "I arrived late last night at Yeocomico church 3 or 4 miles from Kinsale. I have six hundred and fifty men and I am expecting a detachment of men from Essex momentarily". The British did have a great number of large ships and tenders and barges in the Potomac. The enemy landed twenty-two barges and three tenders with their men at the "Narrows" near the mouth of Machodoc Creek. The notorious Admiral Cockburn and his 1200 men went on a pillaging expedition up Nomini Creek. They burned Mr. Thompson's

64a. Ibid., 157.
64b. Westmoreland County Recordbook.
65. *Westmoreland County, Virginia*, Norris-Editor, "A Military History: War of 1812," pp 354–357.

house at Nominy ferry and carried off the Nomini Church communion silver. They fired on Nomini church and almost destroyed it, burned "Bushfield," now the home of Bushrod Washington and "Walnut Farm," home of Corbin Washington. They also plundered the farms, taking a large booty of slaves.[66] Because General Hungerford's troops were stationed at Yeocomico Church, they have received the blame for the Holy table being used for a chopping block and for otherwise defacing the church.[67]

On August 5, 1814, General Hungerford wrote another report in which he told of the burning of Kinsale and the deplorable situation there. Finally a detachment from the Virginia Militia arrived. Four complete companies of Infantry and one of Artillery were organized into a battaliom for the defence of the area between the Rappahannock and Potomac Rivers and it was ordered to rendezvous as early as possible at Cox's house near Yeocomico Church in Westmoreland County".[68] This description sounds very much like "'Elba," the Cox home which is still standing today at English's Corner.

After one hundred and fifty years, 1664–1814, the Parish had gone through many phases. Now this: Kinsale, her only town, ravaged by war, with homes and warehouses burned to the ground, both churches in ruins, Yeocomico abandoned and being used for a storeroom and barracks; Nomini wrecked by the shelling of Admiral Cockburn's gun boats;[69] the Parishioners demoralized and without an ordained minister to lead them. There was only one way to go and now the greatest challenge for Cople Parish lay ahead!

---

66. Ibid., page 358.
67. *Old Churches and Families of Virginia*, Bishop Meade, pp 156–157.
68. Ibid.
69. *Westmoreland County, Virginia*, "The War of 1812," pp 358–359.

THE LIFE OF COPLE PARISH 1814–1864

by BERTHA NEWTON DAVISON*

In his Preface to *The South Lives in History*, Wendall Holmes Stephenson says, "History is too much a record of conflict; too little a matter of harmonious living; of affairs, great and small, that affect daily lives more tangibly than political and constitutional issues."[1] Well, the daily lives of the inhabitants of Cople Parish, that geographical bit of territory in Westmoreland County, were certainly disrupted by the conflicts that raged around them during the War of 1812. They were just becoming accustomed to the changes brought about by the Revolution. The greatest difference in the life of the Parish was the lack of church services read from the familiar litany of the Anglican Church which now was anathema to a large segment of the population because of the connection with England. The two churches were in deplorable shape, with no Glebe for a resident rector and no shepherd to lead the members to restore the Churches.

The parishioners had a choice of attending the Methodist meetings which were held in private homes, or they could attend the Baptist meetings held in a comfortable frame meeting house which had been erected on land donated by Captain Joseph Peirce (a former Cople Parish vestryman) near Templeman's Cross Roads. Sometimes the Baptist meetings were held in private homes. In the minutes of Nomini Baptist Church for January 1824 is recorded the following: "At a Church meeting held at Sister Mary Porter's the Saturday before the 4th Sunday, business of the Church was attended to." Henry Toler was their first preacher. He had been sent to Pennsylvania by Councillar Robert Carter for three years, 1779–1781, to be educated for the ministry and became the first minister at Nomini Meeting House. In 1810 Samuel Templeman, having been converted by Mr. Toler, began to preach and, after Mr. Toler left, became the second pastor to serve Nomini Baptist Church.[2]

Bushrod Washington, the son of John Augustine and Hannah Washington, was born June 5, 1762, at BUSHFIELD on Nomini Creek in Cople Parish. He had followed in the footsteps of his illustrious family and was taking his place

---

*This is the fourth in a series of articles about this historic parish. See Vol. XL, p. 4578–4612; Vol. XLI, p. 4703–4733; Vol. XLIII, p. 5017–5038.

1. Wendall H. Stephenson, *The South Lives in History*. Baton Rouge, La: Louisiana State University Press, 1955, p. 4.

2. Col. John Smith, *The History of Nomini Baptist Church, Templeman, Virginia*. Fredericksburg, Va: Fredericksburg Press, 1986, pp. 11–12.

Miss Mary Porter's namesake, Miss Mary Porter Hall and her family are active members of the present Nomini Baptist Church.

in the affairs of the Church, State, and new Nation. He attended the College of William and Mary, was a member of Phi Beta Kappa Society in 1778, and studied law in Philadelphia under Mr. James Wilson, one of the leading lawyers of that city. He joined Mercer's Calvary Troop in 1780. He returned to Bushfield with his wife, Anne Blackburn of Prince William County, and practiced law for several years in Cople District. He represented Westmoreland County in the General Assembly and in the Convention which ratified the Federal Constitution in 1788. He moved first to Alexandria, then to Richmond where he was appointed to the Supreme Court by President John Adams and served with great distinction until his death in 1829.[3]

Judge Washington was a strong member of the Protestant Episcopal Church and was actively interested in the affairs of the Diocese of Virginia. With Edmund Randolph and John Wickham, he tried to prevent the Episcopal Churches and Glebes from being seized for common use. In 1816 Judge Washington was President of the American Colonization Society which was organized under the leadership of the Episcopal Church in the District of Columbia, which, at that time, included Alexandria and the present County of Arlington in Virginia. The purpose of this society was to assist those free blacks to return to Africa to the new country of Liberia. Judge Washington was a distinguished son of Cople Parish. He inherited Mount Vernon from his uncle, President Washington, and moved there in 1802 after the death of Mrs. Martha Washington.[3a]

The 1813 Convention of the Diocese of Virginia has been called the "turning point" in the Life of the Episcopal Church in Virginia.[4] It was agreed at this time to call a rector for the new Monumental Church in Richmond from outside the Diocese. A committee consisting of a native of Cople Parish, Bushrod Washington, was chosen to approach The Rev. Richard Channing Moore, rector of St. Andrew's, Staten Island, New York. Bushrod Washington, then living at Mt. Vernon, and Edmund J. Lee of Alexandria were successful in persuading this fine clergyman to come to Virginia, and he was elected Bishop of The Diocese of Virginia in May 1814.[5]

Bishop Moore was a great preacher and an able leader of men with a lovable character and "an unflagging" zeal to preach the gospel. "He came to a 'cowed'

3. T. R. B. Wright, *Westmoreland County, Virginia.* Richmond, Va: Whittet and Shepperson Printers, 1912, pp. 20–23.
3a. *The Encyclopedia Americana, Vol. 28,* New York, N.Y., 1938, pp. 773–779.
4. G. MacLaren Brydon, *Early Days in The Diocese of Virginia.* Richmond, Virginia: Virginia Diocesan Library, 1935, p. 3.
5. Mary Newton Stanard, *Richmond and Her People.* Philadelphia, Pa: J. D. Lippincott Co., 1923, p. 107.

life of the old Episcopal parishes in Virginia and brought a message of hope and courage."[6]

In 1815 at the meeting of a Convention of the Protestant Episcopal Church of the State of Virginia held at the Monumental Church in the city of Richmond, "Mr. Peter Presley Cox and Maj. John Turberville, for Cople Parish Westmoreland County" were the delegates.[7] (This was the first record of Cople being represented at a convention since 1799 when the Rev. James Elliott is listed as "Clergy for Cople.")[7a] The Committee, appointed to examine the parochial reports, gave a condensed report which included, "Cople, in Westmoreland County," and stated: "In the Parish of Cople the number of communicants is considerable, and an earnest desire is manifested among the people to revive the church. A hope is confidently entertained that soon the former character of the church in that parish will be supported by making provision for the permanent and respectable establishment of a minister."[7a] Sad to say, this was slow to come to pass.

The economy of Cople Parish was suffering. The land could no longer yield tobacco in great abundance. The land was exhausted because the topsoil had been overworked and washed into the rivers. People were moving away. The old life of the Lees and Carters was no more. With the decline of the international trade, the wharfs began to welcome regional trade routes between Baltimore and Norfolk. In 1815 the steamboat *Washington* joined the other small sloops and schooners on the Potomac River that brought supplies to the merchants: i.e. kerosene, molasses, and household wares and hauled away grain, lumber and produce to the markets in the cities."[8]

In 1815, an "epidemic, variously designated as epidemic influenza, catarrhal fever, typhus pleurisy, pneumonia typhoides, peripneumonia notha, catarrhal quinsy, and winter fever, was extremely fatal and took a heavy toll of life in Virginia."[8a] Dr. Thomas Gray of Tappahannock published an account of the fever in 1814 which stated: "In the Northern Neck, pneumonia was a frequent complication so fatal that it carried off whole families in a day or two." Dr. Grey felt "the prophylactics in this disease, as in all other infectious disorders, should begin and end with cleanliness, but, he added, 'The effluvia arising

---

6. Brydon, *Early Days in The Diocese of Virginia*, p. 24.
7. Francis L. Hawks, *Ecclesiastical History of the United States of America.* New York, N.Y.: Harper and Brothers, 1836, p. 96. (1815 Convention of the Diocese of Virginia)
7a. *Ibid*, pp. 98–99.
8. John C. Wilson, *Virginia's Northern Neck*. Norfolk Virginia: The Dunning Co., 1984, p. 49.
8a. Dr. Wyndham Bolling Blanton, *Medicine in Virginia 19th. Century.* Richmond, Virginia: Garrett & Massey, 1933, pp. 246, 247, 367.

from the volatile particles of camphor, asafoetida, onions, garlic, tar or sulphur, confined in bags and worn about the neck, have no doubt some effect in keeping at bay, or neutralizing the acrimonious infectious particles, which circulate in the room of sickness".[8b] Whether or not Cople Parishioners were visited by this epidemic is hard to tell. The Westmoreland County Record books show that "Thomas Bundell of Cople Parish" died and his will was probated in 1815.[9]

The widow of Dr. George Thompson lived above Nomini Creek on "Ferry Hill" and may have been suffering with this disease when she wrote her last will and testament with Dr. Robert Murphy in attendance:

> "In the name of God, Amen, I, Elizabeth Thompson of Westmoreland County, being in a weak and low condition of body, but sound and disposing mind and memory, do make, constitute and ordain this to be my last will & testament. Imprimas (?) my will and desire is that all my property be equally divided amongst my children whither real or personal, but, if my son Thomas shall receive payment for his property destroyed by the British, then my will is that (my son Thomas) have only one fourth of my property, the other three fourths be equally divided between my daughter Betsy & my son George Thompson. My will is that my daughter Betsy have the furniture in my bed chamber except the desk which I give to Tom. I also give to Betsy the damask Table cloth & napkins that belonged to my grandmother. All the rest of my bed & Table furniture it is my desire, shall be equally divided amongst my three Children. My will and desire is that my Executors, hereafter named, shall *shall* make good and sufficient deeds of conveyance for my lots sold in Alexandria & the money arising therefrom be applied to the payment of my debts, except one Hundred Dollars which is my will and desire be equally divided betwixt my Sister Sally & my niece Emily Griffith—and whereas I alone qualified as Executrix of the will of my Husband, Doctor George Thompson, and John Murphy & Charles Leland were my only securities for my Conduct of the Estate according to the will of my said Husband. Knowing I have done nothing wrong as Executrix, but also believing that securities are sometimes injured notwithstanding the best intentions and conduct of their principles—nothing doubting the honour of my Children or either of them—I do hereby make Known and declare that if either of my Children or their Legal representatives shall at any time claim or demand recovery or receive of either of my said securities or their representatives, any sum or sums of money for or on account of the Securityship aforesaid—Then that the said child so doing recovering and receiving as aforesaid Shall forfeit, *forfeit*, all benefit.
>
> Signed:
> Eliza. G. Thompson

8b. *Ibid,* page 367.

9. *Westmoreland County Records,* Montross, Virginia. Wills 1815, Book 3, p. 10.

In presence of
Emily C. Griffith
Anne Murphy
Dr. Robert Murphy[10]   28th day of July 1817: Jos. Fox

This will is full of information concerning the role of women in this period in history. Mrs. Thompson was certainly a firm character and well educated. She wrote the will in her own hand and underscored, by repeating a word, her forceful nature. It is interesting also to note that Dr. Robert Murphy was present probably because she was so ill. Also, one wonders if son Thomas was paid for the damage done to his property by the British? Mrs. Thompson's will was probated July 28, 1817.

We know that Dr. Robert Murphy was practicing in the area and was listed as "Surg. Mate." in the 111th Regiment Virginia Militia at Westmoreland County during the War of 1812–1814.[11]

Sarah Richardia Lee and Presley Cox were married June 8, 1815.[12] They were probably married at "Lee Hall," home of her mother. No record of the officiating minister has been found. The Cox family had lived in Cople Parish since the earliest times. "Elba," the brick house still standing on land patented by Vincent Cox in 1667, (according to Eton's Atlas) may have been the home of Presley Cox at this time, or they may have lived at "Locust Farm," just across the road to the east of "Elba." This land remained in the Cox family for many years. "Elba" and "Locust Farm" are among the oldest brick houses in Westmoreland County.

Stephen Bailey died and his will was presented to the Court and proved to be wholly in his hand writing and ordered recorded on the 26th day of February 1816. He lends to his "wife Ellen during her natural life, the place I now live" and describes the boundaries of the property which, along with his mother's dwelling, are on the main road leading from Yeocomico warehouses and Church, etc. He mentions his brothers Sydnor, John, and Robert, whom he wants to manage his children and to "bind out my sons to some trade."[13]

In 1816 Lt. William Rogers returned to Ayrfield and was married to Anne Ballentine Murphy, daughter of Mr. and Mrs. John Murphy, on June 16, 1816,

10. *Westmoreland Wills and Deeds 1818.* Book 23, page 301.
**Mrs. Thompson was Elizabeth Griffith, daughter of the Rev. David Griffith. Information from E. Colville Griffith, "Washington, Hungerford, Griffith Families of Virginia." Charlotte, North Carolina.
11. Walter Norris, Editor, *Westmoreland County, Virginia 1653–1983.* Wadsworth Pub. Co., Marceline, MO, 1983. Militia Rolls, 111th Regiment of Virginia Militia. 1813–1814, p. 360.
12. *Westmoreland County Marriage Book,* Vol. 4, July 8, 1815. Montross, Virginia.
13. Stephen Bailey's Will, Westmoreland County Court House Montross, Virginia. *Will Book 23,* p. 160.

at least that is when the license was recorded.[14] (Mr. Rogers neglected to mention this connection to the Parish in his letter to Bishop Meade in 1857!) This romance was a most fortunate thing for Cople Parish and Yeocomico Church in particular.

In 1817 the Rt. Rev. Channing Moore, in his report to the Diocesan Convention meeting in Fredericksburg on May 6, told of visiting and preaching at the Court House in Westmoreland County. (Montross was part of Cople Parish at this time). Mr. McGuire, who was rector of St. George's in Fredericksburg, accompanied the Bishop. The Bishop remarked that there was a flourishing congregation at St. George's. When Bishop Moore came to the Diocese in 1814, there were only seven clergymen, and he was earnestly working to remedy this. Visiting clergy, like Mr. McGuire, were unselfishly going to the shepherd-less flocks, and it was no easy task in those days. Crossing rivers on ferryboats, fording streams and driving through sandbeds, over roads not too much better than cowpaths made travel slow and difficult. But, little by little, they were building up the vacant parishes. Bishop Moore, in an eloquent address to the 1817 convention, thanked the faithful by saying, "In your zeal I have perfect confidence. Our number, it is true, is small; but we may be confident of success. Unborn generations will enjoy the benefit of our labours, and embalm our memory with the tears of gratitude and affection."[15] This prophesy has certainly come true.

"April 26, 1819, Peter Presley Cox, Gent. is appointed to Superintend an election of the Overseers of the Poor in the lower District of Cople Parish. John Harvey, Gent. is appointed to superintend the election of the Overseers of the Poor in the upper district of said Parish.[16a]

May 25, 1819, "The Court doth appoint the following persons Overseers of the Poor of this County: Vincent Edmonds, Thomas Spence, and Richard T. Brown for the upper District of Cople Parish. John Bailey, George Glascock and Wm. Wright for the lower District of Cople Parish."[16b]

Mr. Rogers, in a letter to Bishop Meade, tells of his visit to Cople Parish in 1820 when he undertook the work of repairing the old church with the help of Mr. Murphy of "Ayrfield."

"Mr. Murphy gave his money, labour and his personal service. The gentleman of the neighborhood subscribed cheerfully and liberally, so the work was pushed forward by

---

14. *Westmoreland County Marriage Book*, Montross, Virginia; Book 4, Jan. 16, 1816.
15. Francis L. Hawks, *Ecclesiastical History of United States of America.* New York, N.Y.: Harper & Brothers, 1836, p. 120. From Bishop Moore's report to the Diocesan Convention 1817.
16. *Westmoreland County Marriage Book 1818.* Montross, Virginia.
16a. *Westmoreland County Records Order Book B.* 1819–1823, page 38.
16b. *Ibid,* p. 119–120, Helen C. Tayloe Research.

employing suitable mechanics and importing from Alexandria lumber, shingles, paints, and seven or eight barrels of tar for the roof which had not had a shingle put upon it since the year 1788, at which time, I heard Mr. Murphy say, 'the gentlemen of the surrounding estates were assessed to meet the expense'. It is true as you state, the font, 'a beautiful marble one,' as you describe it, had been taken away and used for unholy purposes, and by him restored; also the plate, with a damask tablecloth and napkins marked 'Yeocomico Church' in the center, had been safely kept at "Lee Hall," and were gladly restored, by the pious and excellent lady, the late Mrs. Sarah Newton, who at that time lived and occupied the mansion and estate." The letter continues:

The first thing we did was to open a double gateway in front, with a wide gravel-walk up to the porch or apex of the cross, the pavement of which I laid with my own hands, none there being familiar with such work. If the narrow opening in the wall was a symbolic of the 'narrow path,' the one we now opened was illustrative of 'free grace;' a truth to which I feel myself indebted for a knowledge of salvation through the interceding blood of a crucified Redeemer.

It is also true, as you state, I presented the church with a large stove and ample pipe to warm it thoroughly, it having stood for upward of a century without one. It is also true I had the great pleasure to place a Bible and Prayer Book both on the desk and in the pulpit, and I rejoice to know the church is still protected and cared for, although I have not seen it in more than twenty years."[17] It is wonderful to have the record of men of different denominations working together to restore the old church.

In spite of the fact that Lt. Rogers of Princeton, N.J., and Mr. Murphy, "The Scotch gentleman from Ayrshire, living at Ayrfield, a Presbyterian of the 'Covenant' school whose estate of some thousands of acres surrounding the Church," and the men of the Parish had restored Yeocomico, the Parish was still without a resident pastor.

There is an ancient wrought-iron "dipper" which at one time was chained to a tree by the spring at the foot of the hill behind Yeocomico Church. It was placed there many years ago by Presley Cox to be used by thirsty parishioners to get a drink of cool, pure water. Mr. Cox's initials, "P.C." were impressed on the bowl of the ladle.[18] This was probably done when the Church was repaired in 1820 because Mr. Cox was active in the Parish at that time. The dipper is now in safe keeping in Ameslee Hall, but there are still people in the Parish who remember when the dipper and Spring were in use! It probably accounted for the spread of many germs! No mention is made of the Sun Dial by either Bishop Meade or Mr. Rogers.

Presley Cox in his will, which was probated June 28, 1824, named his children, his wife and his friend Robert S. Bailey. He divided up his "worldly

17. Bishop Meade, *Old Churches, Ministers and Families of Virginia.* Vol II. Philadelphia, Pa.: J. P. Lippincott, 1857, pp. 151–157.
18. Wat. Tyler Mayo, *A Sketch of Yeocomico Church.* Washington, D.C.: Sudwick Printers, 1936, p. 10.

estate" among them with the specific orders: "not to move any of the negroes out of the neighborhood or in any wise sell any of the said negroes, but shall at all times use them with the Greatest humanity and should any of the aforesaid negroes become infirm it shall be the duty of the said Robert S. Bailey to furnish said negro or negroes with a 'House and Garden' and shall furnish them with provision and clothes and treat them well in every respect"[18a] We notice the concern Mr. Cox displayed for the human property of which he wrote and also he did not refer to them as "slaves."[18a]

There is no record that Nominy was a total ruin after the British shelled it in 1814, or that it was completely destroyed by fire. The legend in the Parish is that the Methodists used Yeocomico Church for their meetings, and that occasional Episcopal services were held by visiting ministers. The families of the Parish used the Book of Common Prayer which was distributed by the Prayerbook and Tract Society to instruct their children in the liturgy of the Church, which was a canon of the Episcopal Church.[19]

In 1819 when the Convention of the Protestant Episcopal Church met in Petersburg, the Rev. William H. Wilmer was appointed to prepare an address to the Hon. Bushrod Washington, President of the American Colonization Society, to be read to the assembled Clergy and Layman assuring Mr. Washington of the support of the Church in this Society "over which you preside, and is one which cannot fail to awaken the sympathy of every humane mind. The forebodings of the politician, the regrets of humanity, and the prayers of Christians, have long been turned upon the question of providing a remedy for the evils growing out of the slave population in this country," and the long discourse ends with "In the name of God and of humanity, we wish you good luck. May Heaven prosper and reward your labour of love."[20]

In February 28, 1820, the Westmoreland Court Records showed that "Gerard Hutt and Thomas Hutt were appointed processioners for the upper District of Cople Parish and William Wright and Benedict Lamkin were appointed processioners for the lower district of Cople Parish"[21] The County government still referred to Cople Parish in many Court records, a habit hard to break.

In 1820 the popular reading of the day was William Cullen Bryant's "Thanatopsis," Washington Irving's *Sketch Book*, and The works of James Fenimore

---

18a. Westmoreland Co. Clerk's Office. *Will Book 1824.* pp. 56, 57, 58.
19. Hawks, *Ecclesiastical History of United States of America*, p. 169.
20. *Ibid*, page 137.
21. *Westmoreland County Records.* Order Book 1819, pp. 119–120. Research of Helen C. Tayloe.

Cooper. The money from the sale of the Glebe Lands had been put into a Literary Fund for support of the education of Poor children and for "the advantages to society which must ever please from a dispersion of knowledge among all of our citizens."[22] In 1823 Westmoreland County commissioners from Cople Parish were John Murphy, Robert Murphy, Thomas Stowers, Daniel Payne, and John Campbell.[22a]

At the time Yeocomico Church was being restored, several marriages were taking place in the Parish. Eliza Bland Newton, daughter of the "Pious lady" of Lee Hall, was married to Dr. Robert Murphy.[23] Her half sisters, Richardia Lee and Lettice Lee were the wives of Presley Cox and John Augustine Smith respectively. The Cox's daughter Elizabeth married Edward Colville Griffith, son of The Rev. David Griffith of Alexandria, and lived at "Locust Farm" near "Elba." Both houses are still standing and in wonderful state of preservation.

In 1822 the Convention of the Diocese of Virginia met in Charlottesville. Mr. John Nelson, who had been appointed to solicit subscriptions throughout the Diocese for the support of the Theological School, reported that he had "met with success beyond his expectations." Twenty-three ministers of the gospel attended this convention, and, with the beginning of The Theological School in Alexandria, the problem of vacant parishes would be solved in a few years. When the Seminary opened in Alexandria in 1823, classes were held at the home of The Rev. William H. Wilmer, rector of St. Paul's Church, Alexandria, Va.[24]

When Willoughby Newton II died in 1812, Dr. John Augustine Smith took his wife's half-brother, Willoughby Newton III, who was ten years old at the time, under his wing and gave him the opportunity to be educated in New Jersey where the Smiths lived. On his return to Virginia, he attended the College of William and Mary where Dr. Smith was then President. When he returned to Hague in 1825, he began the practice of Law and he lived with his mother at "Lee Hall" and helped manage her large estate. The region roundabout Mr. Newton's birthplace and residence was one of the most impoverished and wretchedly cultivated in Virginia".[25] Mr. Newton was married to Miss Elizabeth Holt of Williamsburg and began to build a home across the road from "Lee Hall," but his wife died in childbirth and the baby also before

---

22. Norris, Ed., *Westmoreland County VA.*, pp. 508–509.
22a. *Ibid.* School Commissioners from Cople Parish, April 27, 1829.
23. *Westmoreland Marriage Book* 1818. Montross, Virginia.
24. Francis L. Hawks, *Ecclesiastical History of United States of America.* pp. 153–154.
25. Obituary of Willoughby Newton, copied from Newspaper clipping found in scrap book found at Kelvin Grove, Hague, Virginia.

anything but the brick kitchen was built. It is assumed the work on the home at "Linden" was stopped for awhile.[25a]

Roads were a problem but were being constructed or improved by the county May 24, 1824: William King is appointed Overseer in the precinct of road from Sandy Point Woods to Tucker's Run and from Courtney's run to Sandy Point from thence to Tucker's Run, thence to Yeocomico Warehouse, thence to Garner's Shop and Bailey's Mill." May 24, 1825: William Beale is appointed Surveyor for the precinct of road from Lee's Cross Roads to Newton's Mill and from thence to Turberville's Mill, from thence by Appleby to the beginning. May 24, 1825: William H. Sanford is appointed Surveyor of the precinct of road from Stratford to Chilton's Cross roads going the way of Chantilly in the room of William Doleman. Benedict Wright is appointed Surveyor of the precinct of road from Presley Cox's power Mill to Kinsale, in the room of Daniel Mealy. October 24, 1825: Gordon Forbes is appointed Overseer of the precinct of road from Sandy Point gate to the cross roads leading to Yeocomico Warehouse, from thence by the church down the neck to the beginning".[26]

October 8, 1825, the Post Office at Hague was opened with Mr. Orson Ingram named Postmaster. David B. Taylor was Post Master at Kinsale at this time.[26a]

Mrs. Sally Bland Lee Newton died at "Lee Hall" in the summer of 1828. Her will was probated August 16, 1828. The first paragraph states:

"1st I give to my son Willoughby and to my daughter Eliza B. Murphy and Agnes A. Smith all the property of every description left me by my son Thomas F. Newton to be equally apportioned amongst them. (Thomas had died while a student at Princeton).

2nd. The remainder of my property of every description I wish to be divided equally among my children Mary Jones, (grandmother of Congressman William Jones of Richmond County.) Willoughby Newton, Eliza B. Murphy and Agnes A. Smith, of *Mantua*, Northumberland County, and my grandchildren, the offsprings of my daughter Lettice Smith, deceased, and Elizabeth and Sarah Cox, children of my daughter Richardia Robinson (in any way that they may think best) my said grandchildren taking their respective mother's portion only."

3rd: I wish my negro woman Fanny to have the privilege of selecting

25a. *Ibid.*

26. Excerpt from *Westmoreland County Orders Book 1823–1827*, Montross, Virginia; pp. 46-163-171.

26a. Mary R. Miller, *Place Names of The Northern Neck of Virginia*. Richmond, Virginia: Virginia State Library, 1983, p. 61.

for herself and family the master or mistress to whom she may wish to belong."[27]

Mrs. Newton was buried in the graveyard at "Lee Hall" with her first husband. She had lived to see her son elected to the State Legislature but not to have the pleasure of seeing the homes of her descendants erected all around the Parish and the area brought back to its former prosperous economy and feeling of well being.

On May 12, 1829, Willoughby Newton III was married to Mary Stevenson Brockenbrough, daughter of Judge William and Judith Brockenbrough in Monumental Church, Richmond Virginia.[28] During his time in the State Legislature, he met Edmund Ruffin, a large land owner from Hanover County. Together they formed the Virginia Agricultural Society and worked to improve Virginia farm lands by introducing new types of crops and fertilizing the worn out fields with guana brought from South America. This proved a boon to the area and before long the economy had shown great improvement. Virginius Dabney, writing about this period in *Virginia—A New Dominion*, states: "Willoughby Newton, a leading citizen of Westmoreland County, pioneered in introducing Peruvian guano to Virginia, and the results were sensational. Newton stated that the 'introduction of guano, was an interposition of Providence to save the county from total ruin.' Guano was relatively expensive, whereas marl was ready at hand and cheap, but those who could afford the Peruvian fertilizer profited greatly from its application to exhausted lands. The farmers of the Northern Neck, fellow citizens of Willoughby Newton, were said to have become the richest agricultural population in America."[28a]

An EXTRACT found by Mrs. Virginia Brown, the wife of J. Dall Brown, great grand-nephew of G.F. Brown, referred to in this paper, tells an interesting story:

"Journal of the United States Consulate General at Algiers: March 12th. 1830, a courier from Oran brings packets of papers and letters from Dept. of State to the Consul Genl. Among them is one for Mr. G. F. Brown from his father announcing the death of his mother, Mrs. R.T. Brown of "Windsor," a lady for whom the Consul General felt sincere esteem, and friendship. It appears that excessive grief for the loss of her eldest child, a son, had preyed upon her mind so severely as to shorten her days, although she had seven other sons and two daughters surviving. This shows that mother love is the most acute and unchangeable of all human affections." This was

---

27. *Westmoreland County Wills Book 1828*, Montross, Va. pp. 95–96.
28. Brockenbrough Family Bible in possession of Mrs. William B. Newton, Summer Hill, Hanover County, Va.
28a. Virginius Dabney, *Virginia, The New Dominion.* Doubleday, 1971, p. 280.

copied from a paper found in Mrs. G. F. Brown's trunk by a granddaughter of the lady (Mrs. R. T. Brown) 71 years after it was written in Algiers, where Mr. G. F. Brown was assistant to Major Henry Lee, Consul. Genl."[29]

Lovely homes were being built from Nomini ferry to Kinsale. "Laurel Spring," the home of Thomas Rice, was enlarged in 1844; "Spring Grove," home of Dr. and Mrs. Robert Murphy, was completed in 1834; "Green Hill," was the home of the Jackson family who had moved up "on the ridge" from Wilton; "Boscobel" was built circa 1850 by Dr. B. Franklin Brown; "Cabin Ford" was built by Richard Lee Turberville Beale circa 1835; "Buena Vista" was built by Thomas Brown circa 1849; "Afton" circa 1840; "Linden", circa 1834, was built by The Willoughby Newtons; "La Grange," circa 1850, was built by Robert H. Chowning; "Auburn" was built about 1830 by the Campbells; "Centreville," built circa 1849, was the home of The William Carey home; and "Woodburne," built circa 1840, was a Bailey residence. All of these homes were built up on "The Ridge Road." In place of the worn out land and "unsightly, neglected District, farms were now neatly enclosed, highly improved and producing crops of wheat, corn and clover that would vie with those of the most favored regions of the state." "The Grove," built in 1832 on Kinsale Creek by David Ball Taylor a merchant in Kinsale, was one of the few brick homes erected on the water at this period. "The Great House" was rebuilt in 1827 by Major Robert Bailey and is said to be copied from the floor plan of "Kirnan," at Hague.[30]

Mary Stevenson Brockenbrough Newton had been raised in the shadow of Monumental Church, Richmond, where her family attended services. There she had heard the wonderful sermons of Bishop Channing Moore that were meant to inspire and challenge his listeners to rebuild the Episcopal Church in the Diocese. The words had not been lost on Mrs. Newton. When she came to live in Cople Parish, she was appalled at the lack of practicing Episcopalians and distressed not to have a minister to hold regular services. In 1834, following her husband's example of encouraging the revitalization of the farms in the area, Mrs. Newton managed to have the Bishop appoint her cousin, The Reverend George Washington Nelson newly graduated from the Virginia Theological Seminary, as Rector in charge of Cople Parish, together with Farnham and Lunenburg Parishes in Richmond County.[31] These parishes had also been vacant for some time.

---

29. Extract of Journal in possession of Mrs. J. D. Brown, Spring Grove, Mount Holly, Virginia.
30. Norris, Editor, *Westmoreland County VA.*, pp. 277–317.
31. Francis L. Hawks, *Ecclesiastical History of United States of America.* p. 308.

As there was no Glebe or Rectory, and because there were not enough people to support an Episcopal rector, Mr. Nelson and his wife were guests at "Linden." Mr. Nelson, accompanied by Mrs. Newton, rode on horse back all over the Parish calling on the families and announcing the good news that Cople Parish was back in full time business. In this way the Parish was rejuvenated. Mr. Nelson held regular services and gradually strengthened the Old Parish.

In October 26, 1834, the Rt. Rev. Channing Moore visited Cople Parish, and with the new rector, George Washington Nelson (a familiar name in the Parish!) held services at Yeocomico. "I preached at Yeocomico Church, Westmoreland County, administered the Lord's supper, and confirmed one person."[31a]

In May 1835, Mr. Nelson gave this report of his work to the Diocesan Convention which met in Lynchburg, Virginia:

"A Sunday School has been established in Yeocomico. A flourishing Temperance Society in each County; and the cause of temperance is manifestly gaining ground. Services in the afternoon of the Sabbath have been held in each of the churches for the coloured people which have generally been well attended. A Female Society, for general religious purposes, has recently been organized in Lunenburg and Yeocomico".[31b]

According to recollections of his childhood, John Brockenbrough Newton remembered the family prayers and regular reading of the Bible held at the homes of kindred and friends during the week; the regular attendance at church services were a matter of course. There was a pleasant social life in the Parish, happy and hospitable with visits to the spa Springs in the summer. Young people were taught either at home or at the home of neighbors until old enough to go to boarding schools. Episcopal High in Alexandria, Edgehill in Caroline, and Washington Academy near Oak Grove in Westmoreland County were some of the academies of the day.[32]

The close fellowship with the Methodist at this time accounts for the affection so many members of the Methodist congregation have always felt toward the "Old Church." The two denominations lived in "Christian harmony and good will."[32a] They shared Yeocomico Church building for worship. In 1838 Ebenezer Methodist Protestant Church was built at Oldhams Cross Roads; Carmel Methodist Episcopal Church congregation was formed in 1850.

31a. *Ibid.* page 317.
31b. *Ibid.* page 328.
32. Mary Newton Stanard, *John Brockenbrough Newton: A Biographical Sketch.* Richmond, Virginia: The Virginia Churchman, 1924.
32a. Robert A. Lancaster, *Historic Virginia Homes and Churches.* Philadelphia, Pa: J.P. Lippincott, page 332. (Research of Miss Ethel Thompson, Virginia Writers Project)

In 1856 a Baptist Church was built at Machodoc Cross Roads. This was a wooden structure known as "Machodoc Meeting House," under the pastorship of Mr. George R. Northern.[32b]

In The year 1839 two baby boys were born at "Linden." One, the son of the Rector and named for his father; the other, John Brockenbrough Newton, named for his mother's uncle who was President of the Bank of Virginia. These little boys would grow up to become very active members of The Diocese of Virginia. George W. Nelson, Jr. served as deputy to three General Conventions of the Episcopal Church and John B. Newton became Assistant Bishop of Virginia.[32c]

After only six years, Mr. Nelson died in the fortieth year of his age and was buried near the northeast corner of St. John's Church, Warsaw. The gravestone which was erected by his parishioners reads, "In the triumph of the faith of that Gospel which he preached for six years as rector of Lunenburg, North Farnham and Cople Parishes."

Mr. Nelson served faithfully as rector of the three Parishes under his care. It was during his rectorship that St. John's Church at Warsaw was built and the Parishes were inspired by "his energetic faith and preaching" to build up their fallen churches.[33]

The next rector of Lunenburg, North Farnham, and Cople Parishes was the Rev. William Norvell Ward. He was born in Lynchburg, the son of Seth and Martha Norvell Ward. Mr. Ward entered the U.S. Military Academy at the age of twenty and was a classmate of Robert E. Lee. He left the Military Academy to enter the ministry of the Protestant Episcopal Church and was graduated from the Seminary in Alexandria in 1834. He was minister of churches in Harrison and Kanawha Counties (now West Virginia) 1835–1836. Mr. Ward married Miss Martha Smith Blincoe in Leesburg, August 9, 1836, then moved to become Rector of Berkeley Parish in Spotsylvania County and St. Margaret's in Caroline from 1836–1840. The Wards came to Cople Parish in 1840, and there is no record of where they resided until 1847. The legend is they lived at Bladensfield until the owner, Mrs. Lucias M. Davis, a descendant of Anne and John Peck, died in 1847, and then Bladensfield became the property of the Wards. Mr. William Ward, grandson of Cople's 11th Rector, said the deed was recorded in Richmond County Clerk's Office dated April 26, 1847.[34]

32b. Smith, *History of Nomini Baptist Church*, p. 126.
32c. Stanard, *John Brockenbrough Newton*. p. 8.
33. Elizabeth Ryland, Richmond, Editor, *Richmond County, Virginia*. Richmond, Virginia, Whittet and Shepperson, 1976, pp. 260–261.
34. Ward Family Records at Bladensfield, Richmond County, Virginia.

Mr. and Mrs. Ward were very popular in the Parish, and when Mr. Ward started a school at Bladensfield several young ladies from Cople Parish were pupils there. Among them was Miss Camie Forbes.[34a]

In 1841 The Rt. Rev. R. Channing Moore died after thirty-seven years of distinguished service. His successor was The Rt. Rev. William Meade who had been Assistant Bishop.

During Mr. Ward's rectorship of Cople, a controversy arose concerning the ownership of Yeocomico Church. The "peaceful Harmony" between the Methodists and the Episcopalians had hit a snag, and a petition was presented to the General Assembly of Virginia in 1844 by members of the Methodist congregation. The petition, in so many words, asked that the Yeocomico Church property be put up for public sale. This was not met with enthusiasm by the Rector or other members of the Episcopal congregation, and a counter petition was presented to the General Assembly on behalf of the Episcopalians. The Rev. Mr. Ward stated in his petition that he had "seen with profound regret a petition from certain citizens of the said County, presented to your Hon. body praying, among other things, for the sale of the said church, and holds it to be a duty to himself and to the people whose place of worship is thus sought to be taken from them, to remonstrance against any such act. In so doing your petitioner is desirous to avoid everything in the least degree calculated to give offense, or to recite those feelings which unfortunately ever attend upon controversies connected even remotely with the subject of religion."[35]

Apparently the Legislature had avoided dealing with this touchy subject until Mr. Ward's counter suit. The following letter from Judge McComas of the Virginia Courts of Justice settled the matter:

"Richmond, January 20, 1844

To the Rev. Wm. N. Ward:

  Dear Sir: You will remember that I objected sitting as a member of the Committee for Courts of Justice, whilst it was acting upon the petition in relation to Yeocomico Church, because I was a member of the Methodist Episcopal Church, and understanding that it was the subject of dispute between that Church and the Episcopal Church; but at your instance I did sit, but, being chairman of the committee, its action made it unnecessary for me to vote. I take this mode, however, of saying that I perfectly agreed with the committee, and even desired to go further than the committee in this. I wished to pass a law giving the Episcopal Church all churches that it is now in possession of to which it had a right before the Revolutionary War. I think the con-

---

34a. Taylor Papers in Dupont Library, Stratford Hall, Virginia.
35. Edward R. Earle, Virginia General Assembly Records, Richmond, Virginia; *Northern Neck News*, Warsaw, Virginia, August 11, 1977 and February 16, 1984.

struction given by the committee to the Act of 1802, or at least my construction of it is, that the General Assembly claimed for the Commonwealth the right to all the real property held by the Church, but that Act expressly forbids the sale of the churches, etc. It is true, the proviso to that Act does not confer upon the churches the right of property in the houses, etc. But it intended to leave the possession and occupancy being in the Episcopal Church, it had a right to retain it until the Legislature should otherwise direct. I believe that the Committee was of the opinion that the Episcopal Church had a right to the use and occupancy of the church now in question: It certainly is my opinion. I hope my Methodist brethren will see the justness of the determination of the Committee, and with cheerfulness acquiesce in its decision.

Yours very respectfully
David McComas.[36]

Apparently this put an end to the matter and peace was restored to the community.

During Mr. Ward's rectorship Nomini Episcopal Church was rebuilt by October 18, 1848. According to a deed, Miss Sally Griffith of Alexandria gave one acre of land to the trustees of the "Protestant Episcopal Church of Cople Parish lying on the northeast side of the main road near Nominy Ferry in the said county of Westmoreland immediately around and adjacent to the NEW CHURCH LATELY ERECTED NEAR THE SAID FERRY."[37] This deed in the Westmoreland Court House names as the trustees at this time of Cople Parish: Robert Mayo, Jr., John T. Rice, J. Jett, Geo. F. Brown, and Willoughby Newton. Because of this document there is no question as to the age of the present building standing on the property given by Youell Watkins in 1703 for a church to be built *over* the graves of his grandparents.

A Vestry Minute Book beginning in 1849 "came to light" after being missing since the Rectory at Hague was burned in 1913. There was great rejoicing in the Parish. Apparently it had been tucked away on a shelf and forgotten.

Mr. Ward resigned in 1849 from Cople Parish after a busy and fruitful ministry. He continued as rector of Lunenburg and Farnham Parishes. On May 10, 1849, at a meeting of the vestry at Hague with Mr. Ward present as rector, "Thanks were voted the Rev. William N. Ward for his services as our minister for the last nine years." The vestry expressed "undiminished confidence in his ability as a man and a minister, and regret that the condition of the parishes in

---

36. Bishop Meade, *Old Churches and Families of Virginia.* Philadelphia, Pa.: J. B. Lippincott, 1857, p. 153.
**There was great rejoicing when the Vestry announced one of the Parish Vestry Minute Books (1849) was safe and had not been burned in the fire which had destroyed the Rectory and all the other Parish records in 1913.
37. *Westmoreland County Deed Book. 33.* Page 60, Oct. 17, 1848.

which he officiates, render it impossible that he can perform services sufficiently often to advance the interest of the church.

"Resolved, that the parish ought to support a minister to officiate weekly in the churches at Yeocomico and Nominy alternately."[38]

On June 9, 1849, the vestry again met at Hague.

The rector was not listed as present. It was understood that Mr. Ward took offense at the resolution of the May 10 meeting and sent in his resignation, which was accepted; although the vestry had passed the said resolutions in good faith and "think the resolutions of the 19th are not susceptible of any construction injurious to him."[39]

Mr. Ward opened a school at his home "Bladensfield" in 1855 with an advertisement in the *Richmond Enquirer*: Bladensfield Female Academy, The Rev. William N. Ward, Principal. Mr. Ward was a colorful and interesting man. "At the opening of the war, he yielded to the solicitations of General Lee, and other friends, who knew that he had received a military education. He entered the Confederate Army, and was by Governor Letcher, appointed Major in the 55th Virginia Infantry, in which capacity he served as commandant of Fort Lowery near Tappahannock until after two years, he was forced by feeble health to resign."[39a] Mr. Ward's family still lives at Bladensfield.

At the June 9, 1849, meeting Gordon Forbes and Dr. John Jones were elected to the vestry but Gordon Forbes withdrew from the vestry. George F. Brown resigned. P.T. Chandler was appointed in his place.

August 25, 1849, Vestry meeting at "Linden" Resolved, that the Rev. Theodore S. Rumney, "with whom an arrangement has been made by the Bishop for that purpose," be called as minister of this Parish.[40] Dr. John Jones resigned by letter.

November 14, 1849, Vestry meeting at Hague with the new Rector present. Mr. P.T. Chandler resigns because he expects to leave the parish in a short time. (Montross Parish was being formed at this time. Mr. Chandler would not be living in Cople Parish when this was completed.)

The next minister, (he was still a Deacon), and twelfth clergyman in charge of Cople Parish was The Rev. Theodore S. Rumney, an 1849 graduate of the Seminary in Alexandria. Very little is known about Mr. Rumney except he wrote to the Rev. John B. Newton from Germantown, Pa., in 1894 when Mr. Newton was elected Assistant Bishop of the Diocese of Virginia, to tell him

38. Cople Parish Vestry Minutes. May 10, 1949.
39. *Ibid* June 9, 1949.
39a. G. B. Goode, *Virginia Cousins*. Richmond, Virginia: J. W. Randolph and English, 1887, pp. 204–205.
40. Cople Parish Vestry Minute Book. August 25, 1849.

"when reading of the Virginia election, my thoughts traveled back over many years to my diaconate where, in my room in your good father's house, I gathered the children on Sunday afternoons to teach them the Church Catechism. Those were pleasant days to me, and it is ever a joy to recall them, and you were one of those children."[41] Apparently Cople still did not have a Rectory in 1850.

At a vestry meeting Feb. 27, 1850, in Hague, Mr. Rumney was present when the vestry received a request for an alteration of the bounds of Cople Parish so as to enable the Episcopalians to erect a new Parish, called Montross, out of the territory granted them. The Cople vestry did not agree to adopt the Nomini River as the boundary line as proposed in the communication, but resolved "to adopt as the eastern boundary of the proposed new parish a line beginning at the mouth of Nominy River, thence up said river to the mouth of Peirce's Creek thence up the same to the head thereof thence along the road passing Mrs. Peaks to the fork of Oakville," (Where Miss Mary Porter Hall lives today, 1994).) thence up the main county road passing Templeman's X Road to Nomini Baptist Meeting house, thence to the line of Richmond County".[42]

Mr. Rumney signified his intention to resign at a meeting of the vestry on May 4, 1850. The resignation was to take effect in July.[42a] The same month on May 15, Mr. Rumney attended the convention of the Diocese at St. Paul's, Alexandria and voted for the 19th canon which says, "All offenders are to be repelled from the Lord's Table." This was reported by T. Grayson Dashiell in "A Digest of the Proceedings of the Councils in the Diocese of Virginia." pp. 207, 208.

Resolution of the vestry June 12, 1850: "That this vestry receive the resignation of the Rev. T. S. Rumney with regret; and in severing the relations between them and him, they tender him their thanks for the devotion to the welfare of his charge and for the efficient manner in which he has discharged his pastoral duties, and to express their high appreciation of his Christian character and offer their good wishes for his welfare in the future."[42b] Mr. Rumney went on to be rector of St. Peter's, Germantown, Pennsylvania, for thirty years and died in 1903. In 1905 the eagle Lectern at the Virginia Theological Seminary Chapel was given by Mr. Rumney's daughter in memory of her father.

---

41. Stanard, *John Brockenbrough Newton*, pp. 40–41.
42. Cople Parish Vestry Minute Book, February 27, 1850. Parish Lines Diocese of Virginia. Richmond; authorized by Virginia State Library. 1967. p. 305.
42a. *Ibid* May 4, 1850.
42b. W. S. R. Goodwin, *History of the Theological Seminary in Virginia and Its Historical Background*, Centennial Edition Vol. 1, p. 293. Research of Bessie Tiller for Virginia Writer's Project.

At the June 12, 1850, Vestry meeting it was unanimously decided to call The Rev. Edward B. McGuire to the rectorship of the parish to take effect in July.[42c] The Rev. Edward Brown McGuire (1818–1881) was the son of the Rev. Edward C. McGuire, Rector of St. George's Church, Fredericksburg for forty-four years, and his wife Judith Carter Lewis, granddaughter of Col. Fielding and Betty Washington Lewis.

The 13th Rector of Cople Parish graduated from the seminary in 1842, was ordained by Bishop Meade to the diaconate in Fredericksburg Feb. 22, 1842, and ordained to the Priesthood by Bishop Meade at Grace Church, Sussex County on May 14, 1845. He had been rector (1842–1846) of Meherrin Parish, Greensville County, and officiated during this period in Sussex and Southampton Counties. He was Rector of St. Paul's in Hanover, and St. Peter's in New Kent (1846–1850) and had services for St. David's, King William County. So he came to Cople with plenty of experience in country parish work.[43]

The new rector attended the Nov. 2, 1850, vestry meeting at the Hague. At this meeting a recommendation was offered, and signed by the members of the vestry present, to the society of young men, for the purpose of educating Mr. Justin P. Peale in order that he may prosecute his studies as a minister of the Prot. Episcopal Church. A Committee was appointed to adopt a means to prevent the church at Nomini ferry from smoking. Committee appointed to consider the propriety and cost of removing the gallery and pulpit in Nominy (sic) Church. Members of the Cople Vestry at this time were Willoughby Newton, John T. Rice, Thomas Brown, Robert Mayo, Jr., William D. Nelson, Edward C. Griffith, Landon C. Berkley, James Jett, George F. Brown, Col. Gordon Forbes, P. T. Chandler, and Dr. John Jones.[44]

A vestry meeting was held November 30, 1850, at Rice's store with the rector present. At this time the proposed alterations to be made in Nominy church, reversing the pulpit and pews and taking down the gallery, were approved and a resolution was drawn up concerning the changes.[44a]

In October 1850, A land mark of Cople Parish, "Nomini Hall," burned to the ground. This was one of the most beautiful houses in the country and well described by Philip Fithian in the Diary he kept while a tutor for Councillor Robert Carter's children at Nomini Hall in the 1770's. It was built by Robert (King) Carter for his son Robert Carter II, and was inherited by Robert Carter

---

42c. Vestry Minutes Cople Parish, Hague, Virginia, June 9, 1950.
43. William Stanard, *The McGuire Family in Virginia*, Richmond, Virginia: The Old Dominion Press, 1926, pp. 23–55.
44. Vestry Minutes Cople Parish, Hague, Virginia, Nov. 2, 1950.
44a. *Ibid.* Nov. 30, 1851.

III when his father died quite young. Councillor Carter's descendants, Dr. John Arnest's family, were living at Nomini Hall at the time of the fire.[45]

Mr. Hannibal Chandler of "Windsor" near Montross kept a wonderfully helpful diary. He attended services regularly at Nomini Church at the Ferry. He described going down to the Glebe to visit his mother and recorded in his diary on December 1850, "The Rev. William McGuire at Ferry preaches first "regular" sermon, "Christ is All." Also Mr. Chandler attended services on January 12, 1851, at the Ferry. (Nomini) and again January 26th he notes, "Good weather, All the world goes to Church to hear Mr. Edward McGuire who preaches a very fine sermon." It seems the McGuire brothers, both ordained Episcopal priests, often exchanged pulpits. Services were held in Montross and at Nomini on a regular schedule at this time." On March 2, 1851, Edward McGuire changed pulpits with his brother William at the Court House."

In Mr. Chandler's diary is this note: "Sunday, April 13.1851.Poor Mrs. Griffith died . . . buried today. She stays at Afton". Could this have been the mother of Dr. Frederick Griffith and Mrs. Eleanor Griffith Fairfax? On August 13, 1851, Mr. Chandler reports that he has been to Albany and "has a very good wheat crop, 2100 bushels!"[46]

April 26, 1851, it was announced at the Vestry meeting held at the Hague that the alterations to Nomini Church have been completed and a resolution adopted for a plan to alter and repair Yeocomico Church and a committee was appointed to supervise these repairs.[47]

August 25, 1851, Mr. Edward McGuire, the rector of Cople Parish, and Miss Mary L. Murphy were married at her home "Spring Grove;" the ceremony was performed by the Rev. William McGuire, brother of the groom. He was rector of Washington Parish.[48]

October 27, 1852: The Vestry held regular meeting at Hague with Rector present and at this time Mr. McGuire resigned by a letter to the vestry, dated Oct. 2, 1852. Mr. McGuire had accepted a call to St. Anne's Parish, Essex County.

"Resolved: That the Vestry has received this intelligence with profound regret, and cannot permit the occasion to pass without expressing the deep concern which they feel at parting with a pastor, who has officiated among them for more than two years, most acceptably to the whole parish, and by his many acts of kindness has endeared himself to his parishioners."[49]

---

45. Thomas Tileston Waterman, *The Mansions of Virginia*, 1706–1776. Chapel Hill, North Carolina: University of North Carolina Press, 1946, page 420.
46. Hannibal Chandler, *Diary*. Windsor, Montross, Virginia 1850–1855.
47. Vestry Minutes of Cople Parish. Hague, Virginia, April 26, 1851.
48. *Westmoreland County Marriage Book*, Clerks Office, Montross, Virginia, 1851.
49. Vestry Minute Book of Cople Parish, Hague, Virginia, Oct. 27, 1852, page 11.

At the same meeting a "Committee appointed to confer with the vestry of Montross Parish to see if an arrangement can be made to call a pastor to minister in that parish, together with Cople Parish." This committee was further empowered to call the Rev. William McGuire to the Rectorship of the Parish.[49a]

February 3, 1853, the following notice appeared in the *Southern Churchman*, Alexandria, Virginia:

"The Rev. William McGuire, having taken charge of Cople Parish, requests that letters and papers intended for him be directed to Hague Post Office, Westmoreland County, Virginia." Mr. McGuire did not stay in the Parish very long and by February 18, 1854, the Vestry met at the Hague with no Rector present. A committee was appointed to raise funds for the purpose of buying and fitting up a parsonage for the use of the parish. Committee was also appointed to confer with the vestry of Montross parish in regard to "connecting with them in calling a minister". Also at this meeting Fleet William Cox, William F. Chandler, and Benjamin Franklin Brown were elected to the vestry.

Here are excerpts from a letter "S. E. B to Mary. Kirnan, Dec. 20, 1853": The scribe was Sarah E. Bowie, daughter of the late Walter Bowie, (who died June 23, 1853) and his second wife, Mary Todd of Kirnan. Sarah wrote to her little sister Mary who was attending school at Mr. Hallwell's in Alexandria. She told all the news that had taken place in the Parish since she returned from a visit to Northumberland. "We got here just about supper time and found brother W. and Ella had gone to a party at Dr. Mayo's, which being a dancing party, Gillie (Walter's wife) declined attending. The Tuesday before Mr. Tom Brown gave a party to which only brother W. and Ella went from here, making in all, three large parties we have had in the course of as many weeks!. Hurrah! for old Westmoreland, you will think she is 'turning out' when I tell you we are all invited to a Cotillion Party, (a lively dance of French origin) to be given at the Court House on Thursday evening, I expect after that everything will be as quiet as usual. Col. Brown and Dr. Mayo's parties were both, I presume, given to Wm. Newton and his bride". (The bride and groom came down to "Linden" from "Summer Hill," the bride's home in Hanover County, the week after they were married to visit his family,) the letter continues, "We called on Mrs. Newton and she returned our visit and we were very much pleased with her. Ella, who met with her at all the parties, became very well acquainted and was perfectly charmed. The bride and groom left "Linden" on Dec. 21 and expected to have a large party given them in Tappahannock that night."

The neighborhood was a bustling place and the household at "Kirnan" was right in the middle of it all. Sara was twenty-two at the time she was penning the epistle, and showed her dislike of "Hog Killing Time" which she managed to miss by overstaying her visit to Northumberland and was "sorry" she had forgotten it. (Reading between the lines gives us an idea that she was a perfectly normal young lady!) Her sister Margaret was married June 16, 1853, to Col. Roderick Lawrence who conducted a school in Northumberland. "Brother Walter" was married to Gillie Jones. Ella, their sister, and brother Eddie were still single and they were all living at "Kirnan" with their mother. Walter had assumed the role of head of the house. It was almost Christmas and Sara told of going to visit Mrs. Cox and the Browns and from there to the Hague. "It was the first time I had been there since the store house was altered and can't say I think much improved in anything except the comfort of the place. Brother 'R' does not seem to have a very large assortment of goods." She added. The only mention of Christmas presents is when she told her little sister she was "making a cap for mother" and hoped she can finish it. She is looking forward to Meg and her husband coming for Christmas. There is no mention of Church preparations probably because the Rector was absent. Their half-brother James has been to Alexandria and the family had sent Mary a cake which they hoped James delivered. There is also the news that Brother Walter and Brother James have "concluded" to take Coles Point at the appraised value of $16,000. "I suppose before long the servants will be divided—I dread that time very much, not only on my own account but theirs, I know it will be a trying time to them. Christmas is rapidly approaching, Mary, I hope you may spend it very pleasantly and happily and live to see many returns." Sara said she wished Mary could be at home, "each and all join me in best love to you, particularly Ella Jones. The servants very often ask me to 'give their love' or 'tell Mis' Mary Julio', How-dy."[50]

In the August 1854 minutes of the vestry show that Mr. McGuire had resigned "after officiating as pastor for the parish for the period of one year". The vestry directed the secretary to address a letter to The Rev. T. Grayson Dashiell and invite him to accept the pastoral charge of this parish. Mr. Dashiell accepted by October 21, 1854. Mr. Dashiell was present at the regular vestry meeting and a committee was appointed to contract and to make all necessary arrangements for the building of a rectory.[51]

---

50. Taylor Papers, Sara E. Bowie letter, in archives of Dupont Library, Stratford Hall, Virginia, Dec. 1853.
51. Vestry Minutes Cople Parish, Hague, August 1854.

In His memoirs, "A Pastor's Recollections," written in 1874, Mr. Dashiell told of Bishop Meade telling him just before his ordination "Well, I shall send you to Cople Parish in Westmoreland County, they will give you plenty of work, and I hope will take good care of you".[51a] Mr. Dashiell neglects to mention the fact that he had just been married three months to Wilhelmina Sparrow, daughter of Dr. William Sparrow, D.D., the dean of the Virginia Theological Seminary in Alexandria.[51b] He does "thank God for the privilege of remembering the brotherly love of Colville Griffith (a descendant of one of the first bishops of the American Church), under whose hospitable roof my family found a home for more than twelve months". We have no record in the vestry minutes of the building of the long awaited rectory, but it was built across the road from "Linden" on a slight rise in a grove of oak trees. Here was born, we can assume, several of the Dashiell's four children. Mr. Dashiell's memoirs tell us of the "Ladies holding their meetings every week and by their regular gatherings, for counsel and work, were stimulating their own zeal and were provoking the gentlemen to the commendable effort of raising the funds for the rectory." He also told of the three old ladies, the Emily and Mary McGuire and Mrs. Davis, who lived "above the ferry" and told him some remarkable stories of parish life when the parish had no minister. This is well worth reading.[51c]

Mr. Chandler's diary for Sunday March 24, 1855, told of going to Nomini for service and said "there is a large congregation". Another time in the diary he noted "Went to Ferry to church. Mr. Dashiell gave a most excellent discourse on aiding Foreign Missions. Fine attendance."[52]

At the April 2, 1856, vestry meeting, Dr. W. H. Tyler of "Wilton" and James B. Bowie of "Kirnan" were elected to the Vestry. Mr. Bowie's son-in-law, Roderick Starling Lawrence, was elected to the vestry at the November 2 meeting and at the April 7, 1858, vestry meeting was appointed as a lay delegate to the Diocesan Council to be held in Winchester on May 19, 1858; F.W. Cox was named alternate. At this meeting James W. English was elected to the vestry, R. S. Lawrence resigned as Treasurer of the vestry, F. W. Cox "chosen to fill that place".[53]

The Marriage Records for 1856 in the Westmoreland County Court House

51a. T. Grayson Dashiell, *A Pastor's Recollections.* New York, N.Y.: D. Appleton and Company, 1875. pp. 9–10.
51b. Benj. Dashiell, *Dashiell Family Records.* Vol. 3. p. 647.
51c. T. Grayson Dashiell, *A Pastor's Recollections.* pp. 10–29.
52. Hannibal Chandler, *Diary,* Windsor, Montross, Virginia, Unpublished. March 24, 1855.
53. Cople Parish Vestry Minutes, 1856–1858.

show Sarah B. Bowie and Thomas N. Murphy received a marriage license Dec. 11, 1856.[53a]

Services were held at Nominy, on the day after Christmas 1858, by Mr. Dashiell, which was well attended according to Mr. Chandler's diary. He also reported attending March 13 and March 27, 1859, and on July 10th when he remarks "Mr. Dashiell most uninteresting preacher, not worth riding down to ferry to hear him preach in hot weather!" This was the remark of a tired old gentleman.[53b]

> The Vestry meeting May 4, 1858, was held at the Hague
> (No Rector reported in attendance.)
> "Present: W. Newton, R. Mayo, F.W. Cox, J.T. Rice, W. D. Nelson, W. H. Tyler and Thomas Brown. Mr. Newton was called to the chair. The following resolution was offered and adopted. Resolve that Thomas Brown, John T. Rice and Ro. Mayo be a committee to examine the accounts of this vestry, with the Treasurers and report to a meeting to be held at the Hague on Saturday next: Nelson, Lawrence and Cox, the late and present Treasurers be requested to attend the said committee with their books and papers. The vestry then adjourned to meet again on Saturday". No minutes of the proposed meeting have been located. There are no records of vestry meeting between May 4, 1858 and September 17, 1865.[54]

Mr. Dashiell was in the Parish as late as July 1859. We do not have a record of his resignation to the vestry. He served the Parish for at least five years. Mrs. Dashiell died in 1862 leaving him with four children. In 1864 he married her sister Katherine who died in 1888 leaving eight children. During the Civil War, he was Chaplain with General Lee in his West Virginia campaign. Mr. Dashiell was the founder of St. Mark's Church, Richmond, and was Rector for more than twenty-five years. He died in Colon, South America, Mar. 18, 1893.[54a]

Another interesting letter found at "The Grove" in the Bowie, Forbes and Taylor Papers are more information about life in Cople Parish. This is a letter from Anna Forbes Bowie to her son, Gordon, dated "Home, October 27th. 1860. (Home was "Fort Hill", near Hague, where the James Bowies lived). Mrs. Bowie was the daughter of Col. Gordon Forbes of Sandy Point; her son Gordon was apparently teaching. His mother told him, "I hope you will make friends where ever you go, always act the gentleman in every transaction, never forget that, and be polite and kind to every one and you will be sure to have

---

53a. *Westmoreland County Marriage Book*, Clerk's Office, Montross, Virginia, 1856.
53b. Hannibal Chandler, *Diary*. Windsor, Montross, Virginia; Christmas 1858—March 1859.
54. Cople Parish Vestry Minute Book. May 4, 1858.
54a. Benj. Dashiell, *Dashiell Family Records Vol. 3*, pp. 647–648.

friends, try and make your scholars love you by your patience and kindness towards them, you will have less trouble in teaching them." Among other things she told of the death of Frederick Brown and Mr. Nelson (the husband of Lettie Chandler whose family owned the "Glebe"). Mr. Brown was buried at Pecatone and Mr. Nelson at "The Glebe." They were stricken with a fatal illness just after Mr. Brown's daughter's wedding and reception. Mrs. Bowie reports, "these deaths have cast a gloom over us all." Gordon's brother Walter is a student at VMI and wrote home about attending a Fair near Lexington. In this chatty letter, Mrs. Bowie tells of "Phil and George Brown breaking a colt "they put the rope around her neck and I rode with her yesterday for the first time. They behaved very well indeed." she adds, "I don't believe Phil Mayo will go any where to school this fall, his father keeps so unwell that I don't think he wants to leave him." These letters show a very affectionate concern for all family members and neighbors in Cople Parish.[55]

The next Rector of Cople Parish was the Rev. Charles P. Rodefer, a 1861 graduate of the Va. Seminary. He was born Dec. 10, 1839, in Abington, Virginia. He was ordained a Deacon Whit-Sunday 1861 and "assigned to this parish by Bishop Meade, entered upon the discharge of his duties here on the 29th of May 1861; served the churches regularly as rector until the 16th of March 1862."[56] Mr. Rodefer was married October 12, 1864, to Miss Anna Lee Johnson in Lynchburg, Virginia. She was the daughter of Mr. and Mrs. William H. Johnson. Her mother, Louisa, was the daughter of William Taylor of Caroline County.[56a]

Mr. Rodefer did not resign from the Parish but took a leave of absence to serve as Chaplain in the C.S.A. on March 16, 1862.

Once again Cople and her people were in the throes of war. It had been almost fifty years since the devastation of 1814. Gradually her congregation had pulled themselves up and were enjoying the fruit of their hard work, coupled with an active Parish and pleasant living. This was all swept away. Services were once again read in the homes from The Holy Bible and The Book of Common Prayer by the women who were left at home alone to care for their families. Now this awful conflict ripped apart the families, and completely changed the fabric of their society. Very few homes in the area were not stricken by the loss of sons and fathers killed in battle or maimed for life. Cople was raided by the Yankees several times. The rivers and creeks were used by

---

55. Taylor Family Papers. In archives of Jessie Ball Dupont Library, Stratford Hall Virginia. 1860. File Box 426.

56. Cople Parish Vestry Minutes Book, May 1861.

56a. R. A. Brock, *Virginia and Virginians, Vol. II*, page 753.

foraging parties from the Gun Boats in the Potomac to frighten the women
and children and old men who were trying to keep the farms and homes together. The family at "Wilton" was visited often by raiding parties. Dr. Tyler
was not in the army and so spent his time eluding the Yankees when he wasn't
riding over the Parish tending the sick. Lots of stories have been handed down
in the Parish about the raids on the area from land and sea, but we have the
official report from Headquarters First Army Corp. of Captain Craig W. Wadsworth, Aide-de-camp. Here is one story from the Yankee prospective.

> " *'Headquarters, First Army Corps.*
> *Near Belle Plain, Va. Feb. 17, 1863*
>
>   *Sir: I have the honor to report that, in pursuance of verbal instructions from the
> major-general of Eighth New York Cavalry, under command of Captain Moore, on
> the 13th instant.*
>
>   *We reached Westmoreland Court-House at 12 noon. Learning that a mail was
> received at Warsaw Court-House from Richmond every Tuesday and Friday evenings,
> and that it was quite a rendezvous for smugglers, I pushed on to that place, arriving
> there at dusk. As we were entering the town, I arrested a citizen of Maryland, who
> was returning from Hague in a sulky, and had with him several hundred yards of
> dress stuffs. He came from Maryland about the 1st instant with two other citizens.
> They brought with them three wagonloads of goods, which they took to Richmond. He
> has also been in the habit of carrying the mail between the two rivers. At Warsaw I
> got a Richmond mail, which was brought across the river that afternoon. I searched
> several of the houses, and also the hotel, which was used as a depot, but found that
> everything had been removed two days before. William E. Callaban, the postmaster,
> and the proprietor of the hotel, both escaped into the woods. I found there was a regular
> line between this place and Hague, and that a large amount of goods had been brought
> through during the last month. They have two large boats and several small ones at
> the ferry, which is about 3 miles from Warsaw. They can bring over 16 horses at a
> time on the large boats.*
>
>   *General F. Lee's brigade of cavalry is stationed in Essex County, opposite Richmond
> and Westmoreland Counties. We left Warsaw at 11 P.M., and went 6 miles to the
> direction of Hague, where we bivouacked.*
>
>   *On the morning of the 14th we went to Hague. There were quite a number of
> citizens and several soldiers in the village as we came in. We took 4 Prisoners, 1
> belonging to the Ninth Virginia Cavalry, 2 to the Fortieth Virginia Infantry, and
> the other to the Signal Corps. The later was on duty, watching the Potomac River,
> the other three were on furlough.*
>
>   *The afternoon of the 14th we spent in searching the houses and country in the
> vicinity of Machodoc Creek. A large quantity of contraband matter had been landed
> at this point and sent forward to Warsaw. Dr. (Samuel E.) Spalding, of Leonard-
> town, Md. had crossed the Potomac the night previous. The doctor is the wealthiest
> and largest trader in the Neck.*
>
>   *On the 15th, instant we came back as far as Millersville and on the 16th returned*

to camp. I took for the United States Government 17 horses and a mule. Turned over to Captain Moore, Eighth New York Cavalry, 13 horses and the mule and the other 3 horses to Captain Myron H. Mandeville, quartermaster First Division of this corps. Four horses were taken from Mr. Newton's farm, at Hague. Mr. Willoughby Newton is a member of Congress in the so-called Confederate States. Five were taken with the prisoners and the balance from farms of citizens who were in the army or had sons there".[57] *(This same story is related in Mrs. Judith McGuire's* Diary of a Southern Refugee *in a letter from her sister Mrs. Willoughby Newton, written at "Linden" the night after the raid with a Southern point of view!)*[57a]

The 200th anniversary of the Parish was not celebrated in 1864. No one was in the mood! The Parish was without a shepherd again, but the faithful were reading their Bibles, teaching the children The Lord's Prayer, The Catechism and the Ten Commandments and praying for the war to cease. There was something about the people of Cople Parish, even when they were "too poor to paint and too proud to white wash," they always had enough to share with their neighbors. After all didn't they live in God's Country where the rivers were full of fish, hedge rows full of quail and rabbits and wild turkeys waiting for the hunters? The emancipation proclamation changed the way of life for everybody. It took 200 years to bring an end to the slave trade. For many both black and white this was a blessing. The Parishioners will learn to live in a new world.

---

57. *Official Records of the Union and Confederate Armies in the War of the Great Rebellion.* Chapter XXXVII, page 14. Researched by Charles Hutchinson Jr. 1970, St. Christopher's School Library, Richmond, Virginia.
There is also an account of this action in *The Iron Brigade, A Military History,* by Alan T. Nolan, Printed by the Historical Society of Michigan, Hardscrabble Books, Berrien Springs, Michigan, 1983. Researched by Dalton Mallory.
57a. Mrs. Judith McGuire, *Diary of a Southern Refugee.* New York, N.Y.: E. J. Hale & Son, 1867, pp. 192–194.

THE MAYFLOWER PILGRIM AND THE VIRGINIA ROYALIST

The Allertons, Father and Son

by MARTIN H. QUITT*

Isaac Allerton II, born and reared in Puritan New England, became one of the busiest and most influential public officials in the last third of the seventeenth century in Anglican Virginia. As a militia officer, he was involved in a controversial incident that inflamed the Indian crisis that escalated into Bacon's Rebellion. As a Burgess, he was instrumental in shaping the assembly's relationship to royal governors in the aftermath of that insurrection. And as a Councillor at the time of the Glorious Revolution, he dramatized the capacity of some Virginia leaders to stand for principle when he relinquished his seat rather than abandon his oath to the Stuart monarchy. His career as a Crown loyalist in Virginia was not a predictable progression from his roots as the son of Mayflower Pilgrims.

Like his father, Isaac Allerton I, he has not received favorable treatment from modern historians. Both Allertons have been depicted as having abused their public places to advance their private interests. Another review of the sources, however, suggests that both deserve a more balanced consideration.

Allerton was born when his father was in his mid forties. His mother died when he was about three years old. The two most significant adults during his childhood were his father and his maternal grandfather, William Brewster. No two role models could have been more dissimilar.

Isaac Allerton I, was born in Suffolk county, England ca. 1585. He trained as a tailor in London. He moved to Leyden, Holland around 1611; whether for religious or commercial reasons is not known. Similarly the origins and basis of his association with the Separatists who founded Plymouth are open to conjecture. What is clear, however, is that his experience in overseas trade was highly valued by the Pilgrims, as Governor William Bradford made him his first assistant and entrusted him with five political and commercial missions to England for the new colony. To the gratitude of Plymouth's leaders, he negotiated a buyout of the colony's London partners. He did not succeed, however, in obtaining a charter similar to that granted to Massachusetts. Following this failure, Allerton's relationship with Bradford deteriorated, and the latter's *His-*

---

*Martin H. Quitt is Professor of History at the University of Massachusetts, Boston.

THE LIFE OF COPLE PARISH   1864-1964

by BERTHA NEWTON DAVISON*

As Josh Billings* an American humorist of the 1880's, remarked, "It's better to know nothin' than to know what ain't so." Therefore, I have tried to tell Cople's story as factually as possible by using Vestry minutes, old diaries and Court House records; but, in this the fifth and last article, I may tell a story or two which was "passed down" in my family.

The Rev. Charles Rodefer, fifteenth rector of Cople, served the Parish from 1861-1862. He took a leave of absence to serve as Chaplain in the Confederate army. In 1865 Mr. Rodefer returned to the Parish and lived in the rectory with his family.[1]

At this time veterans of the "Lost Cause" were returning to a saddened parish. Among them was Dr. John Brockenbrough Newton who had served as a Surgeon during "The War." After four long years of a hard fought struggle, the glamour was gone and those returning were in all states of disarray.

September 17, 1865, the following members were elected to the Vestry of Cople Parish: Willoughby Newton, Sr. of "Linden," Robert Mayo, Jr. "Auburn," John T. Rice, "Laurel Spring," James B. Bowie "Fort Hill," Fleet W. Cox, "Elba," John N. Murphy, "Peckatone," Willoughby Newton IV, "Mount Pleasant," John H. Norris, "Level Green," Dr. Benjamin Franklin Brown, "Boscobel," Robert M. Mayo, "Kelvin Grove," Dr. John B. Newton, "Cabin Point," and Col. Thomas Brown, "Buena Vista." The Westmoreland County Deed Books given an idea of the difficulty faced by these men and all their neighbors to meet payments on their homes. Taxes could not be paid. Very little cash was seen in Cople Parish at this time. Records in the County Deed Books from 1866 through the 1880s are full of land changing hands, much of this due to foreclosures. As an example, when the war began, Willoughby Newton was a wealthy land owner who borrowed on his holdings to support the Confederacy. When the war was over, he was expected to meet his obligations. He was bankrupt, and after long court battles his land was sold at auction to pay his debts.[2]

Miss Hallie Brown, daughter of Mr. and Mrs. G. F. Brown and sister of Mrs. John Newton Murphy, was married at "Peckatone" on November 28, 1865. This was the last family wedding held at "Peckatone" as not long after this,

---

*Mrs. Davison, a native of Cople Parish in Westmoreland County, concludes the first three hundred years in this historic parish. See Vol. XL, p. 4578–4612; Vol. XLI, p. 4703–4733; Vol. XLII, p. 5017–5038; Vol. XLIV, p. 5125–5151.

*Henry Wheeler Shaw (1818–1885).

1.   Cople Parish vestry minute Book 1849-1902. September 17, 1865.

2.   The portion of land with the dwelling house and 150 acres known as "Linden" was bought back by Mrs. Willoughby Newton, using funds she received from the sale of her family farm in Hanover County, Virginia.

"Peckatone" was purchased by Mr. Samuel Hardwick and the Murphys moved with their children to "Spring Grove" at Mount Holly to stay until their new home "Kenmore" was built.

Most of the members of Cople Parish were in the same financial straits as the Newtons. Since cash was very scarce, the barter system kept households going. Most families had chickens, a pig and a cow or two. Eggs and butter were used to buy sugar, coffee, tea and spices at local stores while corn and wheat were taken to the mill to be ground into cornmeal and flour with the Miller keeping a portion as his share. Horses and oxen were the tractors of that day and there were no electric, gasoline or telephone bills. Most of the ante-war carriages were dilapidated and buggies and farm wagons were the mode of transportation, if you were fortunate enough to have a horse. The roads were almost impassable to Tidwells, Coles Point and Sandy Point in the winter. The former servants and slaves had to find shelter and work to support their families now that they were no longer legally dependent on their white neigh-bors. A system of share cropping was arranged with the former slaves working the land of their former owners for a share of the crops because there was no other way they could make a living. In most cases the families were allowed to live in their former homes or were given land to build their own homes. "I cannot pay you wages, but if you wish to stay and work I will share with you." It was at this time that Potomac Baptist Church and Zion Baptist Church were organized by the colored members of Cople Parish and were led by the Rev. Tommy Johnson and the Rev. Charles Russ, Jr.

Times were hard but the Spirit of Cople Parish was still at work! In spite of their personal troubles, the vestry tried to meet the financial needs of the Parish and keep the churches open for services. It was not easy.

"The vestry of Cople Parish met at the Hague on January 13, 1866. All of the vestrymen had seen service in the Confederate army and were now trying to put their lives back together. To their credit they began to look after the affairs of the Church. Mr. John Rice, was chairman and the following resolutions were adopted:

> "Resolved: that the members of this vestry and the congregation generally are much gratified by the return to the Parish of their esteemed Pastor, the Rev. Mr. Rodefer. Resolved: that whilst we regret our inability to do all that we desire, we will do whatever may be in our power, in the changed condition of the country, to promote the comfort of himself and family:
>
> "Resolved: that the Wardens be instructed to use all diligence to increase the subscription list and to procure contributions of provisions, etc. for the support of the minister.
>
> "Resolved: That a copy of these resolutions be handed by the secretary to Mr. Rodefer." Mr. R. M. Mayo was unanimously elected treasurer of the Vestry, Dr. John B. Newton, Secretary. The Vestry determined to collect a

sufficient amount of corn to supply the Rector's family with meal, and deposited it with Mr. Thos. Brown to be sent regularly to mill for him. Apparently Mr. Rodefer's family could not subsist on these meager terms and at the April meeting of the Vestry at Hague a letter, from the Rev. Mr. Rodefer resigning from Cople Parish was read by the Secretary. Upon a motion, the resignation of Mr. Rodefer was accepted and the treasurer was directed to collect all of his salary which was due and pay it over to him. These vestry minutes tell volumes by what they do not say. It was an humbling time for a group of proud people, but they did not give up. Nothing daunted the Vestry who realized the importance of a pastor in their parish, and the need for regular church services. The Vestry met on Sept. 3, 1866, and the Rev. Andrew Fisher was invited to become Rector of Cople in connection with his present charge (Richmond County Episcopal Churches). The Vestry offered him $250.00 and the use of the Rectory. Mr. Fisher accepted the offer to become the sixteenth Rector of the Parish in December 1866,[3] but he would live in Richmond County. The Vestry records report the difficulty the Parish had in raising funds for the minister's salary and drastic measures had to be considered.

Meanwhile cupid helped brighten up spirits in the Parish when wedding bells rang out on January 15, 1867, for Judith Newton and Edwin Claybrook; on Feb. 26th, for Dr. William H. Fairfax and Miss Eleanor Griffith of "Locust Farm;" and on December of the same year for Colonel Robert Mayo and Lucy Claybrook. Mr. Fisher performed these marriages.[4]

The Vestry met at Hague in May 1867 to consider selling the Rectory. It was determined that it should be sold to the highest bidder with a limit of $200. J. T. Rice, Thomas Brown, and W. Newton, Jr. were named as a committee to see about the sale.[5]

February 29, 1868, the vestry met at the Hague with Mr. J. T. Rice in the chair. At this meeting it was "Resolved that the Treasurer be instructed to collect the remaining subscriptions to the minister's salary as speedily as possible and pay them over to Rev. Mr. Fisher to the amount of $250, and that when the "interest on the fund from the sale of the Rectory falls due," the treasurer collect as much of it as accrued up to the 1st. day of Jan. 1868, and pay the same over to the Rector. "Resolved, that the Vestry has never before had the question of what should be done with the interest on the Rectory fund, but very cheerfully make this disposition of it."[5a]

"Resolved, that we sincerely regret that any circumstances should have occurred to render the resignation of Mr. Fisher which this vestry is constrained to accept, with best wishes for his health, happiness and continued usefulness in the ministry." Mr. Fisher continued as Rector in Richmond County Parishes until 1871. He was a very effective leader according to the records of St. John's Church in Warsaw. "Mr. Fisher, among

3. Cople Parish vestry minute Book 1849-1902.
4. Cople Parish Marriage Register 1861-1892.
5. Cople Parish Vestry Minutes, page 23.
5a. *Ibid.* February 29, 1868.

others, was not wanting in intellectual equipment or spiritual power; yet they chose to devote the greater part, and many of them the whole, of their parochial ministry to the upbuilding of country parishes."[6]

February 29, 1868: Vestry "Resolved, that the Secretary be instructed to communicate with the Rev. Dabney Wharton the desire of this Vestry to engage his services as Rector of this Parish in connection with his present charge (Montross) at a salary of two hundred dollars per annum." Mr. Wharton became the **seventeenth** Rector of Cople. He had been ordained by Bishop Moore July 10, 1834, was experienced and a good choice for Rector to help a struggling parish. In 1871 the Diocesan Missionary Society had greatly contributed to the relief of the Parish treasury by assisting with Mr. Wharton's salary.

There was a Ladies Sewing Society in the Parish and at the February 5, 1871, meeting a letter, addressed to the Vestry from Mrs. Bessie Newton, secretary of this organization was read, stating "their society had raised $800, which, with the addition of $200, they wish to apply to the erection of an Episcopal Chapel at the Hague on a lot of land which they have been informed will be given by one of your body for that purpose. Said Chapel to be under the control of the Vestry."[7] The minutes do not record any discussion by members. This was the beginning of plans to build a Cople Chapel in Hague, the center of the Parish.

In June 1871, Dr. John B. Newton, who had been registrar of the parish, had practiced medicine and had studied for the ministry since 1866, was ordained to the Priesthood in St. Mark's Church in Richmond by Bishop Whittle. Soon he became pastor of St. John's Church, Tappahannock. At this time, Dr. Newton asked the Vestry of Cople to release him from his bargain to buy the rectory when it was for sale. He had occupied it with his family for approximately four years. He also resigned from the Vestry, and Mr. R. S. Lawrence, Treasurer, was appointed Registrar in his place, and Willoughby Newton, Jr. was appointed Treasurer.

In the minutes of September 30, 1871, the Vestry appointed a Committee to rent the Rectory. Also the Vestry minutes report "Whereas Dr. John B. Newton has submitted a proposition to the vestry,

> "Resolved that this Vestry accept the said proposition upon the condition, however, that Willoughby Newton, the holder of the legal title to the strip of land recently acquired and added to the former Rectory lot, and now enclosed, adjoining C. Harrington's est., convey the same to the said Trustees to be held as a part of said Rectory lot for and of the P.E. (sic) Church of the Parish. Upon execution of which conveyance the said Trustees, the Treasurer of the Vestry is ordered to deliver up the bonds aforesaid to be cancelled, and upon further consideration that Dr. J. B. Newton shall pay the taxes on said property for the time he had possession thereof, including those of 1871".[8]

The minutes of the vestry February 7, 1872, tell a sad story. In a letter ad-

6. Copied from *The History of Theological Seminary*, Vol. II, pp. 488, By W. A. R. Goodwin Published by Edwin S. Gorham, N.Y., 1923–24.
7. Vestry Minutes of Cople Parish 1849–1902, February 1871.
8. *Ibid.* 1849–1902, pages 34-35-36.

dressed to Mr. Wharton, the vestry had to admit that they just could not pay the salary they had promised him because their "extreme regret in being reduced to pecuniary embarrassment to take such a step, yet they deem it due both to him and themselves to inform him of their utter inability to raise the salary agreed to be paid him in the future, at least until the amount now due him can be collected. The Vestry would express to Mr. Wharton their sincere thanks for the kind and Christian manner in which he had discharged his duties to the Parish, and they assure him that their failure to pay regularly the salary agreed to be paid has not resulted from lukewarmness on the subject, but from the severe pecuniary distress of almost every contributor to the support of the Church. The vestry pledged themselves to use their utmost endeavors to raise, as soon as possible, the amount which they now owe Mr. Wharton, and beg him to believe that he will always retain their esteem and affection of the entire Parish. Resolved that the Registrar be instructed to send a copy of this resolution to Mr. Wharton" Mr. R.S. Lawrence Registrar noted in the minutes that this was done.[9]

During this time Mr. James Dall Arnest, who had left "Nomini Hall," his ancestral home, in 1849 to seek his fortune in Philadelphia, returned a wealthy man and bought "Wilton"[10] and moved his family back to his roots. In November 1872 he became a member of Cople Vestry.

Mr. Wharton performed the wedding of William Mayo and Miss Lizzie Brown December 19, 1872. The Mayos would live at Coles Point and become active members of the Parish.[11]

At a vestry meeting early in 1872, Mr. John N. Murphy offered a resolution to the effect that the vestry adopt a proposition of Mrs. Sara Fessenden of Philadelphia[12] and other non-residents to allow them to restore Yeocomico Church upon the original plan of the church, and she pledged herself to have the work properly done without calling upon the citizens of the Parish to contribute anything towards the expense . . . "the work to be done in approved style".[13] However, the vestry at the December 7, 1872, meeting resolved that the former resolution of the vestry be revoked and the whole question of repairs be left to the discretion of the Committee: namely, Col. Thomas Brown, James D. Arnest, and C. U. Unruh.[14]

At this time it was ordered that the Registrar write to the Diocesan Missionary Society for aid in raising the deficit due the Rector. **(Times were still**

---

9. *Ibid.* Dec. 7, 1872, Westmoreland County Wills and Deeds book.
10. Westmoreland County Records Deed Book, 1871.
11. Cople Parish Marriage Register, December 1972.
12. Cople Parish Vestry Minutes page 37. Cople Parish Marriage Register, 1861–1892, page
17. Mrs. Sara Richards Fessenden was Sara Anne Murphy, daughter of John Ballentine Murphy of Ayrfield.
13. Cople Parish Minutes Book, 1872. Page 37.
14. Cople Parish Vestry Minutes, Page 39.

difficult!). In answer to this request, the DMS notified the vestry that it authorized the Rev. D. M. Wharton in January 1873 to draw on the Treasurer of the Diocese Missionary Society for $100.00.

Services were held in the newly restored Yeocomico Church July 27, 1873. The Rev. Grayson Dashiell, a former rector, assisted Mr. Wharton. The church had been "beautifully repaired and restored." At a meeting of the vestry August 25, 1873, a report of the building committee of Yeocomico was received and "thanks were voted to them for the taste displayed and to the Gentlemen and Ladies of Philadelphia for liberal contributions of money to help repair said church sent to the Parish through Mr. Jas. D. Arnest and family".[15]

John N. Murphy, of "Kenmore," reported in his diary, July 27, 1873, "Took Mary and the children to Yeocomico Church to hear Mr. Dashiell preach. The work of repairing the Church has not been quite completed but is an exceedingly nice job as far as it goes. My preference was for restoring the Church to its original style and plan, but failing to convince the Vestry of this I abandoned the scheme, tho' reluctantly, yet without bad feelings. I was dropped from the Vestry at the last election because of my opposition on this question and I am glad that I was. In the plan of the interior the committee had returned somewhat to the original plan: the pulpit has been put back in its old place; the reading desk is a poor imitation of the original; and chancel is in the original place; the aisles are as they originally were. The general appearances of the Church is very nice and shows the touch of a master workman. Mr. J. Clark, an Englishman, who has settled here was the contractor, and his son came from Philadelphia and did the work. Mr. Wharton prayed for rain today and before we reached home from church we had a shower, and in the evening two fine showers . .".[15a]

In December 1873 The Rev. Dabney Wharton resigned as Rector of the Parish but said he would act as a "Missionary" in the Parish.[16] Mr. Wharton had been a wonderful and faithful pastor wherever he served. While a "Missionary" in Montross and Cople Parishes, he began holding services in the Nomini Grove area once a month in any vacant house that was suited for that purpose about the years 1876–77. These services were brought about by the kindly and earnest solicitations of the zealous and untiring efforts of the saintly and noble church worker, the well known and ever remembered, Mrs. Susan J. Hutt. Through her influence and efforts, she secured one acre of land from Mr. John Crabbe, who donated the land for the erection of the first Episcopal Church at Nomini Grove, Virginia. After holding services once a month by the Rev. D. M. Wharton, the interest seemed to manifest itself more in earnest and the attendance was such as to awaken the thought and arouse the move to

---

15.   Cople Parish Vestry Minutes, Page 39.
15a.   John Newton Murphy's unpublished diary — July 27, 1875, page 64. The Diary is in West Virginia with the great-great-granddaughter of John Newton Murphy.

build a house of worship."[16a]

Mr. Wharton lived with his family at "Lawfield," Montross, Virginia and died there in 1887. He is buried in St. James Church, Montross, churchyard, and a beautiful plaque to his memory was placed in the church by the congregation he served there. It must be remembered that Mr. Wharton traveled by horse and buggy over the rough roads of that day. He had to cross Nomini Creek by the Ferry that ran west to east from Nomini landing to Mount Holly landing and vice-versa.

There were celebrations in the parish in spite of the difficult times. The Rev. John Newton returned to the parish October 26, 1875, to perform the marriage of his younger brother Edward C. Newton and Lucy Yates Tyler at "Kelvin Grove." Right after this happy occasion, Miss Charlotte Claybrook was married to Thomas Brown, Jr. of "Buena Vista," in Yeocomico, on December 7, 1875. The ceremony was performed by the bride's brother, F. W. Claybrook.[17]

During the time the Parish was vacant 1873–75, The Rev. John Peyton McGuire of South Farnham Parish, Essex County supplied services for Cople when he could. (He was not a stranger; his wife, Judith Brockenbough McGuire, author of *Diary of a Southern Refugee* published in 1867, was sister to Mrs. Willoughby Newton. Several records of his official acts for Cople are in the St. John Church, Tappahannock Record Books which are in the Virginia State Library, Richmond, Va.)

At the vestry meeting at Hague August 16, 1875, it was announced that after trying for over a year to secure a rector for the Parish, Mr. John Lloyd had accepted the call to come to the Parish as a Lay reader until his ordination for the salary of $400.00. A committee was appointed to have the rectory prepared and Messrs. Lawrence and Newton were appointed a committee to apply to the DMS for aid. At the January 8, 1875, meeting of the Vestry, a letter was read from the DMS which refused the request for help because **that Society was also having problems raising money!**[18]

Meanwhile, the Vestry decided to appoint Col. Fleet Cox, J. D. Arnest, and R. S. Lawrence as a committee to try to raise an additional $100.00 or more, if possible, by subscription for the salary of Mr. Lloyd. On January 21, 1876, Col. Cox reported the Committee had added up the subscription list, and Mr. R. S. Lawrence selected to "inform our Paster, Mr. Lloyd, that we could guarantee to him $500.00 per annum as the Vestry of Cople Parish and there may be still something from the DMS, and, whatever that may be, it will be given him in addition." (What courageous men. They just weren't about to give up!)

---

16. Cople Parish Vestry Minutes, December 1873. pp. 39.
16a. St. Paul Church Register, Nomini Grove, Virginia.
17. Cople Parish Marriage Register 1861–1892.
18. Cople Parish Vestry Minutes August 16, 1875 pp. 46.

At this same meeting, it was reported that St. Phillip's Church in Philadelphia had sent the Parish a lot of Books (supposedly Prayer Books.) The Registrar was instructed to acknowledge the receipt of the gift and "request the Church to give us any other books they may have to dispose of." There was no public library in the parish.[18a]

Mr. John N. Murphy noted in his diary August 26, 1876, "I went today in my wagon with Mary [his wife] to Nomini Church and took to my office the pulpit taken out of the church which has been sold to Zion Church (the colored Baptists) for $6.00. The building committee, which was appointed by the vestry to draw a plan of repairs for Nomini church and to have the repairs made, sold the pulpit and invested the money received from it as they thought best. They proposed to spend it in putting a solid partition down the center of the pews which were made for $6.00. The plan upon which the church has just been repaired was drawn by Rev. John Lloyd, the rector, and adopted by the committee. It consisted in removing the pulpit and chancel and erecting in its stead a platform furnished with two lecterns, two chairs, a communion table, painted a dark oak and a baptismal font. The center aisle was changed into two side aisles and making the pews a solid body with a partition down center, two stoves, one in each aisle, were put in. I was much opposed to this arrangement of the stoves, but was opposed by Mr. Lloyd and Mr. Claybrook, Mr. Rice agreed with me but noted in favor of Mr. Lloyd's plan to gratify him. The ladies who cleaned up and fixed the church were the Misses Rice, Sally and Bettie, Miss Louise Harwood and Mrs. M. S. Murphy assisted by their servants. No other ladies of the congregation came near the church during the time of repairing it and never rendered any assistance, not even Mrs. Lloyd. Mr. Lloyd seemed much interested in the work at first, but his interest seemed to flag. He did not come near the church for a week or more before it was finished. Mr. John R. Clark and his two sons, William and Charles, did this work charging for the entire job $69.00. Mr. Albert Jenkins made the lectern gratis, charging for the material $1.00. The North wall was battened and plastered. Total cost of repairs $70.00"[19]

The Rector's daughter, Miss Nellie Lloyd, was married by the Rev. Beverly Tucker in Yeocomico Church August 8, 1876, and James Dall Arnest gave his niece in marriage to George Fulton Brown at Yeocomico on November 21, 1876.[20] The Browns would live first at "Drum Bay" and then "Poplar Hill". (The neighborhood around the old Lee Hall estate was well represented by descendants of the Lee family but the name only survived in "given names." "Lee Hall" house had fallen into decay after a fire and Col. Thomas Brown,

---

18a. *Ibid*, page 47.
19. Diary of John Newton Murphy.
20. Cople Parish Marriage Register, November 21, 1876, Yeocomico Church.

the heir, had moved "across the road" to "Buena Vista" many years before. However Col. Brown, as well as his wife and son Arthur, was buried in the graveyard at "Lee Hall."[21]

In February 1871 at the Cople Parish vestry meeting, a Committee was appointed to negotiate with George Murphy for purchase of land for a cemetery for Yeocomico Church. All the space within the wall had been used. They were considering five acres. At the May 1878 meeting, an announcement was made that Miss Millie W. Murphy had given the Parish a gift of one acre of land adjoining Yeocomico churchyard for the cemetery. The Registrar of the Vestry was directed to express the appreciation of the Church for this generous gift.[22]

Mr. Lloyd, the eighteenth rector, served the Parish until Sept. 30, 1878,[23] after having had a fruitful, if not lucrative ministry. The Parish had been represented at all the Annual Councils in spite of the difficulty in arranging the delegates' travel expenses. During Mr. Lloyd's rectorship, Cople Parish Branch of the Rappahannock Valley Convocation Missionary Society was organized in the Parish to support the Rev. Curtis Grubb, a 1878 graduate of Virginia Theological Seminary, who was sent to Africa as a missionary.[23]

The nineteenth rector of Cople was the Rev. Pendleton Brooke who accepted the call extended to him on April 14, 1879.[23a]

On Tuesday November 5, 1879 "Linden," home of the Newtons, was gutted by fire. According to the *Northern Neck News* the fire started in the roof and was not detected until it was too late to extinguish the flames. Since it was election day, there were many people gathered at the Hague, and they went to help save what they could. The story is told that Mary Brockenbough Newton (Mrs. Willoughby Newton) went into her downstairs bedroom, got her family Bible and the Cople Parish Communion silver which had been entrusted to her by her mother-in-law, Sally Bland Lee Newton, when she died in 1928. She then went out under the large poplar tree and sat quietly until the fire had consumed her home. She had no place to keep the furniture which was saved, so she gave it to neighbors who had room to keep it out of the weather. Among the furniture was a large mahogany side board which was charred by the fire on one side which she asked her former coachman, The Rev. Thomas Johnson, if he would take care of it for her. He took it to his home and kept it safe. In 1929 his descendants sold it to Blake T. Newton when he built a house at "Linden" on the site of the old one.[23b]

Colonel Thomas Brown of *Buena Vista* died April 11, 1880, after serving his

21. Cople Parish Burial Register in Parish House at Hague.
22. Cople Parish Vestry minutes, May 1878, page 53.
23. *History of The Virginia Theological Seminary*, Goodwin, W.A.R. Rochester, N.Y.: DuBois Press, 1924.
23a. Cople Vestry Minutes, February 26, 1879. page 56.
23b. *Northern Neck News*, November 7, 1879.

Parish as vestryman for twenty-five years. He also represented the county in the Virginia Legislature and was a popular and trusted member of the life of Cople Parish. The Vestry offered a resolution in recognition of his service to the parish and of the distress felt by the community over his passing which was written in the vestry minute book and sent to the *Northern Neck News* and *The Southern Churchman.*[23c]

Nomini Church was the scene of the wedding of Robert Bruce Massey and Lucy R. Jackson of "Green Hill" November 1881. Mr. Brooke, rector of the parish, performed the ceremony.[24] The Masseys lived at Mount Holy on the land originally owned by Thomas Youell whose grandson gave the land for Nomini Church. At this time the farm was called "Peach Grove Farm" but was later called "Liberty Hall."

During Mr. Brooke's charge, the rectory porch was repaired and Mr. Eugene Tubman was given permission to use Nomini Churchyard as a place of recreation for his family and as a lot on which to turn his horse or calf to graze, "provided he enclose it with a good plank fence with gate to be kept locked."[25]

At this time there was an amendment to the Church Canons concerning the duties of the Church Warden, defining his duties, to wit: "Watch over the Church property; prepare it for every occasion of public worship; see that the sexton and other employees properly discharge their duties; collect offerings; accommodate congregation with seats; maintain order and decorum in the time of public worship."[26] These changes were adopted gradually by the vestry.

Mrs. Fisher Howe of Princeton, New Jersey, the former Mary Willoughby Brown, born 1878, great niece of James Dall Arnest of "Wilton," daughter of Mr. and Mrs. George Brown (nee Mary Estelle Arnest) grew up in Cople Parish, lived first at "Popular Hill" then "Wilton" and inherited "Spring Grove" from her first husband, John Rogers Williams, grandson of Jane Murphy Rogers. Before her death in 1940, Mrs. Howe wrote a wonderful booklet, "This I Remember," for her family. In it she describes so vividly the Rev. Mr. Brooke's daughter, May Lou Brooke, who was about twelve years old when she took part in a "tableaux" depicting the seasons. She said "Louise Murphy (later Mrs. Robert Beale of "Sunny Side") was *Autumn* with red leaves in her hair; May Lou was dressed as *Winter* with holly in her dark hair. This affair was held on the Porch at "Cabin Ford," the home of the Beales near Hague. "I was about six and wore a white dress with a wreath of rose buds in my hair." Also she

23c. Cople Parish Vestry Minutes, pp. 60. April 13, 1880.
24. Cople Parish Marriage Register 1862–1892 November 1881.
25. Cople Parish Minutes 1849–1892. pp. 62. Mr. Tubman lived at the Mount Holly house which he built. He was the grand father of the present benefactor, F. H. Tubman, of Nomini Church.
26. *Ibid*, page 64.

recalled the ladies of the Sewing Society meeting at "Wilton" to make clothes for the needy families in the Parish and attending school in the little public school house at the gate to "Popular Hill." Mrs. Howe also describes her teen years growing up with her brother, James Dall Brown, and the fun they had riding her father's horses around the race tract across from the *Rectory* and between "LaGrange" and "Linden."[26a]

In 1881 The Rice family moved from *Laurel Springs* to Cherry Point, their farm in Coles Point Neck, when Mr. and Mrs. E. Poinsett Tayloe moved their large family from Middleburg to *Laurel Springs* in Cople Parish.[26b]

July 23, 1881, minutes of Cople Parish Vestry meeting reported "on motion the Vestry resolved that a committee be appointed to receive and hold any money given by the Good Society of Templers for expending the same on Yeocomico Church according to their wishes." Money appropriated by the Ladies Sewing Society was voted to be used for the roof repair at the Rectory.[26c]

On April 5, 1882, a special committee was appointed to solicit subscriptions and put in operation the Duplex Envelope System whereby members of the Parish would pledge yearly to the Parish and honor the pledge by placing a portion of the pledge in numbered envelopes in the offering each month or Sunday as they had designated. This would hopefully make a big improvement in the Treasurer's ability to pay the minister's salary each month. This also shows the economy was improving![26d]

The Church lost a valuable member when Mr. John T. Rice died in March 1887. He had been a member of Cople Parish all of his life, and a member of the Vestry from 1849 until 1884. He was buried in the family graveyard at "Laurel Spring," Mount Holly. The old order was changing.

In the April 28, 1882, minutes of the vestry, it is recorded: "Congregation met at the chapel." This was an annual meeting of the congregation at which time they elected the vestry.[27]

The rector's salary was still a matter of concern when the vestry met October 31, 1882; however, the main order of business was making arrangements to provide entertainment for the Rappahannock Valley Convocation which was scheduled to meet in the parish on Wednesday, November 8, 1882.

March 26, 1883, at a called vestry meeting those present voted to reduce the vestry membership to seven. At the meeting on April 7, 1883, Mr. J. Arnest was elected Senior Warden of the Vestry. The condition of the floor of the

---

26a. *"This I Remember"* a memoir by Mary Willoughby Brown Howe.
26b. Tayloe Family papers compiled by W. Randolph Tayloe.
26c. Cople Parish Vestry Minutes, July 23, 1881. pp. 65.
26d. Cople Parish Vestry Minutes, pp. 66. April 5, 1882.
27. Cople Parish Vestry Minutes. pp. 67. Congregational Meeting *Cople Chapel* is mentioned as being in use for first time. April 28, 1882.

vestry room at Yeocomico was discussed. A motion was made and seconded that the Senior Warden get a carpenter to inspect Yeocomico to examine the floor of the church, report to the rector, and he will take up an offering to have necessary work done. Junior warden was instructed to investigate cost of whitening the walls of Nomini Church and report findings to rector who will take up collection for these expenses. The vestry agreed to pay for repairing the porch at the rectory.[28]

The vestry minutes record a meeting was held February 2, 1884, when a committee was appointed to consider the matter of the cemetery at Yeocomico and to make arrangements with George W. Murphy concerning the lumber and wood on the said lot.[29]

August 25, 1885, the Rev. Pendelton Brooke offered his resignation, which was accepted with regret and best wishes for his success in his new field.[30]

The Congregational meeting was not held in the parish at the usual time that year because of no rector and lack of spirit after a sad year. But on May 25, 1886, the congregation met at the chapel and elected the new vestry. E. C. Claybrook was elected Senior Warden. On June 30 a letter was received from the Bishop stating he had secured the services of a Seminary graduate, R. A. Castleman, to be in the Parish by July 20, 1886. The vestry was instructed to correspond with the Diocesan Missionary Society about an allowance and to learn what sum would be appropriate for the salary for "our new Minister." The vestry contacted the Montross Parish vestry about sharing Mr. Castlemen to which they agreed.[31]

Another fire destroyed one of the show places of Cople Parish when *Peckatone* was burned in 1886. This was a great loss to the architectural and sentimental treasures of the Parish.[32]

The Rev. Mr. Castleman came to the Parish as a deacon with the blessing of Bishop Whittle on July 2, 1886. He was ordained priest in 1887.[33]

October 27, 1886, the vestry appointed R. B. Massey to look into the condition of Nomini Church and see if it was safe for use. As a result of this, at the February 16, 1887, Vestry meeting, a committee was appointed to have a brick mason give an estimate of the cost of repairs to Nomini Church. The committee was also instructed to find out if it was advisable to sell part of Church lot in order to obtain two or three hundred dollars for the repair to Nomini Church.[34]

On April 19, 1887, the vestry met "at the Chapel" and again on April 26,

28.   Cople Parish Vestry Minutes, pp. 69. Congregational Meeting March 26, 1883, pp. 69. Reduced Vestry.
29.   Cople Parish Vestry Minutes, pp. 71. February 2, 1884.
30.   *Ibid.* August 25, 1885. pp. 76. Mr. Brooke's resignation accepted with regrets.
31.   Cople Parish Vestry Minutes, May 25, May 26, and June 30th, 1886. pp. 78, 79, 80.
32.   *Northern Neck Historical Magazine*, Vol. XXIII, pp. 2433, Elizabeth H. Dos Passos.
33.   Cople Parish Vestry Minutes for October 27, 1886.
34.   Cople Parish Vestry Minutes Congregational meeting for April 19th, 1887.

1887. This was six years after the first mention of building a chapel and the strange thing is that no mention of the construction appears in any of the minutes for those years.

July 17, 1887, Thomas Jerome, infant son of Mr. and Mrs. William N. Carey, died and was buried at the Carey home, "Centreville."[35] Mr. Castleman read the burial office. Children's funerals were not an unusual task for the pastors at this time. The doctors had very little to prescribe for childhood illnesses. Only the strong could survive the poor sanitary conditions of that period. Death of babies in the summer time was a sad, but almost an expected condition. The ice used to cool drinks during the hot months had been cut into slabs during the winter when the ice on the mill ponds was about six inches thick, put on wagons and carted to ice houses. (Big holes in the ground usually dug under a large tree and lined with saw dust about two feet deep) This ice would last almost all summer and the butter and milk were kept in these ice houses. All transportation was via buggies, wagon or horseback and all farming was done with the aid of a plow drawn by horses. Every farm had livestock, so you can imagine the swarms of flies which had to be kept away from the kitchen where all the meals were prepared. Therefore, diseases were readily carried from one household to the other in spite of all the care taken to prevent contamination. This was truly the day of the survival of the fittest. Some families, in spite of this, raised large numbers of children.[36]

The Rectory property ownership was cleared up when a deed dated November 10th, 1887, was recorded in Westmoreland County Court House.[37] The Deed to Cople Parish for The Rectory land from Robert M. Mayo, assignee of Willoughby Newton, deceased, who had *donated* the land on which to build the Rectory in the year 1854. However, before 1887 no deed was ever made or, if made, was never recorded. The action of Robert M. Mayo on November 12, 1887, in behalf of the Parish rectory property cleared up a big mystery as to how the rectory land was acquired by Cople in the first place. All vestry records from 1858 to 1866 are missing from the Vestry book!

On October 1, 1887, the Rt. Rev. Alfred M. Randolph consecrated Cople Chapel at Hague. Assisting ministers were the Rector and The Rev. A.B. Kinsolving. "The Church was erected, at a cost of about $900.00 midway between Nomini and Yeocomico Churches and was used for services at the irregular times such as the fifth Sundays, holidays and Thanksgiving days, at night when convenient to the Rector, for Sunday School of the Parish, for Union Prayer meetings, and by the Young Men's Christian Association. NOT

---

35.   Cople Parish Burial Records, July 17, 1887.
36.   Letter from Mrs. Richard Lee Griffith to her father Col. Thomas Brown tells about harvesting ice in the Hague area in the winter of 1912.
37.   Westmoreland County Court House Clerk's Office, Montross, Virginia. Deed Book 47, Page 414. 1887.

for lectures except those of a clearly religious character, and for no other purpose whatsoever. The earnest rector finds it most valuable for these purposes."[38]

Another "purpose" for the Chapel not mentioned by Bishop Randolph took place on November 28, 1889, when John Westley Evans and Clara Warren were married at the Chapel. This was the first recorded marriage in the new chapel. The marriage of Charles Grant McCrea and Maggie Flew followed on January 10, 1890, and on October 12, 1891, Miss Ella Lawrence Murphy and Gilbert Cox were married "at the Chapel at Hague."[39]

John Poyntz Tyler, a native of Cople Parish, was graduated from the Virginia Theological Seminary in June 1887.[40]

In his diary on August 23, 1888, Mr. John N. Murphy tells of the excursion the "ladies of Cople Parish took to Colonial Beach on the steamer *I. W. Thompson* for the benefit of Nominy (sic) Church". A supper was had in the Church just before embarking. The steamer left Mount Holly about 8 o'clock P.M. and returned about 3 o'clock A.M. Net profit of the venture was said to be $100.00. Two days later August 25, 1888, the vestry met at the Chapel and the committee on Nomini Church was directed to sell one-fourth acre of the church lot for $150.00 to Mr. F.E. Tubman and to expend the money on repairs to Nomini Church.[41]

Mr. Castleman officiated at many baptisms in each church of the parish, but one especially stands out in the Parish records on October 10, 1888, when John Howell was immersed at "Nomini Run Bridge" on the road near Nomini Grove with Mrs. Susan Hutt, Mrs. John Howell, of St. Paul's Church, Nomini Grove and B. B. Atwill of Cople Parish, as sponsors and witnesses.[42]

Christmas Day 1888 was a bright, warm lovely day. The Murphys of "Kenmore" attended church at the Hague Chapel. Mr. Castleman held the service . . . "went in old carriage, renewed at home, a job no one is proud of! The house was merry with lots of visitors after church. Brother Frank, his wife, Lill, and two little boys from "Afton," Mary and Tom Jackson, brother and sister, from "Green Hill," Frank Tubman and his cousin from Maryland (Mr. W. Lee), and John T. Beale also came." During the Christmas season another benefit for Nomini was held at "Afton" on New Year's Eve. "Frank and Lill gave up the hall for the stage and audience and their old kitchen for the supper room. This bright and delightful weather is very favorable, and when the proceeds are counted will doubtless be a gratifying sum to the ladies who got it up. It is principally a children's exhibition of private theatricals with

38. Notes on Bishop Randolph visit to the Parish.
39. Marriage Register of Cople Parish 1861–1902. November 28, 1889. Marriage Register Cople Parish 1861–1902. January 30, 1890, also Oct. 12, 1891.
40. *History of the Theological Seminary in Virginia*. Goodwin, W.A.R. pp. 156. 1887.
41. John Newton Murphy's Diary, August 23, 1888.
42. Cople Parish Baptismal Register, October 18, 1888. Baptism at "Nomini Run Bridge" of Mr. Howell.

some tableaux of grown girls. My little girls Freddie, Louise, and Gawina take part."[43]

Cople Parish Vestry Minutes for January 4, 1889, reported the Vestry met at the Chapel. Col. R. M. Mayo was directed to negotiate with J.E.R. Crabbe for the repairing and painting of the Chapel. A committee was appointed for the cleaning up and surveying of the cemetery at Yeocomico, and authority was given them to sell lots and make deeds to the same.[44]

According to the vestry minutes during his time here, Mr. Castleman was a very energetic, innovative, and dedicated minister to his people. He extended his service to the more isolated Tidwells and Machodoc Neck area. The roads were almost impassable in winter and difficult all the time so that transportation was limited, but the people implored him to hold some services in that area. The story is told that the first service was held beneath a sail that was stretched over some poles in Mrs. James Evans's yard. This was very symbolic since most of the families in this part of the parish lived on the water and made their living fishing, crabbing or oystering. Mr. Castleman managed to get a congregation started. The Boyce, Evans, and Chatham families got together with other Christians in the community and the Methodists and the Episcopalians built a community chapel that is referred to interchangeably in the minutes as Edgewater Mission, Boycetown or the Mission Chapel. It is not until 1924 that the name St. James is used to designate the church at Tidwells.

To indicate that the economy was improving, Mr. Castleman was able to have printed schedules of parish services that indicated first and third Sundays AM at Yeocomio and PM at the Hague Chapel; second and fourth Sundays at Nomini. Regularly scheduled meetings of the vestry, Missionary Society, Ladies Sewing Society, Little Helpers, and Communicants Prayer meetings are indicative of a working parish a long way in their Christian life, and it also shows the improvement in their financial affairs.[45]

Mr. Castleman wrote to Vestryman Thomas Brown, Registrar of the vestry, from the Rectory, June 21, 1889, saying there were seventy-eight communicants in the Parish, and Mr. Castleman wanted each one of them to feel a part of the workings of the Parish. Since he had to be out of the Parish at the time of the regular vestry meeting due to a funeral that he had to conduct in Montross, he wrote Mr. Brown, in great detail, instructions for the business meeting:

> *"Three matters of importance I wish to bring before the Vestry: Many who would give have never been asked to give. It will greatly increase their interest in the church, if they are induced to contribute to its regular charges especially salary of minister (let it be clearly understood that I desire no increase in salary; for I do*

---

43.   John Newton Murphy's Diary, Christmas Week, 1888.
44.   Cople Parish Vestry Minutes, January 4, 1889. pp. 92.
45.   Edgewater Mission was in the present day Tidwells area and Boycetown area is known today as Chatham Village.

*not need it.) But I do want every member of our congregation to have a share in
the support of the parish. I wish it for their own sakes and for the good of the
parish, especially do I wish it for all communicants."*

"1st: "The application to The Diocesan Missionary Society for help with Ministers salary expires July 1, 1889, and the rules require renewal yearly. Please
attend to this. He suggested a committee on the minister's salary be appointed "one
from lower end (Carey's to Kinsale) one from middle (Carey's to Gen'l Beale's X
Roads), and one from Ferry neighborhood to be appointed, not to interfere with
Treasurer's duties in this matter, but to assist him by soliciting from every member
of our several congregations who is not now a contributor to the salary, a subscription to the salary for coming year, (large or small according to means of each
person) to be paid in quarterly installments, on first day of each quarter; said
Committee to be careful that each subscriber be urged to give not more than he can
afford and is reasonably assured that he can promptly pay the annual subscription
even as little as $1.00 or .50 or .25 cents. In this way the burden of Parish support
will be less unequally distributed; in this way I will be able to feel that I am, more
than ever before, the minister or pastor of the whole people and not a pastor selected for the congregation and* supported, for them, by a few members thereof;
*in this way the zeal of many will be quickened and the parish take on new life; and
this way I feel confident that $50. (and more likely $100.00) more than heretofore can be easily raised.*

"2nd: The great need for repairs on the Rectory and Church buildings is appar-
ent to us all. We have upon us the burden of necessary repairs neglected now for
many years. The people have been willing, but the system used for such purposes
has, besides other objections, been unsystematic and spasmodic in its operations.
Fairs and Festivals are bad financing for there is no steadiness or growth or per-
manence in the system, though I do not at all believe in them, as I have not hesi-
tated to say — still — I am not prepared to forbid them, or even actively to oppose.*

*But yet it must be remembered that we, the Vestry — are the selected and
authorized financial agents of the parish, and we are each pledged to use our best
efforts for its prosperity; moreover, we are in the eyes of the world responsible, and
rightly so, for the financial course of the Parish. I suggest then, a Church Repair
Fund, the same to be raised by monthly contributions from man, woman, and
child within our bounds who are willing to aid in the restoration of God's house.
The collection of this, the ladies will attend to. Its expenditure should be in hands
of a committee of Vestry, of which, if deemed expedient by Vestry, I am willing to
be one. Such a fund will, at present be at once consumed as fast as raised. In the
future it may accumulate so that the interest therefrom be used to maintain repairs. It is a good plan, it is a sensible plan; it is a business plan; and it is the* right
*plan, on Christian principles. I hope its adoption. I will give .50 per month to this.
In both cases I will ask the vestry to determine the number of men to be put on the
committee and to permit me the naming of the members thereof.*

"3rd: The Stable of which I spoke is an immediate necessity. I cannot afford to
raise pasture as I have no place to store it. I cannot afford to buy provender by the
load (the present loft will hold but one load) and pay advanced prices as the spring
comes on. I have no granary. I must buy grain at a constant advance when I might
buy it at low rates in the Fall. My buggy, which I keep solely for benefit of parish,
had as well be outdoors as the shed in which I must now keep it. When called here,*

I was offered a Rectory. Fair outbuildings supposed in such a case unless otherwise clearly stated. Has the vestry fulfilled its contract? (I write plainly, but this is a simple matter of business) An inexpensive stable with buggy shed and granary, is all that is needed. I hereby subscribe $5.00 to said stable.

If you prefer you can read this to Vestry, as it is what I would have said, if present. I am anxious to get the parish on a sound financial basis (and its affairs in good business) I am sure the vestry will earnestly second me in this effort and the people will loyally second the vestry.

Very truly yours.
R. A. Castleman To Thomas Brown, ESQ.
Registrar of Vestry Of Cople Parish.

P.S. Don't you think a note of thanks to Mr. J.E.R. Crabbe for his material aid and personal attention to the repair of Chapel would be timely and graceful? Next regular meeting of vestry 1st. Saturday in July, 4 P.M. Would it not be well to postpone 'til same day in August and same hour? Bishop Whittle will be Montross that day so I will be absent besides this meeting so near to that date."[46] *(Mr. Castleman was also Rector at St. James, Montross, at this time).*

The Vestry tried to carry out their rector's suggestions and requests which were very helpful to a sincere but inexperienced vestry.

The Vestry met at the Chapel Aug. 6, 1889. *The committee on minister's salary* reported that as yet they had taken no action but would be ready to report by next vestry meeting. It was resolved that if the Diocesan Missionary Society restore to $200 the amount of their aid that the vestry will make up the amount of the minister's salary to $600 without the aid of the Montross Parish and that our Rector be relieved of his present work in *that* Parish.

October 5, 1889, Cople Parish Vestry Minutes report Mr. Castleman has resigned as rector of Montross Parish and The Rev. Mr. Latane has accepted call to that field. The Vestry thanked Mrs. Howe and Miss Kipper Webster and Co. of Baltimore, Md. for the very handsome chancel chairs presented by them to the Parish Chapel. Report recorded December 1889 in the minutes says "Little Helpers' money will be used to repair the roof at Yeocomico Church."[47]

At a called meeting of the vestry, 5th. of March, 1890, at "Mount Pleasant" it was resolved that the vestry proceed to put a new roof on the Rectory and that they give their obligation with interest at twelve months to Mr. J.E.R. Crabbe who advanced the money for that purpose and that the sect'y be empowered to execute a note to Mr. Crabbe for the cost of same.[48]

In 1890, the Diocese of Virginia was divided into The Diocese of Southern Virginia with Bishop Randolph, the Assistant Bishop of Virginia, becoming

---

46. Mr. Castleman's letter to Mr. Brown with suggestions for getting the Parish on a good financial and spiritual basis. Letter on file at Parish House.

47. Cople Parish Vestry minutes, October 5, 1889, pp. 98. The chairs referred to are now used at the Cople Parish House in Hague.

48. Vestry Meeting May 5, 1890, pp. 100.

the Bishop of the new Diocese. Bishop Whittle continued as Bishop of the Diocese of Virginia.[49]

Vestry met at the Chapel April 5, 1890, and the committee on repairs reported the contract for putting a new roof on Yeocomico Church had been given to Mr. Augustus Delano, the lowest bidder, and that all necessary material was in place and every thing ready for Mr. Delano to go to work. Permission was granted the Ladies Sewing Society to put a suitable Iron Gate in the wall of the cemetery lot at Yeocomico Church.[50]

"May 14, 1892, the Vestry suggests that all members assemble at the cemetery on May 25 and give a day's work toward cleaning up the Cemetery."[51]

In spite of having difficulty receiving his salary, Mr. Castleman put up with that problem and managed to stay in the Parish until 1892. The Parishioners were very sorry to see him go. During his stay he was a "very efficient and zealous Priest, one whose indefatigable labor and Christian spirit are manifest in the growth of the membership and general prosperity of the Parish."[52]

In July 1893 the vestry minutes show that "the Parish being now supplied by the Rev. David Funston Ward (a 1893 graduate of the Virginia Seminary, assigned by The Bishop to our work). In order to devise ways and means by which to provide for his salary, it was resolved that the Vestry obligate itself to pay four of the six hundred dollars promised him, the remaining to be paid by the Diocesan Missionary Society, and that salary be paid quarterly beginning July 1, 1893.[53]

Vestry meeting at "Mount Pleasant" December 27, 1893. At this time it was announced the Ladies of the Parish will get up an entertainment sometime during the month to raise money to pay for the repairs done to the Rectory.[54]

January 17, 1894, the vestry met at the Chapel and elected delegates Robert Murphy and W. R. Crabbe to the meeting of the Council in Richmond on January 31 to elect an assistant Bishop for the Diocese. The delegates from Cople were "instructed to vote for the election of the Rev. J. B. Newton to assistant Bishopric." Also at this meeting, the committee on the cemetery was instructed to make a report of all matters in regard to the Yeocomico Cemetery at a meeting to be held at "Mount Pleasant" in four weeks. On a motion, the Committee on the Cemetery was "empowered to use from the walls of the church lot as many bricks as may be necessary to rebuild the broken wall in rear of the church." On March 17, 1894, the Cemetery Committee was instructed by the vestry to have a book printed containing certificates of ownership of a Lot in the Yeocomico Cemetery.[55]

49. *Southern Churchman* — 1890.
50. Cople Parish Vestry Minutes, 1849–1902, page 101.
51. Cople Parish Vestry Minutes, 1849–1902, page 117.
52. *Ibid.* September 24, 1892. pp, 121.
53. *Ibid.* July 12, 1893, page 125.
54. *Ibid.* December 27, 1893, pp. 128.
55. *Ibid.* January 17, 1894, pp. 130.

On January 31, 1894, a *native of Cople Parish* was elected assistant Bishop of the Diocese of Virginia. John Brockenbrough Newton was consecrated in St. James Church, Richmond, May 1894 at the annual Council of the Diocese.[56]

The Rev. David Funston Ward tendered his resignation as Rector of the Parish to the Vestry at the April 21, 1894, meeting to take effect in July. His resignation was accepted with best wishes of the Vestry for his future.[57]

A special meeting was called on April 30, 1894, and a committee was appointed to solicit subscriptions to the minister's salary.[58] (This seemed to be a never ending problem.)

The twenty-second Rector of Cople was the Rev. Austin Brockenbrough Chinn. He came to the Parish July 1, 1894, with the understanding the Vestry would secure a tenant for the Rectory with whom he could board and keep a room. The Vestry had received a report from the solicitations committee that $400. could be realized from subscriptions, $200.00 from the Diocesan Missionary Society which would enable the vestry to offer $600.00 to the new Rector. He accepted and at his first official vestry meeting he made a "very interesting address" to the Vestry.[59]

November 5th, 1894, The Rt. Rev. John B. Newton made his official visit to Yeocomico and confirmed a class of eight in his home parish.

A called meeting of the vestry was held at the chapel on May 29, 1895, for the purpose of signing the papers of the Rev. A.B. Chinn, Deacon, to recommend him to the Standing Committee of the Diocese for Ordination to the Priesthood. A motion was made and carried at this meeting to give Mr. James Dall Arnest permission to build a fence along the east wall of Yeocomico church lot, enclosing the same and to put in a gate, on the south and west entrances to said lot, the cost of the work to be paid by Mr. Arnest and same to be refunded to him if money is ever available in the treasury but the Vestry is under no obligation to do so, and it was further ordered that the committee on Yeocomico be instructed to so inform Mr. Arnest.[60]

At the July 13, 1895, meeting of the Vestry, "the Rev. John P. Tyler was authorized to solicit and collect contributions for the benefit of Yeocomico Church and such money to be used for repairs and upkeep of the old building."[61]

From the vestry minutes in 1896, we find that the committee on Yeocomico is having the floor of the church repaired and the cemetery fences white-washed and repaired. At the same time the treasurer is reporting once again a deficiency in the payment of the Rector's salary.[62]

56. *Ibid.* April 16, 1894, pp. 133.
57. *Ibid.* April 21, 1894, pp. 134.
58. *Ibid.* April 30, 1894, pp. 135.
59. *Ibid.* July 1, 1894, pp. 139.
60. *Ibid.* May 29, 1895, pp. 147. Mr. Chinn was the nephew of Mrs. Wat Henry Tyler.
61. *Ibid.* July 13, 1895, pp. 149.
62. Cople Parish Vestry Minutes, April 11, 1896, pp. 153.

Bishop John B. Newton died in Richmond May 27, 1897, and there was a called meeting of the vestry to elect a delegate to attend the Special Council held in Richmond June 30th for the election of Bishop Coadjutor to replace Bishop Newton.[62a]

August 7, 1897: A called meeting of the Vestry of August 7 at which time the rector, the Rev. A. B. Chinn "tendered a very kind and feeling letter of resignation to the vestry giving reasons for the necessity of this step and asking that it be accepted to take effect Sept. 15th. next." The Vestry appointed a committee to draft resolutions expressing regret at "severing the relations between us and expressing our high appreciation of Mr. Chinn and of his efficient work, Christian character and of the affection which we feel toward him."[63]

June 1898 Willoughby Newton Claybrook was the third Cople Parish native to graduate from The Virginia Theological Seminary in Alexandria.[64] He was born near Hague, son of Judith Newton and Edwin Claybrook, and was raised in Cople Parish. His father and mother ran a school in the Parish, and his father served many times on the vestry.

The twenty-third Rector of Cople Parish was The Rev. Albert Rhett Walker. He attended the August 6, 1898, Vestry meeting. There are no notes on minutes from November 1897 until August 6, 1898, when those minutes disclose the vestry moved and carried a motion that in the future there will be four regular meetings of the Vestry Viz: on the 1st Saturdays in September, December, March and June. It was moved that except when the regulation of the church required, the amounts received in collections at the various services to be devoted to one special purpose or fund. All collections of the Parish shall be devoted to the general expenses of the Parish and be credited to the general Parish account on the treasurer's books. This motion was carried.[65]

A notice that appeared in 1908 issue of *The Southern Churchman*, the Diocesan monthly paper, stated the wall and sundial was partially restored under the directorship of the Rev. A.R. Walker and neat iron gates were hung at the three entrances. Also noted the Sundial (dated 1717) was kept at the Rectory.[66] Mr. and Mrs. Walker and their family were very popular. A letter to the rector's daughter, "Miss Lila", dated "Linden" May 13, 1899 asking

> *"for the pleasure of taking you to Church Sunday evening. I do hope you have no previous engagement. Thank you for the strawberries, they were simply delicious. Please say to Mr. Walker that I will see that he gets to Nomini tomorrow morning. Thanking you for the berries, I am as ever your sincere friend. W. H. T.*

62a. *Ibid.* May 27, 1897, 162.
63. *Ibid.* August 7, 1897, pp. 163.
64. *History of The Theological Seminary in Virginia*, Vol. II, Goodwin, W.A.R., Rochester, N.Y. DuBois Press.
65. Cople Parish Vestry Minutes, August 6, 1898.
66. *Southern Churchman*, 1908. Publication of the Diocese of Virginia.

Newton — P.S.: You may answer my question tomorrow at Church. Tyler."[67]
The Rectory was a popular place for the young people of the Parish and Mr.
Walker's daughters were very attractive. Mrs. Albert Rhett Walker, wife of the
Rector was the granddaughter of the first Episcopal Missionary Bishop to China,
The Rt. Rev. William Jones Boone D. D. Her father was also missionary to
China and the fourth Missionary Bishop. (Their daughter, Sarah, married Staf-
ford Murphy son of John N. Murphy of "Kenmore.") Mrs. Walker died while
living in the Parish and the beautiful silver wine flagon at Yeocomico Church
was given as a memorial to her memory by her family.[68]
   April 17, 1899, a meeting of the Vestry was called and held at Rectory. "The
Rector handed to the treasurer a check for $100.00 presented by the Society for
the Preservation of Virginia Antiquities for repairs to wall and grounds around
Yeocomico Church." A letter of thanks for this generosity will be sent to the
Society from the Vestry. The Vestry signed a testimonial for James S. Cox, a
native of the parish, to be accepted as Deacon in the Diocese of Virginia.[69]
   Mr. Walker resigned at the June 23, 1900 Vestry meeting. This was accepted
with deep regret. "We recognize our loss will be a serious one and that to him
is due from us, as vestryman and individual members of the parish congregations, our thanks for the efficient, faithful and unselfish service he has tendered the parish as Rector, Preacher and Paster."[70]
   During Mr. Walker's Rectorship a fire at "Mount Pleasant" killed the mother
of "Jotha" Fisher, a young colored boy. Mr. Walker befriended this orphaned
child and when the Walker family left the Parish for a church in Baltimore, Jotha
went too. Mr. Walker procured a position for him with a very wealthy man to
accompany him on his world travels and act as his valet. Jotha was a very handsome, light-skinned young man with oriental features and when he visited Japan
he met and married a Japanese girl and changed his name to Jotha "Nichita".
They were living in Japan when the earthquake of 1923 struck and she was killed.
Jotha never forgot his native country and his childhood playmates at Hague. He
came back for a visit to Hague in 1924, but because he had "passed over" the
color line and taken a Japanese name he was not received in the homes of his
relatives. He stayed in the old law office at "Linden" for a few days then went to
Mexico and married a Mexican, established a good business and became a very
prolific writer of political opinions which were not particularly complimentary
to the social setup of his native countrymen!. Somehow, he did not give credit to
Mr. Walker for giving him the opportunity to make a different life for himself.[71]

67. Letter belonging to the Rev. A. R. Walker's granddaughter, Mrs. James H. Thompson,
Gloucester, Virginia. Tyler was ill with consumption and died in a few years.
68. Wine Flagon belonging to Yeocomico Church of Cople Parish, with inscription.'
69. Cople Parish Vestry Minutes, April 17, 1899, pp. 175–179.
70. *Ibid.* June 23, 1900, pp. 192.
71. Letters and book he wrote in long hand at "Linden" Hague, Virginia.

The twenty-fourth Rector of Cople was The Rev. Franklin A. Rideout. As there are no minutes of the Vestry between April 1899 and June 23, 1900, we do not know just when Mr. Rideout came to Cople from Cyntheand, Kentucky. He attended the Vestry meeting October 6, 1900.[72] The Rideouts lived at the Rectory. Their niece, Mattie Weisger, married a native of Cople Parish, Edward R. Jackson and they lived at "Green Hill," a lovely farm and large house high on the ridge next to "Boscobel" and across the main road from Machodoc Post Office.

A vestry meeting was held at home of Mr. Fred Griffith, March 16, 1901. Special attention was given to the minister's salary. The rector reported that the buggy shed at the Rectory needed repair, a motion was made to have the work done and pay for it with the money left on hand from Yeocomico yard repair fund.[73]

June 1902 another native of Cople Parish graduated from the Virginia Theological Seminary, He was George Pickett Mayo whose family lived at "Kelvin Grove," Hague, Virginia.[74]

Mr. Rideout served in the Parish until 1902. He went to Brandon, Virginia when he left Cople Parish. During W.W.I he served with Y.M.C.A. in France for six months in 1917 and died in 1929 in Norfolk where he served as Rector of Ascension Church.[75]

Twenty-fifth Minister of Cople The Rev. Charles Gross, came to Cople in 1902, a graduate of The College of the City of New York and of The Virginia Theological Seminary in 1902. He was made Deacon by Bishop Gravatt and Priest 1903 by Bishop Gibson, Bishop of Virginia.[76] While he was in Cople Parish he was very active. Journal of the Virginia Diocesan Convention for 1903 lists Mr. Gross as rector of Cople Parish which included St. Paul's Chapel, Nomini Grove, Nomini and Yeocomico Churches, Cople Chapel, and Edgewater Mission. A Receipt from the Diocesan Contingent Fund was found at "Buena Vista" in 1990 among old papers of Mr. Thomas Brown stored in the outside kitchen. It is dated April 5, 1903, and acknowledges $63.00 sent from Cople Parish in Westmoreland County to the Contingent Fund from the 102 communicants of the Parish.[77] Mr. Gross was in the Parish when the finances were in good shape! According to *Potomac Progress*, a newspaper published for a few years by a group of Hague businessmen at Hague, Virginia, Mr. Gross performed the wedding ceremony of Miss Helen Gibson Crabbe, "the charm-

---

72. Cople Parish Vestry Minutes, Oct. 6, 1900.
73. Cople Parish Vestry Minutes 1849–1902. March 16, 1901. page 182.
74. *History of Theological Seminary in Virginia*, Vol. II, page 161. Goodwin, W.A.R. George P. Mayo gave his life to the Mountain missions in Virginia. He built Blue Ridge Industrial School in 1910.
75. Stowe's Clerical Directory 1928–30. Research of H. Ragland Eubank.
76. Lloyd's Clerical Directory 1910.
77. Receipt on file at Cople Parish House at Hague.

ing and accomplished daughter of Mr. and Mrs. Walter R. Crabbe to Mr. Harry Marbery Tayloe, son of Col. and Mrs. E. Poinsett Tayloe of "The Laurels" on April 28, 1903. This was a brilliant and beautiful wedding held at "Mount Pleasant," the handsome home of the Crabbes at Hague.[78] Mr. Gross also performed the wedding ceremony of Miss Mary Willoughby Brown, daughter of Mr. and Mrs. George Fulton Brown, at the Chapel July 2, 1903, to John Rogers Williams of Princeton, New Jersey.[79] Mr. Gross left for Baltimore where he went to take charge of Memorial Church in that city. "Mrs. Gross will remain here for a fortnight or more before leaving for her new home."

The twenty-sixth Rector of Cople Parish was the Rev. Augustus Davisson 1903–1906. He was referred to as "Rector" in the Vestry minutes and also named as member of General arrangements to assist in the celebration in 1906 of the two hundredth anniversary of Yeocomico Church. There is no record that Mr. Davisson graduated from VTS or anywhere else, but it is certain he was "Minister" of Cople because his name is mentioned several times in the Vestry minutes. Stowe's Directory does not list him according to R. Davis in 1940 at the Office of the Bishop in Richmond. Dr. Brydon, Historiographer of the Diocese reported in 1940, found no mention of Mr. Davisson in any of his books and he had no other way of checking on him.[80] Strange!!

In 1906, under the leadership of the Rev. John Poyntz Tyler, Archdeacon of the Diocese of Virginia, The Association For the Preservation of Yeocomico Church was formed to raise a memorial fund for the preservation of "Old Yeocomico Church in Cople Parish, Westmoreland County, Virginia. This fund will be placed in the control of the Diocesan Board of Trustees to be permanently invested and proceeds used to keep the old building and enclosure in repair. In this connection it is proposed to celebrate the two hundredth anniversary of its erection by appropriate exercises, beginning on the 15th day of July, 1906."[81] The members of Cople Parish appointed the following gentlemen as members of a general arrangements committee to assist in this celebration and provide entertainment for visitors: William H. Fairfax, M.D., Wat Tyler Mayo, William J. Carey, S. Downing Cox, Walter E.R. Crabbe, Robert H. Gawen, John R. Gray, Frederick Griffith, and Augustus Davisson.

This Association has been meeting ever since in connection with the Annual Homecoming Service and luncheon held by the members of the Parish, usually in the fall of the year. A news letter is sent out and everyone has an opportunity to support the Yeocomico Memorial Association.

78. April 9, 1903, *Potomac Progress* newspaper on file in Westmoreland County Museum, Montross, Virginia. Contributed to Museum by V.O. Hutt, Kinsale, Va.
79. John Rogers Williams, whose grandmother was Jane Murphy of "Spring Grove," edited Philip Vickers Fithian's *Journal*.
80. Yeocomico Church Sketch Book, 1905, pp. 5.
81. A "Sketch Book of Yeocomico Church," pamphlet prepared by Association Committee in 1906.

July 1906 at a called meeting of the Vestry, The Rev. Augustus Davisson was present because he demanded an investigation of charges against him. The investigating committee reported that after a thorough investigation, Mr. Davisson was exonerated from the charges as there was no evidence to sustain them. The Vestry met at Hague July 28, 1906, and approved the above resolutions. It was further moved, seconded and carried that a copy of these resolutions be spread before the records of the vestry and sent to Mr. Davisson and one sent to the Rt. Rev. Robert A. Gibson, Bishop of Virginia, signed Frederick Griffith Sec. Pro tem."[82]

In 1906 the sudden death of Mr. W.E.R. Crabbe while on a trip to Baltimore shocked the Parish. Mr. Crabbe had been an able member of the Vestry and a very generous member of the community around Hague. A resolution in appreciation for his service to the Parish and community was included in the October 1906 Vestry minutes.[86] He donated the land for St. Paul's Catholic Church which had just been built in 1906 at Hague. Mr. Frank Tubman, of Mount Holly a well known businessman in the area and a Roman Catholic, gave the material needed for this building project[84] and helped enlarge the environs of Hague. At this time there were saloons in Hague.

In 1907 the vestry moved that no more burials be allowed at Nomini because the grounds had been filled up.[85]

July 21st, 1907 the second Annual Celebration of the Association For the Preservation of Yeocomico Church was held at the Church. The Rev. J. P. Tyler, Rev. John A. Moncure and Rev. Heigham presided at the services in the morning and afternoon. After lunch, which was served on the grounds, the Executive Committee opened with a prayer by the Rev. Moncure and the annual meeting was presided over by Mr. Wat Tyler Mayo, President of the Association. Minutes of the last meeting were read and approved. A motion made to elect H. Stafford Murphy, Edward C. Newton and Thomas M. Arnest to the Executive Committee to the three vacancies caused by the death of Walter Randolph Crabbe and Dr. W. H. Fairfax and the absence of The Rev. Augustus F. Davisson, "caused by removal from the Parish". Cople Parish was without a rector once again.[86]

In 1907 Nomini Church, Cople Chapel, Yeocomico and Boyce Mission of Cople Parish reported the pulpits vacant. The Rev. Henry Lane was asked to hold services in the Parish while the Parish was without a minister 1907–1908.[87]

---

82. Cople Parish Vestry Minutes (1906–1949) July 1906. pp. 151.
83. *Ibid.* 1906–1949. October 1906. Resolutions written by Mr. Thomas Brown and Dr. W. N. Chinn, pp. 149–150. Dr. Chinn's brother Austin was a former Rector of Cople, and Dr. Chinn was a faithful member for many years.
84. Westmoreland County Virginia. Edited by Walter Briscoe Norris. pp. 499.
85. Cople Parish Vestry Minutes, May 11, 1907, page 152.
86. *Ibid.* July 1, 1907, pp. 152.
87. *Ibid.* August 17, 1907, pp. 153.

Mr. Lane married several couples. Mary Stevenson Newton of *Linden* and T. Niven Massey of *Liberty Hall* were married at Cople Chapel in February 8, 1908.[88] Mrs. Mary Willoughby Brown Williams and Fisher Howe of Princeton, New Jersey were married at "Wilton" that same year.

At a vestry meeting a check for $25 was sent to Mr. Lane in "appreciation for his kindness." During this time the rectory was rented one month at a time. Aug. 17, 1907, the Vestry authorized the committee on Yeocomico to do any necessary repair work on the Church.

January 30, 1908, The Rev. Arthur P. Gray, the twenty-seventh rector and graduate of V.M.I. and Va. Theological Seminary, accepted Cople's call by stipulating that the rectory be repaired and renovated. The first vestry meeting attended by Mr. Gray was held at the home of Dr. Walter Chinn on March 14, 1908. Noted in the July 11, 1908, minutes was the "general repairs to, painting and papering of rectory completed."[89]

In 1908 the sun dial from Yeocomico Church was kept now at the Rectory according to an article in *The Southern Churchman.*

Among Mr. Gray's experiences before coming to Cople are the following: Assistant Rector of St. Paul's Lynchburg, Superintendent of Schools in Prince William County — where he had Dettingen and Haymarket Parishes for nine years — and Greenbriar Parish, Lewisburg, West Virginia. He was one of the four original trustees of Sweet Briar College and Secretary of the Board of Directors.

Mr. Gray came to Cople from Bromfield Parish, Rappahannock County, Virginia with his wife, the former Wilhelmena Jorden Radford, a son, Arthur Powell Jr. (a graduate of the Va. Theological Seminary in 1910) and daughter Ellen Douglas. According to Blake Tyler Newton, who was a college student at this time, the Grays were very popular and entertained a lot of young people at the Rectory. Mr. Gray became ill with typhoid fever in 1910 and was unable to continue his work in the Parish. He resigned, and he and his wife lived with their son, Arthur Jr. and daughter, Mrs. R. B. Tyler, until his death in 1921.[90]

In the summer of 1910, Mr. James S. Allen came to the Parish as a seminary student and lived in the Parish for three months and returned to the Seminary. He was very popular with all the parishioners. In 1912 the Parish was still vacant and Mr. Allen came back to officiate at the wedding of Miss Mary Lou Sydnor, daughter of Mr. and Mrs. Charles Sydnor of Tucker Hill and Mr. George C. Sanford of Acorn. The wedding took place at Yeocomico Church, October 29, 1912 at *7:30 A.M.* because the couple planned to take the steamer

---

88. Marriage Register for Cople Parish, 1908.
89. Cople Parish Vestry Minutes, 1906–1949, page 155. January 30, 1908.
90. Resumé of Mr. Gray from his granddaughter Miss Elizabeth Gray. Westminster Canterbury, Irvington. His last vestry meeting in Cople was January 30, 1909. Page 151, in Vestry Minutes 1906–1949.

from Kinsale at 9 A.M. and go to Washington for their honeymoon. It took a long time to go by buggy from Yeocomico to the steamboat wharf at Kinsale. Mr. Sanford had a beautiful tenor voice and sang in Cople Parish Choir most of his adult life.[91]

Mr. Allen wrote the well known poem "In The Good Old Northern Neck" after he left the area and went west.[92]

The twenty-eighth Rector of Cople, The Rev. Charles Crusoe, came from St. John's Church, Corbin, Kentucky. He was ordained to the Deaconate in 1910 and to the Priesthood April 23, 1912, by Bishop Burton of Lexington, Kentucky. He did not graduate from The Virginia Seminary. He was married and had three children when he came to Cople in early 1913.[93]

July 1, 1913: The Committee on repairs to the rectory reported progress. A Deed of Trust was given on the Rectory for the amount borrowed for repairs. "After discussion of the financial system the envelope system was adopted and the rector authorized to get it started." August 7, 1913, Vestry meeting at the Rectory. Progress on repairs to the Rectory was reported. The money made by the ladies for the Rectory fund was turned over to the Treasurer of the Church.

A committee was appointed to see if more land could be secured adjoining the cemetery at Yeocomico Church; and to draw on treasurer for funds to pay for removing trees from the cemetery. Insurance on Rectory to be renewed "at best rates possible."

October 3, 1913. The Vestry met at the Rectory.

In September 5, 1913, the Vestry minutes referred to the Mission at Tidwells. A committee report on the State of the Church reported in favor of keeping the work at "Edgewater Mission" and they were appointed to locate the boundary for the land at "The Mission." At the November 6 meeting, the committee announced this had been attended to. The committee was then ordered to employ a surveyor to make the lines. During the winter, the Mission at "Boycetown" was closed. A committee was appointed to visit the Boycetown neighborhood and ascertain what aid the people of that vicinity would give and what is necessary to be done to make the "church" there comfortable for the winter. The committee reported December 5, 1914, that the church needed stove pipe and window panes and at the January meeting it was reported the church "on Boycetown" was repaired and ready for occupancy. (Edgewater neighborhood became Tidwells when a Post Office was established there in 1900. Mr. Irving Daiger was the Postmaster.)

---

91.   Cople Parish Marriage Register and Family History of Mrs. Barnes Rowe, daughter of Mr. and Mrs. George Sanford.
92.   Mr. James Allen is not recorded in the Vestry Minutes. He was remembered by parishioners long after he left.
93.   Page 164 records Vestry Minutes for July 1, 1913, August 7, 1913, The Rev. Charles Crusoe present.

Mrs. Cornelia Hayes remembers when Mr. Charlie Boyce would come across the Machodoc Creek to "Parham," where her father was a store keeper and also a tenant on Parham farm, and pick up her family on Sundays when there would be Sunday School and row back across the creek to the Chapel. Then they would wait on the shore and watch for Mrs. Trader in her large row boat with her children and Mr. Frederick Goodwin coming over from "Meter Post Office" near Coles Point. Then they would have Church. Mr. and Mrs. Horace Bryant were faithful members of the chapel at this time and helped keep the interest alive.

At the November 6, 1913, Vestry meeting at the Rectory, a motion was made and carried to close Yeocomico Church for the winter beginning December 1st.

At the January 3, 1914 the Vestry met at Hague.

Mrs. Charles Taylor's offer of one acre of land adjoining the cemetery at Yeocomico for $30.00 was accepted with thanks. A committee was appointed to develop the Yeocomico cemetery by grading, plotting and marking all lots with prices ranging according to the location of lots.

April 21, 1914, Special Thanksgiving Service at the Chapel at Hague was called for 3 P.M. and conducted by the Rector and the Rev. R. S. Litsinger from Warsaw made the address to the "large audience." The Treasurer of the Parish, Mr. Thomas M. Arnest, conducted a business discussion and reported progress along every line of the Church work under the inspiring leadership of Mr. Crusoe. Mr. Arnest reported as treasurer over twenty five hundred dollars had been raised for the Parish in the past twelve months, every obligation met and discharged to May 1, 1914, and the substantial balance of considerably over one hundred dollars in the treasury. This was music to the Vestrymen's ears. At the vestry meeting held after the service it was decided to open Yeocomico Church for services beginning Sunday, May 3. The schedule for services in the Parish to be: Yeocomico 1st and 3rd. Sunday mornings; Nomini 2nd and 4th Sunday mornings and 3rd Sunday at night: Chapel 1st, 2nd and 4th Sunday nights.

The vestry expressed thanks to the American Wire & Steel Co. of Pittsburgh, Pa. for donating steel posts for fence at Rectory.

A beautiful Hymn Board was given to Yeocomico Church by Mr. G. Dudley Cox as a memorial to his brother, the Rev. James Cox, who had recently died. He was another native clergyman from Cople Parish.

June 2, 1914, THE RECTORY DESTROYED BY FIRE, CHURCH RECORDS DESTROYED ALSO, BUT NO ONE WAS INJURED.

June 3, 1914, Vestry Meeting: Committee appointed to consider plans for restoration of the Rectory. Mr. Brown's offer of school house at "Buena Vista" to be prepared as temporary quarters for Rector and his family was accepted.

The Rector was requested to confer with the Bishop as to taking immediate steps for rebuilding the Rectory and for the Bishop's personal statement to be used to secure funds for rebuilding. A notation to the minutes tells of a motion made and carried "that the rector secure a Bible with fitting inscription and present same to Harry Robbin Anthony from the Vestry as a testimony of their appreciation of his courageous service at the burning of the Rectory."[94]

At the June 15, 1914, meeting, at "Lee Hall," the Vestry was to head the list of contributions to the building fund with a sum of $200.00

At the July 7, 1914, meeting, at "Lee Hall," Dr. W. N. Chinn, treasurer of building fund, received $1000.00 insurance for Rectory fire. Dr. Chinn also reported about two thousand dollars in hand for building fund.

Letters were being sent all over the country asking for donations for the rebuilding of the Rectory. There was much discussion of this, pro and con. At the July 25, 1914, vestry meeting at "Lee Hall," "the vestry decided to send out more letters of appeal at once and any surplus funds over and above what is necessary to complete the rebuilding of the Rectory, be returned to the donors." This motion was adopted with the following amendment, "not over 5,000 more letters be sent out." The vestry minutes from October 13, 1914, to October 9, 1915, give evidence that a lot of controversy took place concerning the handling of the rebuilding project and after much unpleasantness, was finally settled.

On May 3, 1915, the Vestry authorized "The Ladies of Nomini Church to have the grounds of the Church surveyed and gave them permission to have erected a fence enclosing the same." At this time the treasurer was instructed to pay bill due in Dec. 1914 for rental of *phone* in the Rectory. (Phones were not an every day household appliance in Hague at this time!) The Committee for the restoration of Yeocomico was given permission to restore the pedestal on the sundial at Yeocomico. At this time a two-day Annual Spring meeting of The Rappahannock Valley Convocation was held in Cople Parish. The Ladies Aid Society, assisted by other members of the Parish, entertained all who attended. A "Tying Rack" (to tether horse and buggy) was voted to be erected at the Chapel, the chain for the rack to be donated by Mr. T. M. Arnest.

June 5, 1915, meeting at the Rectory it was "moved and seconded that the Sec. be instructed to request the Bishop of the Diocese to send to the Parish a minister to hold a series of meetings for the purpose of arousing the interest of the people to a 'House to House' canvas proposed in the interest of the Duplex Envelope System".

August 7, 1915, a petition of "Edgewater Mission" was presented to the Vestry asking for two services a month and this was granted.

August 7, 1915, the vestry engaged T. B. Mayo to lay off a cemetery at "Boycetown

---

94. Cople Parish Vestry Minutes June 3, 1914, 1906–1949, pp. 181. Harry Robbin Anthony lived next to the Rectory with his father and mother. He was 24 at the time of the fire.

Mission." The name was not settled for the mission until much later.

At the September 25, 1915, meeting at the Rectory, Mr. Crusoe handed in his resignation. It was read and accepted to take effect October 15, 1915.

"Whereas, Rev. Charles Crusoe has determined to tender his resignation and whereas, while accepting his resignation this vestry deems it fitting and proper to adopt suitable resolutions to show Rev. Crusoe our grateful appreciation of his untiring efforts and zeal and his wonderful organizing ability as our Rector." This resolution was sent to Mr. Crusoe.

World War I was declared April 2, 1917, and members of the parish were called up to "make the world safe for democracy." The war did not last long, but took its toll on families in the Parish and when November 11, 1918, came the Parish was thankful. Wat Tyler Mayo of "Kelvin Grove" brought back mementos from Paris and B. Frank Brown of "Kenmore" was with the troops who had to stay overseas for another year. "Over There" was the song of the day, and children in the Parish played with lead soldiers and learned about the flags of the world by coloring them in coloring books. No mention of the war in the vestry minutes. The vestry was too busy trying to secure a Rector!

June 13, 1917, the Vestry meeting was held at "Buena Vista." The Parish was still without a Rector. A committee was appointed "to confer with the vestries of Lunenburg and North Farnham with a view of combining the three parishes and extend a call to a rector to serve the combined parishes."

October 1, 1917: Vestry met at "Buena Vista" and considered a letter from Bishop R. A. Gibson in answer to the letter the vestry wrote the Bishop to ask for approval for the combination of the three parishes. It was decided to invite The Rev. Frederick D. Goodwin to visit the Parish and he became the twenty-ninth rector.

Oct. 8, 1917, the Vestry meeting at "Buena Vista" was opened with prayer by the Rev. Frederick D. Goodwin. The vestry offered Mr. Goodwin $900.00 and $150.00 to assist in paying for a car as rector of Cople. Mr. Goodwin accepted and would take up work November 1, 1917. WHAT A WONDERFUL DAY FOR COPLE!

Nov. 7, 1917, meeting at Buena Vista. Lunenburg, North Farnham, St. Paul's (Nomini Grove) and Cople Parishes extended a joint call to the Rev. Frederick D. Goodwin, "each parish to contribute the minister's salary as follows, Lunenburg $500, North Farnham $150, St. Paul's, Nomini Grove, $100, and Cople $600 with $150, provided the "Diocesan Missionary Society will donate this for the purpose of Cople." In addition to the salary, the parishes offer as follows: Lunenbrug, N. Farnham and St. Paul's $150 and Cople $150 to assist the Rev. Mr. Goodwin with an automobile to be used in the work in the four parishes. Mr. Goodwin shall have his choice between the Rectories in Cople or Lunenburg Parish for his residence. The call was extended and accepted immediately by Mr. Goodwin.

The Rev. F. D. Goodwin and Mrs. Goodwin came to the Parish as bride and groom. They were married October 16, 1917, just before coming to Cople and moved into the Rectory at Hague. Mr. Goodwin was a 1912 graduate of the College of William and Mary and from Virginia Theological Seminary in 1917.

The January 14, 1918, meeting was held at "Buena Vista." Ladies Aid Society lent $75 to help pay for the minister's automobile. Collection will be taken up Sunday, January 27, 1918, and given to the National Commission of the Episcopal Church.

April 9, 1919, the Vestry meeting was held at the Rectory. Ladies Aid Society thanked for contribution of $25 "for improvements at Boycetown Chapel." The vestry decided to hold the Annual Congregational meeting at the 'Town Hall' Hague, to elect the vestry for the ensuing year and to hear reports on the work in the Parish during the past year and present standing of the Parish.

Minutes of the Vestry for 1919 show that vestry meetings were held regularly each month and much interest in Sunday Schools continued in the Parish. Much upkeep to church property was undertaken. Also a committee was appointed on "Nation Wide Day of Convocation" for entertainment of expected visitors to this important meeting. Scarlet fever was in the neighborhood of Nomini in December 1919 which delayed the opening of a Sunday School at Nomini Church.

September 23, 24, and 25, 1919: The semi-annual meeting of the Rappahannock Convocation was held in the Hague Chapel. The Rt. Rev. W. C. Brown, Bishop of Virginia, Bishop J. P. Tyler and sixteen members of the clergy in the convocation were present.

During the 1920's Miss Lily Barber came to the Parish as a Christian Education director to help Mr. Goodwin. She visited the homes and formed a group of the Girls Friendly Society. Miss Barber had been a missionary to China and fascinated the young girls with her stories.

April 9, 1920: The Vestry minutes show that a request had been filed with the Nation Wide Campaign Sub-Committee for a donation of $1,250.00 for the purpose of buying and equipping the "Town Hall" at Hague for a Parish House for Cople Parish at Hague. May 1, 1920, The vestry directed Dr. W. N. Chinn and Blake T. Newton to make all preparations necessary to purchase the Hague "Town Hall." This was a two-story plain rectangular wooden structure built on the right hand side of the road which ran from R. L. Griffith's store at Hague to the St. Paul's Catholic Church where the road forked, with "Buena Vista" farm on one side and "Linden" on the other. The "Town Hall" was built on the edge of "Buena Vista" farm.

A new High School was under construction at Hague to replace the former High School at Kinsale which had burned. The vestry offered "the Parish House to the School Board for the session of 1920–1921 free of rent, provided the School Board enter into an agreement to insure the house for as much insurance as they can get, make such repairs as is necessary for their use, and vacate the premises free of any encumbrances and repair at their own expense any and all damages done during the occupancy by the School Board."

Mr. and Mrs.. Goodwin moved to the Rectory in Warsaw in fall 1920 with their two children, Frederick Jr. and Elbert. Mr. Goodwin divided his time between the three Parishes and he was popular with everyone. Mr. and Mrs. Goodwin had a wonderfully happy approach to life that endeared them to the community and appealed to the teenagers in the Parish.

The Ladies Aid Society was busy raising money for repairs to the buildings. It was at the April Congregational meetings that the custom of the Ladies serving those wonderful meals in the "old Town Hall" began.

The Vestry met April 25, 1924, at Parish House. B. T. Newton was elected Delegate to Diocesan Council with E. M. Penington as Alternate. In these minutes is the first time the name of St. James was used in place of Boycetown or Edgewater mission.

At this meeting it was moved and seconded and carried that Mr. Goodwin be requested to write a letter and have the treasurers of the several vestries involved sign same and forward to Bishop Brown with regard to Mr. Goodwin's two-year leave of absence to work with the National Council of the Episcopal Church on a study of the Rural Parishes and their work. This letter was written and a copy of the agreement between F.D. Goodwin and the Parishes, Cople, Lunenburg, North Farnham and St. Paul's Chapel, was placed in the minute book. During the time of this agreement, the control of the parish affairs was in the hands of the several vestries. The several vestries agreed to provide F. D. Goodwin $25.00 a year during the time of this agreement for travelling expenses to and from the parishes. Mr. Goodwin's study of the Rural Church produced a book called *Beyond City Limits* and was considered a tremendous help to the rural clergy.

In 1927 the Goodwins were blessed with another little boy. He was named Edward LaBaron for his father's brother and all the Parishioners were delighted for the Goodwins. He was born at the Old Rectory in Warsaw and was only three when his father was made Bishop. He looked so much like his father that he was nicknamed "Little Bish."

In 1928 Yeocomico Church was restored again. At this time Wat Tyler Mayo engaged Bedford Brown IV, Architect, of Washington, D.C. for this job. The Rector F. D. Goodwin and Chairman of the Executive Committee of the Association were in charge of sending out an appeal for contributions to the project. The Old Church was beautifully restored at this time and in the process the roof was removed and pictures were taken of the rafters and outline of the original church, circa 1655, was revealed. The brick masons who restored the east wall put their initials above the large round window just as the masons who laid the original bricks had left their initials molded in brick which is now a lost art.

With the advent of cars, new roads were being built. The new road from Carey's Corner to the Hague took away the deep sand bed that was in front of the Rectory, but it also made it difficult to maintain the entrance land for the Rector or whoever was occupying the Rectory. The churches were equipped with pump organs and since Bishop Goodwin had a lovely voice he assisted the Church choirs. Mrs. Robert H. Beale was the organist in all three churches. Mrs. Frank Dobyns was the leader of the choir. The women of the church kept up a lively interest in the Church Missions both at home and abroad with visiting missionary speakers as inspiration.

Each fall there was the "famous" ham and oyster supper held *upstairs* in the Parish House. Since there was no running water or electricity in the building, every bit of water used was carried up the back stairs in large metal cream cans loaned for the occasion by the farmers in the congregation. The wood for the large Home Comfort Range used to cook all the wonderful food was also hauled by the laymen up those steep stairs. Everyone in the Parish worked on "The Bazaar." The walls of the Parish House were cedar tongue and groove, the building was heated with wood stoves and the place was lighted with kerosene lamps. Why there was never an accident speaks well for the congregation. This was also the time the Women's Auxiliary-Aid would put on the Christmas Bazaar downstairs where the air was sweet with the scent of wonderful garland cedar and holly used for decorating the different booths where all sorts of handmade wonders were sold. At the candy booth were stacks of "recycled candy boxes" filled with the most delicious assortment of confections imaginable, homemade by the experts in the Parish. The Fancy Table was presided over by Mrs. John Brown of "The Grove," her specialty was hand crocheted linen table mats and linen napkins to match. There were also beautifully made dresser scarfs, handkerchiefs, etc. all in pure linen. The children's table was full of hand dressed dolls, Christmas tree ornaments, games and toys and the Food Booth with tempting pickles, jams, jellies, cakes, pies and cookies. Everybody stocked up for Christmas and the ladies could send lots of contributions to The Church Missions with the profits. It took a lot of hard work, but the wonderful, happy spirit which filled that old hall was worth it.

Mr. Goodwin stayed in the Parish until he was elected Bishop Coadjutor of the Diocese of Virginia, and he was consecrated at North Farnham Church, Farnham, Virginia, on Thursday, October 16, 1930. He had been Rector of Cople Parish exactly thirteen years. Mr. Goodwin had been a wonderful influence on the young teenage boys in the Parish, and as they grew up and left the Parish they took their places in the churches wherever they went. Two of them served on the Board of the Virginia Theological Seminary. Bishop Goodwin was very pleased about this.

August 1, 1931, the thirtieth Rector came to Cople, The Rev. Clarence Buxton was a 1916 graduate of Virginia Theological Seminary and a native of Bristol, New Hampshire. He was ordained a Deacon in Christ Church Cathedral, Louisville, Kentucky in 1916 and a priest in 1917 in St. Mary's Church, Madison, Kentucky. He served in World War I. The Buxton family came to Cople from Greensboro, North Carolina where he was priest of St. Andrew's Church. The Buxtons had two children: a daughter, Jean Page, and a son, Edward and they lived in the Rectory at Hague. Mrs. Buxton's mother, Mrs. Page, lived with them and was very active with her daughter in the work of the Parish. She introduced "tasting parties" to the Hague community; today we call these affairs "covered dish luncheons or suppers," depending on the time of day. Mr. Buxton was also Rector of Farnham and Lunenburg Parishes and had services in St. Paul's Church, Nomini Grove. He was pastor to all the members of these churches, baptizing, presenting candidates for confirmation, marrying and burying, as well as visiting the sick and shut-ins, and Mrs. Page and Mrs. Buxton accompanied him. Mr. Buxton was interested in history and worked hard on the *Pilgrimage*, a fund-raising house and church tour put on by the members of the Parish in 1932.

Now that the Downing Bridge spanned the Rappahannock River, the Northern Neck and Cople Parish were discovered by Richmonders for recreation purposes. Coles Point and Sandy Point were being built up with summer homes along the bank of the "the river." Bishop and Mrs. Goodwin bought a lot at Sandy Point and spent their vacations there for many years, much to the delight of their former parishioners.

In June 1934 another native son of Cople, the Rev. Frederick Griffith was graduated from Virginia Theological Seminary. He was the grandson of Col. Thomas Brown of "Buena Vista," Hague, and son of Mr. and Mrs. Richard Lee Griffith who were loyal and faithful members of the Episcopal Church.

At the 143rd Council of the Diocese May 5, 1938, Cople Parish reported: Congregation — Families, 63; individuals (not thus included) 54; confirmed persons, 256; church members (all baptized persons) 343.

Mr. Buxton held regular Lenten Services in the Parish at the Chapel on Wednesday nights. Mr. Buxton "exchanged pulpits" with neighboring parishes for Lenten services quite often. Good Friday services were held at the Hague Chapel. Easter services were always held at Yeocomico and Christmas services were always held at Nomini Church at five o'clock Christmas afternoon.

During Mr. Buxton's stay in the parish he baptized twenty persons at St. Paul's Nomini Grove and presented twenty-eight for confirmation there. He administered to his people during the trying times of the "Depression" and during World War II. There was an active Young People's Service League which met on Sunday evenings at Cople Chapel and sent delegates to the summer conferences of the Diocesan Y.P.S.L.

During World War II, 1941–1945, a plaque with names of the members of the Parish serving in the armed services was posted in a prominent place in each of the Churches. April 6, 1942, the vestry passed a motion that a member from the Auxiliary Aid and one from the Vestry be appointed to keep in touch "with all of our men serving in the Army and Navy."

All branches of the service were represented. Everett Anthony of Fort Hill, Hague, was the first casualty from our area. He was lost at sea July 1942 serving with the Navy. Everett was the son of Mr. and Mrs. Marvin Anthony and had attended the Sunday School at Hague Chapel. Everyone in the parish was grieved at this sad news.

Mrs. Anthony was a Gawen whose family had been members of Cople Parish from the earliest times.

In the middle of World War II, Mrs. Hazel Rest's teenaged daughter Emma Lou and her brother were playing on the beach at the mouth of Jackson Creek when they found a bottle washed up on the beach with a note inside. The note gave the name of a sailor and his address stationed across the Potomac at Patuxant Naval Base. Just for fun, Emma Lou answered the note and a correspondence began. The sailor's name was John Flair from Nashville, Tennessee and he and the beautiful beachcomber have celebrated their fiftieth wedding anniversary.

The Vestry accepted Mr. Buxton's resignation in 1944, and the Buxton family moved to Pohick Church in northern Virginia. The Buxtons left a host of friends.

A remarkable group called the Peckatone Circle met once a month for a long time under the guidance of Mrs. William Sanford Tucker Hill. This group was made up of women in Peckatone Neck who found it difficult, for one reason or another, to attend the organized woman's group of the churches in their area. Mrs. Sanford was a member of Carmel Church, but she had grown up in the Tucker Hill area and had attended Sunday School at Yeocomico so that she felt at home with both Episcopalian and Methodist. The Circle flourished for a time and was a great influence.

During World War II, because of shortage of gas, it was decided to divide the Woman's Auxiliary of the Parish into neighborhood groups which would meet each month in homes using the same format as the Auxiliary meetings. These meetings were very successful and when the groups came together once every sixth months at the Parish House, it was surprising how effective this plan was. The minutes of the Mount Holly group from 1944 to January 6, 1954 were located in the home of Helen Palmer after her death and is a treasure trove of information about the work of the Parish in the Nomini area. The following is an excerpt from the little composition book:

"At a meeting of the Mount Holly Group of the Woman's Auxiliary of Cople Parish, held at "Liberty Hall" home of Mr. and Mrs. T. Niven Massey, May 9, 1945 with four members present. The meeting was opened with prayer lead by Miss [Marie] Cooke. The roll was called and minutes read by the secretary, stood and approved. Mrs. R. B. Davis reported that she had sent cards to four sick members of the Aux. Aid. Mrs. T. N. Massey reported that she had a gift given of $5.00 through the kindness of Mrs. J. D. Brown. A discussion was had on our Church property and what to do about them; the vote of all present was to do away with the Chapel and concentrate on the two old churches that we have. This being left to be brought up again in the future. It was suggested that "we talk this up" and then make suggestion at next Aid meeting about what we shall do.

There being nor further business the meeting was adjourned to meet again the 2nd Wednesday in June.

Respectfully submitted,

Lucy Newton Massey Blundon, Secretary"
This tells us exactly when the idea for de-consecration of the Chapel was born. The
ladies were true to their word and "talked it up" at the proper times in the Parish. At
the Vestry meeting June 24, 1946, Joseph Trader made a report relative to the condition of Cople Chapel, stating that in his judgment, the building is beyond repair." It
took over a year to "do away with the Chapel." On September 3, 1946, it was announced to the Vestry in session that the equipment from the Chapel including the
Cross and books had been moved to St. James, Tidwells, except for the rug which
had been sold to Mrs. H. M. Tayloe for $10.00. The Vestry then voted to ask the
Rector, Mr. Rhein, to contact Bishop Goodwin regarding a service of deconsecration
of the Chapel at Hague.

October 1947 Bishop Goodwin came to the parish for two important services. He
confirmed Mr. and Mrs. Hally Tubman and Mr. Hugh Morgan from Warsaw. The
Rev. Ernest De Bordenave presented the candidates for confirmation in Nomini
Church, Mount Holly. It was fitting that Hally Tubman be confirmed at Nomini
Church. He has spent most of his life keeping the church in beautiful repair. The next
service Mr. Goodwin performed that day was to "de-consecrate" the Chapel at Hague.

The thirty-first Rector of Cople was called to the Parish in March 1946. The Rev.
Francis B. Rhein and Mrs. Rhein were a young and good looking couple. They lived
in the Rectory at Hague which they decorated very attractively. Mr. Rhein was a
native of Wilmington, Delaware, graduate of University of Virginia and Virginia
Seminary in 1942 and Rector of Washington and Montross Parishes 1942–1943.
Chaplain in the US Navy from 1943–1945. Mr. and Mrs. Rhein came to Cople as the
parish was recovering and its members were getting their lives back together after
World War II. He had the same busy schedule as his predecessors.

In 1946 the brick walk was laid at Yeocomico from front gate to "porch" of Church.
The one year and a half Mr. Rhein was Rector of the Parish, he presented a Confirmation class when the Bishop came. Mrs. Raymond Sydnor (Frances) was confirmed in that class. He baptized seven adults at St. Paul's, Nomini Grove, September
15, 1946. He is remembered in the Parish for his interest in parishioners who were
having problems with alcoholism.

The Vestry accepted Mr. Rhein's resignation October 13, 1947, and wished him all
the best in his new Parish in Newport, Rhode Island. Mr. and Mrs. Rhein lived at the
Rectory while here although it was in need of a lot of repair. During the four years of
WWII no upkeep had been done and after the war it was difficult to buy the necessary supplies for fixing screens, etc. In December 2, 1946, the Vestry gave permission
to Robert Murphy, Chairman of Nomini Committee to add a room to the back of
Nomini Church for the purpose of installing a furnace. The room to measure 12x20
and not to be used as a Sunday School room.

The thirty-second Rector was The Rev. William Byrd Lee who was a graduate of
the College of William and Mary and Virginia Seminary in 1915. Mr. and Mrs. Lee

moved here from Auburn, Alabama where Mr. Lee was Chaplain of Auburn University before coming 'back' to Virginia. The Lees moved into the rectory in July 1948 and endeared themselves to the community. Their two attractive daughters and two sons were friends with the young people of the Parish. The Rectory was a lively place with a group of teenagers enjoying social times together.

By 1949 Nomini Church had undergone another "face lift." This time the center aisle was restored and new lighting fixtures installed. The old brass oil lamps were sold and the money realized from the sale was used, with the permission of the Vestry, to buy new Prayer Books for Nomini Church. January 11, 1949, the Vestry of Cople Parish wrote Mrs. T. N. Massey of Mount Holly to thank her and "her splendid co-workers for her leadership in the matter of raising funds, in excess of two thousand dollars, for the rehabilitation of Nomini Church. Day after day and week after week, for a period of more than two years, Mrs. Massey's leadership with the cooperation of all others concerned, was something rarely seen and deserves the highest commendation of this body. As a capstone to the work of devotion, in a good cause, is the Bronze Cross now adorning the front of this ancient edifice." This was signed by the Vestry and written by the Registrar of the Vestry, Mr. G. D. Cox.

Mr. Lee was very interested in building a new Parish House and the Vestry agreed. Plans began in 1949 and it was ready for use two years later. This was a big asset for the Sunday School at Hague. There was a large dining room and kitchen on the lower floor and several Sunday school rooms. The top floor had a large assembly room, two restrooms, a stage and another small Sunday school room and an office for the Rector. The Auxiliary-Aid worked hard to raise money for the project and assisted the Committee for the Fourth of July 1950 celebration, to be held on the lawn at "Buena Vista." The big attraction was the Army Field Band for entertainment. Colonel H. C. Bronson, Chairman of the event, announced at the July fifth Vestry meeting a net gain of $500.00 was made and thanked the parish committee, especially the ladies, who voted to give to the Parish House Building Committee the money made to help retire the debt. They also held many rummage sales for this purpose, but continued to support the missions of the church. During this time the ladies of the Mt. Holly group of the Women's Auxiliary sent a box of clothing to a Japanese Mission.

The Korean War began June 25, 1950, and in March 1951 the Vestry minutes revealed that they had the sad task of writing to Mr. and Mrs. Earl Hayes to express sympathy for the news received that their son was missing in action.

The services were held regularly at St. James, Tidwells, where Roy Fagan was Superintendent. Raymond Sydnor was Superintendent for the combined Nomini, Yeocomico, and Cople Sunday Schools. Mr. Lee started training the young boys in the Parish to serve as Acolytes.

In February, 1953, the vestry began to plan for a celebration of the County's 300th anniversary. It was decided to invite the Rt. Rev. H. St. George Tucker, Bishop of

Virginia and Presiding Bishop of the Protestant Episcopal Church in U.S.A., and The Rt. Rev. Frederick D. Goodwin to come for the August 16 celebration at Yeocomico Church. In preparation for this, a committee was appointed to make special arrangements. A utility building was built at Yeocomico to take the place of the wooden facility. Mr. George Lessard did the masonry work, Mr. Robert Carden made the contribution of fixtures, and members of the parish contributed generously and the building was finished in time for the Tercentennial.

Mrs. Lee became ill with cancer and died in the late summer of 1953. After being in the Parish for six years, Mr. Lee resigned. He moved to Richmond in 1954 where he was in charge of *Christ The King Parish*.

The Rev. Edward Morgan III, thirty-third Rector came to Cople in 1955 as a Deacon right out of Virginia Seminary, and there was a big celebration at the Parish House after he was ordained to the Priesthood a year later. The Morgans lived at the Rectory and began their family. Mr. Morgan was a hard working and dedicated priest. St. James flourished under his care.

At the Annual Homecoming, October 16, 1955, Mr. Morgan introduced a "new" idea for the occasion having several babies brought up for baptism after the first lesson. "This emphasized the meaning of the Church family of God as we met to celebrate the occasion of Homecoming, when members of the family of God come from near and far to gather together, it is particularly appropriate for us to welcome into our midst new members of the family. Now every Christian is their brother or sister, and the Church is their new home." Mr. Morgan was a faithful pastor to his large flock. He found trying to serve St. Paul's was a large order, and when he left he recommended that the Rector of Cople not "take on " these additional services. The connection with St. Paul's ceased in 1960.

At the April vestry meeting a motion was made to express thanks to the Ladies Altar Guilds for their loving and unselfish duty to God and the church in maintaining with loving care the altars of three churches.

During the summer of 1957 Macon Walton came to the Parish and assisted Mr. Morgan with his summer work, holding Daily Vacation Bible School and organized summer programs for the young people.

In 1960 Mr. Morgan handed in his resignation because he received "an offer he could not refuse" and moved, with the Bishop's blessing, to a fast-growing Church called St. Luke's in Alexandria.

The thirty-fourth Rector of Cople was the Rev. Lawrence Mason, the first bachelor since 1906. He was a 1960 graduate of The Seminary and was not unfamiliar with the Parish since he also was an assistant to Mr. Morgan while a Seminary student.

Under his guidance the work of the Parish continued to flourish. A new organ was purchased for Yeocomico Church.

In 1963 Bishop Goodwin came to the Parish for a service at Yeocomico Church and surprised Mr. Raymond Sydnor by honoring him with a special plaque for "his thirty-five years of service as Sunday School Superintendent to Cople Parish in the Diocese of Virginia." During this time you have added honor to this Parish by serving on the vestry of the Parish and acting as chairman of Yeocomico Cemetery Committee and as Treasurer of The Yeocomico Association and as member of the Executive Committee of Yeocomico Association. This testimonial bears record of your great and undivided service to the Church and of the respect and love which we hold you. Signed by Frederick D. Goodwin, Lawrence Mason and members of the Vestry of Cople Parish. Mr. and Mrs. Sydnor's son, Charles Raymond, Jr. was preparing to enter The Virginia Theological Seminary on the 300th anniversary of the Parish.

In 1964, when the Parish was beginning its 300th anniversary, The Rev. Lawrence Mason decided to move to "The Church of Our Saviour" at Sandston, Virginia. He handed in his resignation, March 4, 1964, and once more Cople was without a rector, but not for long.

The vestry notified the Bishop that they were interested in calling an Ordained Minister. On June third, 1964, Mr. C. Mottram Sanford, Senior Warden, reported that it was acceptable that the Bishop assign Mr. James Guy here for his "deaconship." Mr. Guy, the thirty-fifth Rector, assumed his job July 1, 1964. Mr. Guy entered the Seminary after he served in the Army of the United States for twenty years and retired with the rank of Major. He was married and had two teenaged children. He came at a time when there were lots of changes brewing.

In 1964 Nomini Church was presented a set of Communion Silver in memory of Mrs. Gladys Hally Tubman by her son and daughter-in-law, Hally and Virginia Tubman, her niece, Catherine Arnest Forsythe, and her friend Mrs. Frances Bronson. The new silver copied as closely as possible the chalice of the old communion set and Nomini had its own silver once more. Since 1814, during the War of 1812, when Admiral Cockburn is reported to have removed the Nomini Church silver, the Communion Silver was carried back and forth by the Altar Guild from Yeocomico Church to Nomini Church and vise-versa.

After three hundred years Cople Parish was still alive and well with Nomini Church and Yeocomico Church still open for services with the addition of St. James to help administer to the spiritual life of the lower end of the County. Through the years Cople has welcomed newcomers to our area. There has never been a stagnant population in Cople Parish. We are an interesting mix of north, south, and west (you can't go east or you'll land in the Chesapeake Bay); farmers, lawyers, watermen, teachers, doctors, blacksmiths, writers, mechanics, masons, boatbuilders, nurses, artists, salesman, merchants, tinkers, soldiers, sailors, and retirees — all are connected to Cople Parish and make it work. We look to our past with thanksgiving for the many saints who have kept the Parish alive in times of great hardships, disappointments, and challenges. We are proud of the many wonderful people who have worshipped with us and shared our lives and especially grateful for the blessings of wonderful spiritual leaders who have kept alive the faith of our fathers, and we look forward to the next three hundred years.

ACKNOWLEDGEMENT

I wish to express my appreciation to Walker Decker who kept my computer working properly; to Katherine Murphy Baltz of West Virginia for the use of John Newton Murphy's diary; to Louise Sydnor for the minutes of the Mount Holly Churchwomen; to C. Mottram Sanford for his counsel; to H. Ragland Eubank for the research project on Cople Parish that he conducted with the help of Mrs. Helen Tayloe; to Mrs. Eudora Ramsey Richardson who stored the project papers in her Richmond home; and to Treadwell Davison for his interest in the history of the Parish.

CPSIA information can be obtained at www.ICGtesting.com
Printed in the USA
LVOW042314220412

278699LV00008B/132/P